About the Author

A. Rahman (b. 1970) took his M.A. degree from Gauhati University in 1995 and later obtained his Ph.D. degree from Dibrugarh University in 2008. He has been teaching in the Department of History at Yingli (Govt.) College, Longleng since 1996. Before joining Yingli College, he was working as a lecturer at Swami Yogananda Girl College, Saktiashram, Kokrajhar. He is a life member of the North East India History Association and has published a few research papers. He also organised and conducted two regional seminars under the sponsorship of the Indian Council of Historical Research (ICHR).

Change and Development in Phom Naga Society

A. RAHMAN

CONCEPT PUBLISHING COMPANY PVT. LTD.
NEW DELHI-110059

ISBN-13: 978-93-5125-096-8

First Published 2015

Published and Printed by

Concept Publishing Company Pvt. Ltd.
A/15-16, Commercial Block, Mohan Garden
New Delhi-110059 (India)
T : 25351460, 25351794, *F* : 091-11-25357109
E: publishing@conceptpub.com, W: www.conceptpub.com
Editorial Office: H-13, Bali Nagar, New Delhi-110 015, India.

Cataloging in Publication Data--*Courtesy:* D.K. Agencies (P) Ltd. <docinfo@dkagencies.com>

Rahman, A., 1970-
Change and development in Phom Naga society / A. Rahman.
p. cm.
Includes bibliographical references (p.) and index.
ISBN 9789351250968

1. Naga (South Asian people)--India--Longleng (District)--Social life and customs. 2. Longleng (India : District).--Social life and customs. 3. Social change--India--Longleng (District) 4. Economic development--India--Longleng (District) 5. Naga (South Asian people)--Political activity--India--Longleng (District) 6. Longleng (India : District).--Politics and government. I. Title.

DDC 305.800954165 23

Preface

Change is the law of nature. No society remains static, though the pace of change and development may differ from region to region. Many of the regions have made rapid progress while some others are advancing only slowly. In pre-independence times the Colonial Government paid little attention for development of the Phom-Naga inhabited areas for poor prospect of revenue collection. Despite this the feeling of tribal solidarity began to develop in the minds of the people of the areas as early as the first half of the twentieth century. The Christian missionaries who were playing a significant role in bringing a major change in other areas of Nagaland, made little break-through in the Phom areas. The continuation of age-old practice of head hunting among the people was another deterrent factor which slowed down the pace of development in the area. It is only after 1947 that the government of free India initiated multifaceted development activities in most of the tribal areas of the north-east. As a result strong winds of change and development began to blow over the Phom-Naga areas along with the other tribal areas of the state. An attempt has been made in this volume to critically analyse and assess the pace of development in the Phom-inhabited areas of Nagaland since independence, and to highlight its impact on the people. Since, the spellings of names of the villages, mountains and rivers differed from writer to writer and in official records, an attempt has been made to maintain a uniformity in accordance with the 2011 Census with the exception of the Bhumnyu village whose residents recently changed the name of their village from Mongnyu to Bhumnyu with the consent of the Home Department of the Government of India.

In recent years a number of books have been written and published on various aspects of Nagaland in general by scholars, Indian and foreign, but no in-depth study has been made on the Phom-Naga tribe. Until now one or two monographs have been published by the Phom scholars and of course, sketchy information on the tribe is available in the form of tour diaries, booklets and paper published on different occasions. Although the Phom is one of the major Naga tribes of Nagaland and has rich cultural heritage, yet the tribe is still known little to the outside people. All these created an enthusiasm in me to undertake and carry on a comprehensive study and prepare an authentic volume on the tribe. My long stay at Longleng, the district headquarters of the Phom tribe and my close relation with the people have enabled me to understand the society from grassroots level.

In the course of my study I was fortunate to receive support, help, encouragement and cooperation from quite a few persons. I thank them all. I am particularly indebted to my supervisor late Prof. S.D. Goswami, Department of History, Dibrugarh University for his inspiring guidance and invaluable help which I received throughout the period of my study. I wish to place on record my deep sense of gratitude to late Prof. K. Borgohain, former Joint Director of Nagaland Higher and Technical Education, and Principal, Yingli College, Longleng for his encouragement to undertake my research work at Dibrugarh University. I am thankful to Dr. Alempa Ao, retd. Principal and all other faculty members and staff of Yingli College for their encouragement and cooperation in completing my work. I am highly grateful to one of my close friends Dr. B. Henshet Phom, Vice Principal, Yingli College, who never hesitate to share my problems and spare his valuable time to discuss on various issues regarding the people of his own tribe. My sincere thanks go to the Indian Council of Historical Research, New Delhi and the Indian Council of Social Science Research, New Delhi for providing financial assistance to me to visit various libraries, archives, etc. My sincere thanks are also due to the Directors and staff of the Archives at Kohima and New Delhi and the Librarians and support staff of the Libraries at Kohima, Guwahati, Kolkata, New Delhi, Dibrugarh University and Longleng where I worked for my research. I shall fail in my duty if I do not acknowledge the cooperation I received from all those whom I interviewed. I am also grateful to my family members for their inspiration and encouragement at every stage of my study. Lastly, no one other than me is responsible for the mistake, if any, found in this humble work.

Longleng

A. RAHMAN

Contents

LIST OF PHOTOGRAPHS

LIST OF MAPS

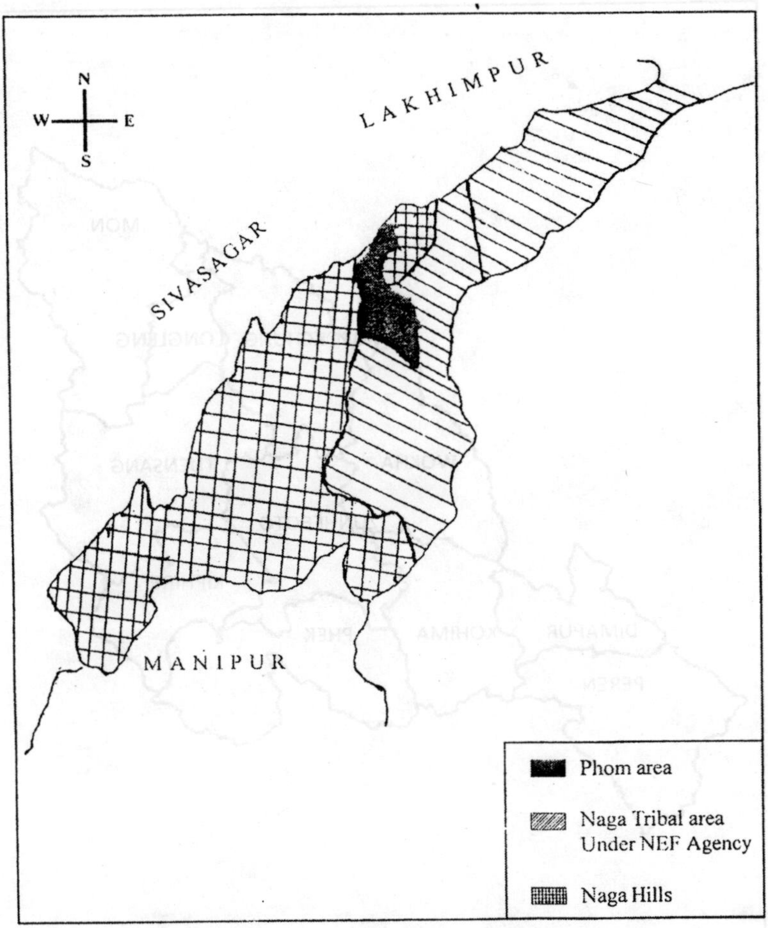

Source: Population and Economic Map Census of India, 1951

Map 1: Nagaland State during NEFA Period (1951-57)

Map 2: Present Nagaland State

1
Land and the People

Nagaland, the easternmost state of India, lies between 25.60′ and 27.40′ north of equator and between the longitudinal lines of 93.20′ and 95.15′[1] with a population of 19,78,502 as per 2011 census.[2] The state which was born on 1 December, 1963 as the sixteenth state of the Indian Union covers an area of 16,579 square kilometres[3] and shares its border with Assam in the north and west, Myanmar and Arunachal Pradesh in the east and Manipur in the south. The topography of the state is very peculiar; full of hill ranges with narrow defile between mountains having terrifying steep terrains full of grass and thickly wooden evergreen forests. Doyang, the largest river navigable for several miles within the state, enters the valley and joins the Brahmaputra river.[4] The state has some other important rivers, namely the Dikhu, the Milak (Jhanzi), the Dhansiri, the Tizu, the Yungnyu (Yangmun), etc. Numerous rivulets drain the hills and usually flow between parallel mountains and also serve as tributaries of various rivers.

The state has now eleven districts[5] in all, inhabited by as many as seventeen Naga tribes as recorded in the 1991 census.[6] The Phek district is the home of the Chakhesangs, the Pochuris and a group of Sangtams. The Mokokchung district is inhabited by the Aos, its headquarters Mokokchung is one of the most important business centres of Nagaland. The Lotha tribe resides in Wokha district and the Semas in Zunheboto district. The Mon district, home of the Konyaks, constitutes the largest single percentage of the total population of the state.[7] The Phoms live in Longleng district. The Sangtam, the Tikhir, the Yimchungre, the Khiemnungan, etc., are found in Kiphire district. Saramoti, the highest peak in Nagaland is situated in Kiphire district and its height is 3,840 metres above sea level.[8] The Tuensang district is inhabited by the Changs, the

Khiemnungans and the Sangtams, the Peren district by the Zeliangs and the Kohima district by the Angamis, the Rengmas, etc. Kohima, the state capital, is an important commercial and transport centre. Japfu is the highest peak of the district. The Kohima town and its suburbs are historically known for one of the most decisive and bloody battles of Second World War fought between the Allies and the Japanese and the INA army in April 1944. The British and their allied forces were victorious in this battle. Some of the legacies of the War are still found here.[9] The Dimapur district, which is situated on the bank of the Dhansiri river, is inhabited by the mixed Naga tribes. A considerable number of non-Naga people, i.e. the Kacharis, the Assamese, the Bengalis, the Kukis, etc., are also found in this district. Dimapur was once the capital of the Kachari rajas, which was sacked by the Ahoms in 1536. The capital was then abandoned, but its ruins are still found here.[10] It has communication and transport links with all the important places of North-East India besides the whole state. The state has only one airport and a rail station situated at Dimapur itself. The town is known as an important commercial centre of the entire state and of the neighbouring state of Manipur.

Over and above Nagaland, various other Naga tribes live outside the geographical boundary of Nagaland. For example, the Tangkhul, the Mao, the Maram, the Kabui, the Zeliangrong, the Maing, the Anal, the Mayan, the Monsang, the Thangal and the Kacha Nagas live in Manipur;[11] the Nocte, the Wancho and the Tangsa Nagas in Tirap district of Arunachal Pradesh; the Rengma and the Zemi Nagas in the Karbi Anglong and North Cachar Hills districts of Assam. The Naga tribes of Burma are the Haimi, the Rangpan, the Htangau, the Tsaplaw and the Somra Nagas.[12] Though the Naga tribes differ from one another in physique, culture and language, yet many things are ubiquitous in them making it possible for us to group them under the generic name of Naga.[13] There were, in the past, some characteristics which were common among the various Naga tribes, viz. headhunting, bachelor's house, trial marriage (premarital relationship), aversion to the use of milk, absence of any powerful political organisation, use of double-cylinder wooden vertical forge, the loom, the shield, the practice of tattooing, etc.[14]

Area and Location of Longleng District

The Longleng district, the home of the Phom Nagas, is situated on the north of Nagaland and lies between 26°17′30″ and 26°47′15″ north of equator and between the longitudinal lines of 94°33′25″E and 94°48′15″E.[15] It covers an approximate area of 566 square kilometres with picturesque mountains and vast fertile land in the foothills.[16] Roughly, the district covers 3.38 per cent of the total land area of the state.

LONGLENG DISTRICT IN 2007

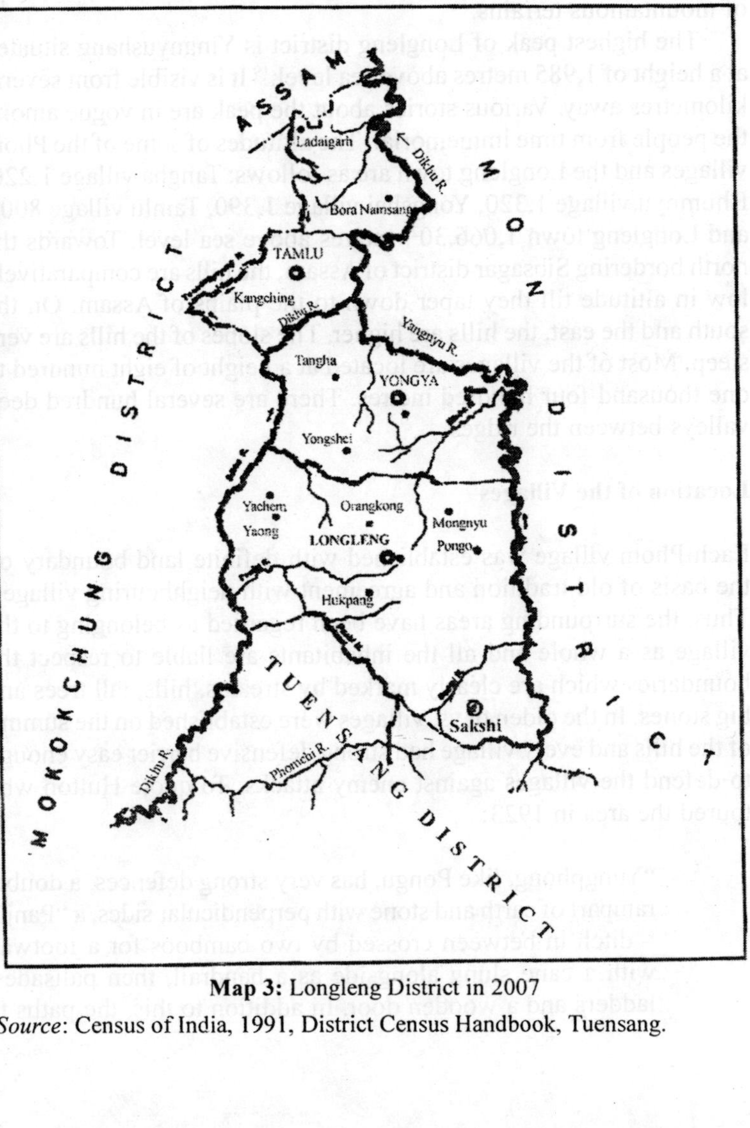

Map 3: Longleng District in 2007

Source: Census of India, 1991, District Census Handbook, Tuensang.

The boundary of the Longleng district touches Assam on its north on a narrow strip between Mon and Mokokchung districts. The other three sides of the district are bounded by the Tuensang district on the south, the Mokokchung district on the west, and the Mon district on the east. The whole area falls on north-western sub-ranges of the Patkai hills comprising three hilly terrains along with deep valleys.[17] Yungnyu, Shemong and Chingmei are the three mountain ranges of the region.[18] Almost the entire land area of the district is composed of mountainous terrains.

The highest peak of Longleng district is Yingnyushang situated at a height of 1,985 metres above sea level.[19] It is visible from several kilometres away. Various stories about the peak are in vogue among the people from time immemorial. The altitudes of some of the Phom villages and the Longleng town are as follows: Tangha village 1,220, Bhumnyu village 1,320, Yongshei village 1,390, Tamlu village 800[20] and Longleng town 1,066.30[21] metres above sea level. Towards the north bordering Sibsagar district of Assam, the hills are comparatively low in altitude till they taper down to the plains of Assam. On the south and the east, the hills are higher. The slopes of the hills are very steep. Most of the villages are located at a height of eight hundred to one thousand four hundred metres. There are several hundred deep valleys between the ridges.

Location of the Villages

Each Phom village was established with definite land boundary on the basis of old tradition and agreement with neighbouring villages. Thus, the surrounding areas have been regarded as belonging to the village as a whole and all the inhabitants are liable to respect the boundaries which are clearly marked by streams, hills, tall trees and big stones. In the olden days, villages were established on the summit of the hills and every village had strong defensive barrier easy enough to defend the villages against enemy attacks. To quote Hutton who toured the area in 1923:

> "Yungphong, like Pongu, has very strong defences, a double rampart of earth and stone with perpendicular sides, a "Panji" – ditch in between crossed by two bamboos for a footway with a cane slung alongside as a handrail, then palisades, ladders and a wooden door. In addition to this, the paths to

> the village were all blocked with branched stumps, sometimes with rows of them, which would entirely prevent anyone from running down the paths."[22]

In the bygone days, the Nagas were known for head hunting and the inter-village feuds were a common practice among them. It was under these prevailing conditions every individual had to lead a life of apprehension of surprise enemy attack. Therefore, the first choice of the founders of a village was the defence of the location where the village was built, while the cultivable land was secondary for them. They also allowed the surroundings of the village to be covered by the dense forest. In case, a village failed to resist the incursion of the enemy, the villagers mostly the women and children took shelter in these jungles in order to save their lives from the hands of the raiders.

Although headhunting is now a matter of the past, village sites have not been abandoned. The people love their ancestral home intensely and do not give it up easily. However, nowadays educated people have started to set up colonies downwards in suitable places around the main villages. Even two or three villages are found on the same spur. The surrounding land area of the two villages Shetap and Ladaigarh, situated near the Assam-Nagaland border, is plain, whereas the land of Ngetchungching is equally flat and hilly. The geographical area and population of the Phom villages vary from village to village. Villagers use the forest products, practise shifting or terrace cultivation, catch fish in the rivers or *nullahs* and use common water sources located within their village boundary. Each village has usually from three to five *khels* and again, each *khel* has a *morung*, i.e. bachelors' dormitory.[23] Many of the Phom villages have well adorned village entry gates.

Soil

The soil of Nagaland is tentatively grouped into four categories, namely entisol, oxisol, mollisol and spodosol. The land bordering Assam is classified as entisol but the major portion of the land of Longleng district is oxisol and a little portion mollisol.[24] Entisol is an important class of soil for cultivation of rice and also for other agricultural crops as the *p*H level of the soil is less.[25] In the higher altitude hills where the *p*H level of the soil is comparatively high, people practise *jhum*, i.e. shifting cultivation.[26] The fertility status of the soil of Longleng district is shown in Table 1.1.

Table 1.1: Fertility status of Soils of Longleng Rural Development Block

pH	*Organic Carbon %age*	*Average*		*Fertility Rating*		
		Phosphate Lbs/Acres	*Potash Lbs/Acres*	*Nitrogen*	*Phosphate*	*Potash*
1	2	3	4	5	6	7
6.30	2.760	18.0	437.5	High	Low	High

Source: Report on Census of Minor Irrigation Schemes in Nagaland, 1987-88, p. 8.

Soils in Nagaland are generally fertile but soil erosion that occurs during the rainy season often affects the people and creates hurdles for farming and also transport system. The land having steeply slope hills is more prone to soil erosion. There are other factors like torrential rain, exclusive practice of *jhum* cultivation, haphazard construction of roads and houses which cause frequent land erosion.

Climate

The climate of the state varies according to season, namely the cold weather season or winter season (December to February), hot weather season or spring season (March to May), the south-west monsoon or summer season (June to September) and retreating the south-west monsoon or autumn season (October to November).[27] In the months from February to April, the sky ordinarily remains clear with the exception of occasional cloudiness and showers. Strong wind blows generally from the south-west during February and March almost throughout the day and occasionally in the night too. Velocity of the wind is so strong that sometimes tall trees are uprooted and thatched leaves or CGI sheets from house roofs are blown away. Rain starts in advance in April but more regularly from May. Monsoon sets in June and continues upto the middle of September.[28] Temperature gradually rises but goes down at once when it rains. Monsoon brings heavy rain and it rains almost every day that makes the *kacha* roads muddy and slippery. The average temperature of the district in summer is 30 degree. During summer the climate is warm rather than hot due to heavy rain. In summer and autumn the sky remains mostly cloudy and the mist rising from the deep valleys often envelops the mountains. The average rainfall of Longleng district is 2500 mm. while the rainfall at Tamlu alone exceeds 100 inches.[29] The temperature of the district starts to come down from September and from November it is severe cold. The sun is scorching in the higher altitude hills because the air is thin.[30] In the foothills bordering Assam temperature is higher than Yongnyah, Longleng and Sakshi areas because of lower altitude of the area. December and January are the coldest months. The average temperature of the district in winter is 17 degree. The sky becomes cloudy at times with smoke in various parts of the district in the months from December to March due to burning jungles for preparing the *jhum* fields.

Drainage

There are two major rivers, viz. the Dikhu and the Yangmun (Yungnyu) which flow through the Longleng district. The Dikhu rises from the north flanks near Nurato Mountain in the Sema territory and turns westward and enters the Ao area, then it flows further northward forming a traditional boundary between the Ao and the Phom areas[31] of Yongnyah and Longleng administrative circles. After that it flows north-eastward across the northern part of the Longleng district marking the natural boundary between Tamlu and Yongnyah administrative circles and finally meets the Yungnyu river near Tamlu. From there it turns towards Assam and once again acts as the natural boundary demarcation between Tamlu subdivision and Mon district. Then it flows north and west through the Sibsagar district of Assam and finally falls into the Brahmaputra river. Its total length before merging with the Brahmaputra river is about 200 kilometres.[32] The river is navigable for a short distance from the confluence of the Dikhu and the Yungnyu rivers to Assam.

A number of tributaries which rise in the north flanks of the Tuensang district and also the southern part of the Mon district ultimately form the Yungnyu river. The river turns northward, then north-westward and ultimately joins the Dikhu river. The river flows past the eastern border of the Longleng district and acts as the natural border between the Longleng and the Mon districts. Both the Dikhu and the Yungnyu rivers are difficult to cross during the rainy season due to the strong current of the water.[33]

Several rills, or *nullahs* passing through the Longleng district act as tributaries of either the Dikhu or the Yungnyu rivers. The ridges separated by deep valleys produce various *nullahs* like Supai, Pochi, Tsubu, Sisha, Tsusangyayung, Phengla, etc. Many of these dry up during the lean season but cannot be crossed without bridge due to strong current during the rainy season.

The springs around the foothills of the Phom villages serve the various needs of the people living in the villages. They catch fish in the rivers and rills with the help of hooks and nets or by the traditional method of using the substances of poisonous plants.[34] Nowadays fish is also caught by throwing and blasting powerful cracker into the water. Community fishing is also done in the rivers and rills in which people of two or more villages take part.

Mineral Resources

Coal and limestone are the two important mineral resources of the district. Coal is found in the areas west of Namsang Chingchang (Bura Namsang). A small quantity of secondary limestone is found at a place 3.2 kilometres to the south-east of Tamlu[35] and also in the areas nearby the Sakchi village. Oil seepage has been reported from the Tamlu-Mon border of Bura Namsang village.[36]

In the olden days the Phom people used to make salt and lime by the indigenous methods of production. After collecting the saline water from brine sources the water was boiled and then stored in the *chunga* (bamboo piece) for a day or two after which a small quantity of salt was found stored at the bottom of the *chunga*. The people also made lime by burning a particular kind of tree or by burning and cooling down the limestone.[37]

Flora and Fauna

The district is almost entirely covered with hills and receives heavy rainfall in the monsoon. The climate is suitable for the growth of various crops. The villages are situated at a distance of four to ten kilometres from each other and the intervening parts are covered by thick jungles. The forest of the lower ranges of Tamlu-Bura Namsang areas is classified as subtropical moist deciduous forest and a small portion as subtropical evergreen rain forest, whereas the rest parts of Longleng district are under degraded regrowth forests (*jhum*).[38]

The wood gathered from the forests is used by the Phom people for construction of houses and furniture, and also as firewood and charcoal. Cane, stone, *agor* wood, bamboo, *dalchini* and varieties of medicinal plants are some of the important forest products of the district. The forest is also the home of different species of wild animals and birds like the tiger, panther, jungle cat, Himalayan bear, bison, *sambar*, barking deer, wild pig, Indian hornbill, jungle fowl, pheasant, green pigeon, doves, etc. Among the reptiles the python is the most important one. Hunting of wild birds and animals is quite common among the Phoms as the Government of Nagaland bans killing of such animals and birds only during the period from 1 March to 31 October.

The Phom Tribe

The Phom is a hospitable Naga tribe scattered over different villages in the Longleng district of Nagaland. Longleng is a new district which was created by carving out the northern portions of the erstwhile Tuensang district. It was inaugurated in January 2004. Milada Ganguli wrote while visiting the Phom villages, "With no other Naga tribe did I experience such a ceremonial welcome and on the other hand such a cold send-off as with the Phoms."[39] The district is now administered by a Deputy Commissioner with the help of a host of other officers. With a view to governing it more conveniently the district has been divided into five administrative units, namely Tamlu, the sub-divisional headquarters, which is looked after by an Additional Deputy Commissioner, and Yongnyah, Sakshi, Kongshong and Yachem the four other administrative headquarters headed by one Extra Assistant Commissioner each.[40] Longleng, the administrative headquarters, is an important centre of commerce and education for the people of the district. Longleng town is situated at a site full of hills, ridges and narrow but enchanting valleys. It is situated in the middle of three Phom villages, viz. Bhumnyu, Hukpang and Orangkong. There are thirty-seven government recognised Phom villages [41] under the Longleng district, namely Alayung, Amosen, Auching, Aboiche, Bura Namsang, Chingong, Dungkhao, Hongnyu, Hukpang, Kangching, Ladaigarh, Lingtak, Bhumnyu, Mongtikang, Namhaching, Netnyuching, Ngetchungching, Nian, Noksosang, Orangkong, Oushok, Pongching, Pongo, Sakchi, Shamnyuching, Shetap, Tamlu, Tangha, Yachem, Yangching, Yaong (Yimchan),

Yimchong, Yongam, Yonglok, Yongphang, Yongshei and Yongnyah.[42] According to 2011 census Longleng district had a total population numbering 50484 souls.[43]

A considerable number of people belonging to other Naga tribes also live in the Longleng district. The Konyaks live in a separate *khel* of Tamlu village and the Aos, among other notable tribes, are engaged in government service and also in business sectors. Ladaigarh, a village on the Assam-Nagaland border, is the only village of the district which has the smallest number of scheduled tribe population.[44] In recent years the village has become an issue of border dispute between Assam and Nagaland. Besides, the Naga people, a small number of non-Naga people from different parts of India as well as from Nepal are residing in this district. Similarly, a few thousand Phom people are currently residing outside the district, in places like Anaki, Tuensang, Kohima, Mokokchung, Mon, Dimapur, Naginimora, etc.[45] Except in Anaki village[46], these people are engaged either in government service or in business. The tribe has been recognised as one of the backward tribes[47] of Nagaland and enlisted as a scheduled tribe.[48]

Migration

No written record is found as to how and from where the Phoms came to this mountainous terrain. However, there are some legends and oral histories which tell about their origin and migration. Generally, the Phom tribe is divided into two groups, each claiming different legends of their origin and direction of migration.

The first group believes that their ancestors came from a place in the east called Pongngaihong (an unknown place on the Myanmar side). They migrated from Pongngaihong to Apaihong and then to Yingnyushang Mountain.[49] While reaching Yingnyushang Mountain they crossed the Phomchi river in the Chang area to the south and the south-west of Yingnyushang.[50] Some linguistic and other evidences help us to believe in their migration from the east to Yingnyushang many generations ago. There are some linguistic similarities between the Phoms and the people of Myanmar. For instance, both the groups call the tiger as *shahnyu* and the bear as *sheptao*. The Phom males had their haircutting style the same as the Burmese while the women had common tattooing custom.[51] At one point of time the ancestors of the Phoms were believed to have lived as a well settled community at Mount Yingnyushang but afterwards they spread all over the present district and even beyond that.[52] A popular folk tale[53], believed and accepted by the Phoms, tells us about the destruction of Yingnyuching and their migration to the present areas. Be that as it may, groups of families migrated and established new colonies which matured into full-fledged villages in the long run. In this way waves of migration continued till the uninhabited lands were available for resettlement. With the formation of new colony or village a close relationship was maintained with the parent village. New colonies or villages presented gifts to the parent villages from time to time. But, in course of time this proximity of relationship lapsed and the gap widened. The people of the new colonies or villages developed a dialect of their own. Yet, they never forgot the tales of their original homeland. A.E. Shuttle Worth, S.D.O. Mokokchung, noted in his tour diary in 1895:

> "Three years ago one *morung* left this village (Bura Namsang) and built a small village at about 5 miles away. This small village still considers itself a *khel* of this village and pays and supplies rice when required within village. There are 20 houses in the new village."[54]

A group of Phoms from Pongching and another group from the Chang tribe mingled together and founded the Mongtikang village presumably in the last part of the nineteenth century. The people of the village, therefore, can speak both the Chang and the Phom dialects.[55] The Konyaks of the Chaklangshu-Mopong group and the Longching group (Upper Konyak) believe that their ancestors migrated from Yingnyushang crossing the Yangmun river hundreds of years ago.[56] Even some families migrated to the Ao areas.[57] William C. Smith wrote that there was a village called 'Mirinokpo' or 'Assiringia' in the Ao area, the inhabitants of which had come from the Phom village of 'Urang Kong' (Orangkong) across the Dikhu, and settled down in the Ao territory many years ago. They largely adopted Ao customs, and most of them spoke the Ao language.[58] About the migration of the Konyak of Tamlu, Christoph von Furer-Haimendrof wrote in about 1936-37:

> "Two different languages are spoken in this village; two of the three *morung* speak a language particular to Tamlu, while the people of the third *morung*, whose ancestors immigrated

from Tanhai only a few generations ago, speak quite a different language. There was difficulty at first, the people told us, but now the villagers have learnt to understand each other."[59]

There is still another group among the Phoms who traces the story of their origin to Longtrok (six stones), near Chungliyimti village, a place where the Ao tribe traces its origin.[60] Probably, this group of Phom people migrated along with the Aos from Chungliyimti village to the different places of Mokokchung district by crossing the Dikhu river. Afterwards being separated from the Aos they again migrated to the east of the Dikhu river in search of new settlements. Yachem and Yaong are the two Phom villages immediately east of the Dikhu and closely allied to the Ao tribe with whom they claim a common origin.[61] However, this group does not reckon themselves as Ao since the bygone days.[62]

It is supposed that among the various Naga tribes the Phoms and the Konyaks were the early settlers in this part of the land. The migration and settlement of these two groups of people might have taken place earlier than the advent of the Ahoms to Assam (1228 A.D.) because the founder of the Ahom kingdom Sukapha was believed to have encountered opposition of the Konyak Nagas while crossing the Patkai Mountains (1215-1228). There were about twenty-three Phom villages at the time of independence, but quite a few new villages came up since then mainly due to the overgrowth of population.

Thus, it goes without saying that the Phom people migrated through two different routes to the present areas. One group migrated from the east to Yingnyushang and then spread to this region while the other group possibly migrated from the Ao area across the Dikhu river. These two groups later merged together as a result of intermarriage and have been living together for centuries. This merging group of people is known as *Yingli Moihiyang*, or the generation of Yingli.[63] It can also be inferred from the above discussion that the Phom tribe has blood relations with the Konyak, the Chang and the Ao tribes.

Origin of the Word 'Phom'

Three distinct spellings, viz. Pohum, Phum and Phom are found in the British records which were compiled at different points of time. It is very difficult to say how the word 'Phom' originated. Firstly, it appears that the word 'Phom' originated from a village name, viz. Bhumnyu. The village was formerly known as Pohum or Phum.[64] In 1909, Chingao, a government interpreter reported to the British authority at Tamlu that the two *morungs* of Wanching (Konyak village) had gone on a raid to Phum and in the process lost 18 heads and a double-barrelled gun.[65] In 1936 Chingyang (a Konyak) reported to Haimendrof:

> "The Chongwe people asked us whether we should like to buy a slave. Where did you get him from? We inquired at first. He was a boy they had captured from Mongnyu – that is a Phom village behind the mountain, and he pointed to one of the mountains to the south."[66]

Secondly, it is also widely believed that the word 'Phom' is derived from the river Phomchi which is in the Chang area of Tuensang district. When interviewed, Apisangpa, a retired *Do-Bhashi* stated that long ago a group of people crossed the Phomchi river from the Chang area and settled down near the Yingnyushang mountain. Afterwards, they moved in different directions and settled down on various hillocks. As these people crossed the Phomchi river, so the Changs called them Phom. Consequently, Pongching village was called Phomching and Hukpang village as Phom village by the Changs.[67] In a report the S.D.O. Mokokchung stated in 1910 that Nake, son of Longkhang, late *Gaon-Bura* of Yongiemdi, informed him that, "Last month the Phum village of Hukpang raided Oranging taking two heads."[68] The name of the village Phomching is found in a report recorded on 20.7.1919[69] and the same name was repeated in the subsequent reports. It was further stated in this report: "Ourangkong, a Phom village, lies between the Phom villages of Mongyu and Hukpong."[70] Hutton, in his report of 1916, mentioned Phom as a distinct tribe[71] and repeatedly used the word 'Phom' to describe the villages of Pongo, Hukpang, Pongching, Bhumnyu and Orangkong in a map showing his tours to the east of the Naga Hills in his Report of 1923.[72]

Thirdly, it is also believed that the word 'Phom' is a corrupt form of *Phum* which means cloud in the Phom language.[73] The Phom areas always remain enveloped in clouds and for this reason perhaps the people came to be called as Phom.[74]

Physical Features

Typical Mongoloid features of snub nose, fair complexion skin, straight hair and brachycephalic head, etc.[75], are found among the Phoms. The people living in the lower altitude villages where the weather is comparatively hot are, however, somewhat darker in complexion. The people are, on the average, neither very tall nor very short. The men have oblique eyes of dark brown colour, thin beards and moustaches. The Census of India, 1891 reported about the people of Tamlu and Bura Namsang as follows:

> "The women, who are very fair complexioned, wear a white petticoat, in some cases striped with red . . . Both sexes chew *pan* and betel, and both have their teeth artificially blackened, a process which does not tend to enhance their beauty."[76]

Steep terrains, hard work, struggle in sunny and cold weather, traditional food habit, etc., made them physically strong and healthy. Earlier, the people had their hair cut squarely round their heads. Women tattooed their legs and wore different types of beads[7] while the men tattooed their body. R.G. Woodthorpe observed:

> "The men here tattoo on the chest after taking their first head. The pattern consists of four lines which spring from the navel, diverging as they ascend, and turn off into two large concentric curves over each breast, the lines broadening out to about one inch in width at the middle of the curves."[78]

Nowadays, however, the Phom people, especially the youngsters, keep their bodies clean.

Family System

The family is an important unit of the Phom village life. They practise nuclear family system which consists of the father, the mother and their children. The father is the head of the family; he is respected and feared by other family members. Properties are divided into equal shares among the brothers, though the lion's share is generally given to the son who lives with the parents.[79] All the sons stay with their parents till they are married. After marriage they are separated from the parental family and live in the houses built by them. After marriage the daughters go and stay with their husbands. Only the sons inherit the family descent as well as the property of their fathers. A Phom scholar, B. Henshet writes, "Phoms practise patrilocal, patrilineal and monogamous family system."[80] Joint family was maintained in some Phom villages in the past. C. Amop Noklang states:

> "In certain villages there were joint families, where one or more married couples lived with their parents. This system was maintained mainly for economic reasons and sometimes because of the parents' compulsion that till they die they want their children to be with them. But nowadays this practice is declining rapidly."[81]

There is a custom among the people of the Phom-Nagas of observing the naming ceremonies for a girl and a boy on different dates. For instance, when a child is born in a family, the naming ceremony is observed on the fifth day for a girl and on the sixth day for a boy along with feasts for villagers and friends.[82] On the occasion of marriage, a grand feast is generally arranged from the bridegroom's family. A married couple never addresses each other by the first name but after the birth of a child they call each other by referring to the father or mother of so-and-so. The parents while writing the name of their child generally adopt the first letter of father's first name. For example, in case of a girl named A. Alin Noklang, the letter 'A' is adopted from the father and Alin is her actual name. Noklang is the name of a clan used by her as her title here. They generally write the tribe's name and in some cases the clan name as their surname. The clan system among the Phom people is an important social entity which consists of certain families and again a few clans constitute a Phom village. Every clan is known by a common name.

Language

The Phoms have as many as five distinct dialects[83], which differ from village to village or area to area. The dialects vary so much so that one group does not understand the dialect of the other group. J.P. Mills wrote about the dialects spoken by the Yaong and Yachem group in the following words:

> "The Yachem dialect is spoken in the transfrontier villages of Yachem and Yong. These villages contain a large admixture of Phom and Konyak blood, and like Konyaks, their inhabitants substitute l for r in words. The dialect resembles Chongli rather than Mongsen, but it has a number of words of its own, and is quite unintelligible to an Ao who does not happen to know it."[84]

From the beginning of the second half of the twentieth century the Phom people developed one dialect out of the different dialects spoken by them as their common language which is now called the Phom language. C. Amop Noklang remarks:

> "Even today, except for the younger generation, most of the older people do not speak or understand any other dialect than their own. But now attempts are being made to overcome this problem. One of the major dialects, one spoken by eight villages called 'Yongnyah Shah' is used as the common language of the Phoms. School text books and other books of literature are published in the common language, and used in the schools and public occasions."[85]

This common language has, however, no script of its own. So the Roman script is now used in writing the Phom language. There were 17,624 Phom speaking people out of 19,423 persons in the present Longleng district according to 1971 census.[86] Most of these people can also speak the Nagamese and the Ao languages. Some of them, especially ex-army and police personnel can speak Hindi. Nagamese is used widely as a link language while conversing with other Naga tribes or non-Naga people. English is the link language of the educated class; it is also the official language of the state of Nagaland. The Phom people living near Assam-Nagaland border can speak Assamese fluently because of the close trade relations they have had with the people of the plains for centuries.

Land Ownership Pattern

All the government recognised Phom villages have lands having boundary demarcation with neighbouring villages. The villagers follow traditional system of land ownership, which slightly varies from village to village. From field study it is found that the individual, clan, community (village), *morung* and the churches possess lands. The land ownership pattern of Sakchi, Pongo, Bhumnyu, Yongam and Bura Namsang villages shows that all these villages have both individual and clan lands, whereas some villages have *morung*, church and community lands too. Major portions of lands of Longleng town are under individual ownership. Village land whether individual or collective has no written records. It may be because of the fact that the Nagas do not pay land tax and therefore, assessment of village land is not felt necessary till now. Farm or forest lands are demarcated by fence, stone, tree, etc.

Clan and village land ownership is collective while the *morung* and church lands can be termed institutional. An individual can acquire land through his own efforts or through lineage. The senior members of a clan distribute clan lands among the needy persons through mutual discussion. A daughter cannot claim a share of her father's properties according to the customary law. If a man passes away without a male issue, all his properties pass on to his brothers or uncles.[87]

Agriculture

Two types of cultivations are usually practised by the Phom people, i.e. *jhum* or shifting cultivation and terrace cultivation. In *jhum* cultivation a plot of land is selected for cultivation and it is done twice and even thrice successively. After that the land is kept fallow for several years depending on the availability of new lands. The jungles excepting the big trees are cleared in winter, then these are dried and burnt. Half burnt logs and branches are kept in lines from top to bottom of the field so that loose earth cannot be washed away by rainwater. By April seeds are sown on the *jhum* fields. In a month or two, weeding is done twice or thrice. Ripened paddy is harvested in July or August. The main crops grown in the *jhum* fields are paddy, millet, maize, pumpkin, cucumber, gourds, chilli, etc.

Terrace cultivation is done by means of irrigation. Most of these lands are steepy, so all the villages do not have abundant water and lands for terrace cultivation. In this system of cultivation, water is channelled out from nearby streams to the terrace field. The field is prepared into several plots of flat land from top to bottom and the side of each plot is raised to retain the water. All the plots are made muddy with the help of spade and also by human feet by supplying water. As soon as the field is ready, the paddy plants are transplanted in the field. It is done in June or July. The crop is harvested in October or November. Unlike *jhum* field, only paddy is grown in terrace field. The implements used in agriculture are the *dao*, axe, spade, hoe, pick, scraper, sickle, rake, winnowing fan, basket, pounding tables, etc.

Dress

The traditional dress of the Phom people varied considerably from village to village or according to their social status. The colour and design of the dress also signified their social status. The man used to wear small waist flap, i.e. loincloth at the hips and it was generally made of woody fibre, woven into coarse cloth.[88] They used a band of cane of three to four strips at the waist[89] as belt. The menfolk left their bodies usually bare but wore cane-made belts around the waists for holding *daos* at the back and loincloths at the front when they went out of home. While visiting Pongching and Hukpang R.G. Woodthorpe recorded:

> "At this village and Siphang (Hukpang) the men tie up their cloths in a most picturesque manner: they are knotted over one shoulder and cover the body, leaving the arms free; they fall to within about six inches of knee, and are tied round the waist by the belt, which carries the wooden *dao*-sheath."[90]

The ordinary cloth for rough use was either white or dark blue. A man who had taken human heads in war used to wear an attractive cowrie shawl called *fanet*. An ordinary Naga was not entitled to put on the bedecked shawl because it was considered a symbol of martial achievement. A rich man used to wear a shawl called *henyu* which was red in colour with narrow white horizontal bands at regular intervals of six cms. In between the white bands there were narrow black lines.[91]

The boys of Bhumnyu village had their hair cut collectively in a haircutting ceremony after they had touched meat, i.e. human flesh taken on raid. It was only after that ceremony that they were regarded as adults.[92] They sometimes kept locks hanging down their necks.[93] The Phom warriors practised tattooing customs with a view to demonstrating their social status and heroism. Many warriors recorded their hunted human heads in the shape of the figures of men roughly tattooed, for each head taken, on their chests.[94] In addition to this, the men of Pongo tattooed the upper arms with the design of buffalo heads,[95] which signified valour.

The women of Pongo, Yongphang and Yangching used to wear a very narrow *petticoat* which can be called waist wrapper, some five inches deep, and above it a belt, or a series of belts, each made of separate threads made up into a bound loop at each end and fastened in front.[96] The women of Tamlu and Bura Namsang generally used to wear white glass or crystal clear ornaments. The breasts were left bare. They wore waist wrapper in some cases with red stripes. The width of this wrapper was only about 12 inches but was long enough for both ends to meet when tied together.[97] Ladies of rich families were entitled to wear a white skirt called *shaka*, although various other skirts were also in use.[98] The women of a few lower Phom villages used to wear a piece of cloth as bodice to cover their breasts.[99] The shawls and short skirts were used not always but on rare occasions. Some women of a few villages including Bhumnyu cut their hair as short as possible, but plucked out the hair from the forehead and also from both sides of the ears by rubbing ashes.[100]

The women tattooed the legs elegantly while many of them tattooed their chins too.[101] They tattooed legs below the thighs before marriage on the belief that they would not be able to bear child if they failed to do so.[102] Tattooing was done either by gashing or pricking with needles to introduce dye. The people of Yachem had a custom of wearing boar's tusk through the pierced lobe of the ears.[103] The people of both sexes wore cotton, brass or cane rings in their ears. A drastic change came off in their attitude towards dress in the post-independence period when they came in contact with the outside world.

Woodcarving

The Phoms were experts in woodcarving art in the bygone days. Verrier Elwin wrote:

> "Some of the finest woodcarving in the entire frontier area is to be found among the Wanchos, Konyaks and Phoms, tribes living close to the Burma border who until recently were engaged in constant inter-village feuds."[104]

This art had close connection with headhunting, the decoration of the *morungs* and the funerary images erected for warriors and other important persons.[105] Much attention was paid to the head while carving the human figure because the importance given to the head was usually out of all proportion to the rest of the body. The *morung* was an important woodcarving centre of a village where all young warriors slept at night. They decorated their *morungs* with various images. The posts, horizontal beams and the wide benches on which the young unmarried men used to sleep were covered with figures of tigers, monkeys, lizards, conventional human heads, deer, birds, fish, gongs, snakes, elephants, etc. The woodcarvings were painted with white, black and brick-red colours. They carved the *mithun*'s (Bos frontalis) head which was a symbol of wealth and the hornbill's head which was considered a symbol of beauty. Elwin observed:

> "At Sakchi, a Phom village, I saw in 1954 a carving of two dogs chasing a tiger; at Pongu there was a tall warrior leading a boy by the hand – I was told that this commemorated an incident when a boy was captured and, after being led through the village, decapitated."[106]

They produced effigies roughly carved out of bits of wood in honour of the dead warriors and rich men. These effigies were ornamented with traditional dress and appropriate tattoo marks, and then placed in front of the tomb.[107] To indicate the *mithun* sacrifices, wealthy villagers set the forked posts in the ground close to the fore walls of their houses,[108] where they carved the figures of hornbill and *mithun*'s head. They made *shem*, or log drum hewn out of a single gigantic log, the two ends of which were decorated and carved with figures of hornbill, buffalo horn or elephant teeth. They also made another instrument called *bushong*, which was carved out of a huge log, upper side of which was made flat but hollowed inside for producing varied notes by kicking it. Both the *shem* and *bushong* were kept in *morung*. In addition to these, they made wooden utensils for cooking and dining purposes, smoking pipe, pounding table, etc.

Regarding the instruments used by the Phom woodcarvers, Milada Ganguli wrote:

> "I was astonished to see how the craftsmen of this tribe managed just with a heavy *dao* and crude mallet to produce such magnificent sculptures of animals, warriors with captured heads in their hands, even whole panels with animal scenes carved in high relief."[109]

With the cessation of headhunting and their aversion to *morung* life, woodcarving skill among the Phoms began to decline.

Traditional Religion

Before embracing Christianity, the Phoms had their own way of life. They believed in different malevolent and benevolent powers of the Almighty, but they had neither worshipped idol nor had a place of worship. The Supreme Being is called *Kahvang* in Phom dialect; a word believed to have originated from two separate words, namely *Kah* and *Vang*. The word *Kah* is derived from *Kahdok*, which means the earth and *Vang*, derived from *Vangsho*, meaning the sky or the heaven. So, the literal meaning of *Kahvang* is "heaven and earth".[110]

And again, the Phoms believed in two other gods, namely *Shang Kahvang* which means the celestial god and *Chong Kahvang* or *Chong Sheb* which means the terrestrial god. They believed that the natural phenomena such as rain, lightning, thunder, sunshine, etc., were the works of the *Shang Kahvang*.[111] The happenings on the earth were believed to be the grace or curse of the *Chong Kahvang*. That was why more attention was paid to the *Chong Kahvang*. Sacrifices were offered to please both the *Shang Kahvang* and the *Chong Kahvang*. Besides these gods, they also believed in other deities like god of home, god of paddy field, god of forest, god of river, etc."[112]

They believed that the heavenly bodies like the sun and the moon were the symbols of god and therefore, they took vows in the event of disputes referring to these heavenly bodies as their witnesses.[113] The Phom people believed in life hereafter. They believed that the souls of the deceased go to a place called *Yimching* where all souls meet one another.[114] After an interval, the souls would be transferred to *Chongching* and again after a long break the souls are finally transferred to *Shiching* where the souls melt away with the dew and vanish.[115]

The Phom people believed in evil spirit which they thought could bring disaster to a family or village in the form of epidemic or other misfortunes. While visiting some Phom villages in 1875-6, R.G. Woodthorpe found bunches of leaves being tied to the door-posts which he believed was done to prevent evil spirit accompanying a stranger from entering a house.[116]

The Priest

Divine rites were performed in the traditional Phom society by the priests, but these practices no longer exist now. The duties of the *thibu* (medicine-man) and the priest overlapped at times in some cases. Divine rituals were performed by means of slicing ginger, making fire by pressing rope, slicing twigs or shrubs or broom, slicing betel or plantain leaf, looking at the intestine of pig or fowl, etc. A priest could tell a person the kind of sacrifice to be offered to God or the spirits through such rites. They were to offer sacrifices like egg, fowl, dog, goat, pig, *mithun* etc., for remedy from natural distresses and diseases. For the inauguration of *morung* human sacrifice was usually recommended.[117] Looking at the sun and the moon and observing other formalities, they used to make prediction about rain, crops, festival, natural calamities, conjugal life, etc.[118]

Healing of Diseases

Before coming in contact with modern medical sciences, the *thibu* played the role of a physician for the treatment of diseases in the traditional methods. The Phom people used to consult the *thibu* regarding their physical, moral and material problems. He followed various methods to cure the disease or alleviate other worries. For example, after studying the nature of ailment the *thibu* would suggest the kith and kin of the sufferer to make sacrifice of certain animals or birds to appease the spirit of *Shang Kahvang* who had allegedly withheld his soul.[119] When the sacrifice was made he would appeal to the evil spirit to set free the soul of the sick man in lieu of the sacrifice.[120] In some cases while performing his duty the *thibu* himself lay on a bed keeping a helper, or the *Yiupa* nearby. He then slowly started shaking his whole body and raised his hands indicating his journey to *Yimching*. There he would consult the departed souls about the sufferings of their sons or daughters who are alive. After that he would come down and disclose the message to the *Yiupa* who then would pass on the same to the sick man's family members. The *thibu* would normally inform that the parents of the sick man had committed wrongs to such and such persons when they were alive and their souls now desire that the wrong committed be rectified.[121] The people offered him *laya* (brass plate), leg of a pig, rice, etc., for his service. A sick man or a child was given indigenous medicine prepared by the *thibu*. A *thibu* could be either a man or a woman. It was believed that he had the spirits of tiger, eagle, cat, etc., and a powerful *thibu* had more number of spirits in him.[122] The popularity and status of the *thibu* began to wane with the spread of modern medical sciences and more particularly with the arrival of Christianity.

Taboo

The Phom people were highly superstitious in nature and practised taboos before embracing Christianity. Taboo is called *genna* in Nagamese, which means forbidden from doing certain works.[123] It was observed in the form of ceremony by the individuals, groups or the whole village. Some of the regular *gennas* had connection with agriculture, which was their chief means of support from time immemorial, whereas some other *gennas* were observed only at times. During community taboo days the village gate was closed and every member of the village spent the day at home without doing any manual work.[124] A six-day taboo was observed by a village when there was an occurrence of an accidental or unnatural death like falling from tree, suicide, drowning, killed by animals, etc. Moreover, one day as a religious day, a day for *Pangmo* festival and eight days for *Monyu* festival were observed by the villagers at different times in a year. When a child was born in a family, six days rest for father and five days rest for mother was observed.[125]

In addition to the above, some other taboos were: women were not allowed to touch or handle the war or hunting weapons; a man would not sleep with a woman before going to war, the husband of a pregnant wife would not kill any animal and the pregnant women or children would not eat cross-bred fruits. In Phom society exchanging drink or other things with the members of an enemy village, cutting hair in the evening and grabbing the property of a person who died in an accident were considered highly immoral.[126] The people also strictly followed the food taboo for certain reasons. Villagers would not take food for a fixed period of time in the house of a person who got injured accidentally or committed suicide. Moreover, it was considered improper to take food in the houses of a murderer's clan for a definite period of time. Some people even did not take a particular fish or animal's meat, and except the owner other people would not take the meat of the animal killed by a tiger. Needless to say that all these taboos were observed either due to ignorance or the belief that similar occurrence might take place in their own family or that they might fall sick or misfortunes might occur in case they violated the taboos. Many of these superstitious beliefs and practices have faded away as a result of the spread of Christianity and modern education although a few are still practised.

Funeral Ceremony

The traditional funeral rituals of a rich man, a warrior and a commoner varied in the Phom society. The corpse wrapped up inside mats was placed about three metres above the ground either in the branches of banyan trees or on platform inside small house within the village precincts, close to the dwelling.[127] In order to obviate any unpleasant odour arising from the corpse, fire was lit in front of the corpse and a plentiful supply of smoke was produced by burning chaff, paddy-straw, etc., which mouldered slowly.[128] The corpse, after being smoked for 10 to 20 days, was put in a wooden coffin and placed in the forks of big trees just outside the village gate. But in case of a distinguished man the body was allowed to rot thoroughly, then the head was wrenched off and placed in an earthen pot which was deposited at the foot of the tree in which the coffin was placed.[129]

They used to make wooden effigies for their dead warriors and rich men. These effigies were placed in front of the tombs but in case of the death of a famous warrior, a row of small figures was made besides his own more imposing image to suggest the number of heads he had cut during his life time.[130] In some cases, the images were not made of wood, but these were of bamboo frames, covered with cloth, decorated with bead and other ornaments, and placed in an open thatched hut.[131] They made wooden or bamboo images probably to please and flatter the ghost or there were some associations between the figures and the soul. As soon as the rites were performed the images could be abandoned there or bundled together and placed beneath a tree.[132] Verrier Elwin mentioned about the prevalence of another practice in the following words:

> "In the Phom country immense bamboo horns, fifty feet or more in length, are erected on a hillside in honour of a dead warrior who had taken many heads."[133]

The erections were made probably with the intention to attract the eye from long distance.

In case of the death of a man, the animals owned by him were killed to arrange a feast and one of the relatives was asked to narrate all the courageous deeds, achievements, etc. of the deceased.[134] Following the death of a warrior or a rich man log drum was beaten to convey the message to far-flung areas; brass plates, i.e. *laya, langnyu, langha, langla* and also the *mithun's* horns were beaten.[135] Villagers abstained from work for a few days. The people of Yongnyah, Tangha and Tamlu buried the hunting dogs by constructing sheds over their graves and offering meat, etc., on the belief that if they did not do so the surviving and the other dogs in future would not hunt well.[136] With the acceptance of Christianity, the Phom people have started burying the dead bodies in the graveyard according to the Christian faith. They now erect memory stone in memory of the near and dear ones.

Feast of Merit

In the olden days a rich man had to give 'feast of merit' to the villagers. The wealth of a person was estimated by the quantity of paddy, the number of *mithuns* and the brass plates he had possessed. When a person produced surplus paddy he used to give a grand feast to his fellow villagers because it was believed that if a person accumulated more wealth without hosting the feast of merit, he might suffer from a dreaded disease known as *Nukdin Nyiamdin* or die untimely or misfortunes might descend on the family.[137] The writings of Verrier Elwin about the Nagas in general are also valid for the Phoms. He wrote,

> "The Feasts bring the donor honour both now and after death and he can henceforth wear special clothes and ornaments, and decorate his house in a special way."[138]

While hosting a feast, the donor killed a *mithun* or, failing that, killed other animals and the heads of the slaughtered animals were kept hanging outside the front wall of the house. On such occasions *mithuns* were usually killed by fastening them at fork posts which were generally kept standing outside the houses in the villages. The posts were decorated with the carved figures of sacrificed animals' heads. While visiting Kamahu (Yongshei) R.G. Woodthorpe observed,

> "Many of the verandahs contain a number of Y-shaped posts, carved with human figures, *methna* heads: these signify that the occupant of the house has been the giver of a big feast."[139]

He was entitled to wear a shawl called rich man's shawl, different kinds of helmets, etc., and anyone could recognise him by looking at his apparels. The age-old feast of merit no longer exists in the Phom Naga society as this custom has faded away under the impact of Christianity.

Slavery and its Abolition

Slavery, a social evil, was prevalent in the Phom society till the middle of the twentieth century. A person of either sex could be a slave. The slaves of the Phom areas can be classified into two categories. The condition of slaves of first category was horrible and they were mostly used for sacrifice. On the other hand the status of the second category of slaves was better than the former but they were usually engaged in manual works or otherwise well treated by their lords. Slaves were purchased by the rich people in exchange of brass discs (traditional coins), animals, etc., in order to enhance their social status. It was up to the lords whether their grown-up slaves would enter into conjugal lives or not.

There were various causes of the existence of slavery in Phom society. Firstly, being unable to bring up the children or orphans due to acute financial difficulty or failure to repay the debt, forced some guardians to sell their children or orphans to rich men.[140]

Secondly, two belligerent villages could arrive at an agreement by delivering slaves.[141] Here the slaves were used to settle the village disputes. If two villages, involved in a prolonged head hunting war, desired to make peace, the village which lost more heads would formally demand one or more slaves from the other village in order to compensate the more heads they lost. Thus, the village which collected more heads would hand over a slave or slaves who were usually decapitated in triumph by the other village.

Thirdly, war prisoners were taken as slaves who were mostly either slaughtered as war trophies or sacrificed for other ritual purposes. Instances of purchasing slaves and beheading them to propitiate the gods were not uncommon among them. People preferred to sacrifice human beings for the inauguration of *morungs* and the sacrificed person was generally a slave.[142]

Thus, the slaves of the Phom areas were born as if with their lucks either for sacrifice or throw themselves on the mercy of their lords. However, this obnoxious practice of slavery gradually came to an end from the Phom region with the introduction of British administration, spread of Christianity and the cessation of head hunting. Steps were taken by the administration to eliminate the practice of slavery and human sacrifice, and punished those who were associated with this cruel practice secretly.[143]

NOTES AND REFERENCES

1. Singh, R.D.N. and Zeliang, T. (ed), *Development Profile of Animal Husbandry in Nagaland*, p.19.
2. *Primary Census Abstract – Nagaland 2011*, Directorate of Census Operations in Nagaland, Kohima.
3. *Basic Facts 1999, Nagaland,* p.1.
4. Saleh, Swabera Islam, *Nagaland's Economy in Transition Since*, 1964, p.2.
5. The eleven districts of Nagaland are Kohima, Mokokchung, Tuensang, Mon, Phek, Wokha, Zunheboto, Dimapur, Kiphire, Longleng and Peren.
6. *Census of India 1991, District Census Handbook, Tuensang*, p. 2. The Naga tribes of Nagaland are the Angami, the Ao, the Chakhesang, the Chang, the Chirr, the Khiemnungan, the Konyak, the Lotha, the Makware, the Phom, the Rengma, the Sangtam, the Sema, the Tikhir, the Yimchungre, the Zeliang and the Pochury.
7. Ao, A. Lanunungsang, *Rural Development in Nagaland*, p. 50.
8. *Basic Facts 2000, Nagaland,* p. 3.
9. Bareh, H. (ed.), *Nagaland District Gazetteers, Kohima District*, pp. 52-53.
10. Allen, B.C.; Gait, E.A.; Allen, C.G.H. and Howard, H.F. (ed.), *Gazetteer of Bengal and North-East India*, p. 585.
11. Horam, M., *Social and Cultural Life of Nagas (the Tangkhul Nagas)*, p. 21.
12. Kumar, B. B., *An Introduction to the Naga Tribes*, p. 1.
13. Devi, Lakshmi, *Ahom-Tribal Relations: A Political Study*, p. 19.

14. Horam, M., *Naga Polity*, pp. 37-40.
15. The figures were worked out from records available in the Office of the Directorate of Soil and Water Conservation, Government of Nagaland, Kohima.
16. *Census of India 2011*, Directorate of Census Operations in Nagaland, Kohima.
17. Bareh, H., *Encyclopaedia of North-East India*, Vol. VI, *Nagaland*, p. 214.
18. Noklang, C. Amop, *Phom Day: A Basis for Peace in Nagaland*, p.11.
19. The information was collected from the Directorate of Soil and Water Conservation, *op. cit.*
20. *Ibid.*
21. *Basic Facts 2002, Nagaland*, p. 4.
22. Hutton, J., *Report on Naga Hills*, pp. 14-15.
23. Henshet, B., *The Phom-Naga Indigenous Religion: A Socio-Philosophical Perspective*, p. 11.
24. Imnayongdang, *Levels of Rural Development in Nagaland: A Spatial Analysis*, p. 23.
25. *Ibid.*, p. 24.
26. *Ibid.*.
27. *Ibid.*, p. 20.
28. Ghosh, B. B. (ed.), *Nagaland District Gazetteers, Tuensang District*, p. 12.
29. *Souvenir 1980-2005*, Commemorating 25 Years of Village Development Boards, p. 102; Allen, B.C., Gait, E.A., Allen, C.G.H. & Howard, H.F. (ed.), *Op. cit.*, p. 469.
    Tamlu is the only subdivision of the Longleng district headed by an ADC (Civil).
30. Ghosh, B.B. (ed.), *Op. cit.*, pp. 12-13.
31. *Ibid,* p. 5.
32. *Ibid.*
33. Michell, John F., *The North East Frontier of India,* pp. 223-224.
34. Bareh, H.M., *Op. cit.*, p. 218.
35. Ghosh, B. B. (ed.), *op. cit.*, p. 5.
36. *Ibid*, p. 6.
37. Interview held with T. Ponglong Phom (52), Chairman of Subdividional Chamber of Commerce Unit, Longleng, at Longleng on 12-10-2003.
38. *Nagaland Forest Statistical Book, 1979.*
39. Ganguli, Milada, *A Pilgrimage to the Nagas*, p. 212. Milada Ganguli, a native of Czechoslovakia was married to a member of the family of the great Indian poet Rabindranath Tagore.
40. *Basic Facts 2004, Nagaland*, pp. 15-16.
41. According to the Nagaland Village and Area Councils Act, 1978, village means and includes an area recognised as a village as such by the Government of Nagaland. An area, designated as a village under this Act, shall fulfil the following conditions, namely:

(a) The land in the area belong to the population of that area or given to them by the Government of Nagaland, if the land in question is a Government land or is given to them by the lawful owner of the land, and

(b) The village is established according to the usage and customary practice of the population of the area. 'The Nagaland Village and Area Councils Act, 1978', *Nagaland Gazette*, 31 March, 1979, Part–V, p. 45. Every government recognised village has a Village Council and a Village Development Board.

42. This information was collected from the DC Office, Longleng in 2012. Village names have been mentioned here in accordance with the spellings recorded in the *Census of India* 2011. Some of these Phom villages were formerly known by other names. For instance, Bura Namsang was known as Namsang Chingchang or Resong or Namsang, Hukpang as Siphang, Ladaigarh as Borhola, Orangkong as Wankhong or Rangkong, Pongching as Phomching, Shitap as Moichangching, Yaong as Chihu, Yongam as Shemmong, Yongphang as Chamba, Yongshei as Kamahu. Mongnyu is presently known as Bhumnyu.
43. *Primary Census Abstract – Nagaland 2011*, *Op. cit.*. Although Longleng was upgraded to a district in January 2004, for convenience of the study the name of the Longleng district has been used now and then by referring to the years prior to 2004 instead of mentioning as Longleng subdivision.
44. *Census of India 1991*, *Op. cit.*, pp. 35 and 155.
45. Each of the places mentioned above has a Phom Baptist Church, *Phom Baptist Christian Association, Golden Jubilee,* 1953-2003, *Bushah Laitap* (History Book), p. 12.
46. The village Anaki is under Mokokchung district and one of its *khels* (subdivision) is dominated by the Aos and another by the Phoms.
47. Government Notification No. OM No. AR/8/9/79 (PT-II), dated 16-8-1979, collected from the Additional Deputy Commissioner's Office, Longleng.
48. 'The Constitution (Nagaland) Scheduled Tribes Order 1970', in Atsongchanger, Mar (compiled), *The Historical Memoranda of the Nagas and Their Neighbours*, p. 120.
49. Henshet, B., *Op. cit.*, p. 9.
50. Interview held with Apisangpa (70), retired *Do-Bhashi*, at Bahok Colony, Longleng on 20-05-2004.
51. *Phom Day, Golden Jubilee*, 1952-2002, 5-6 June, 2002, *Bushah Laitap* (History Book), p. 11.
52. Henshet, B., *Op. cit.*, p. 10.
53. The folk tale runs as follows: Once upon a time, there was a well organised village named Yingnyuching. After some time, the village started missing children one after another. The villagers had become anxious and held a meeting to trace out the miracle. The youth of each *morung* started to keep a close watch on the happenings in the village. Once by chance a youth on duty saw an animal coming towards him and he at once cut the head of the

animal with his *dao* (a large multipurpose chopping knife). The animal was unknown to the villagers and the meat of the animal was distributed among all the villagers but a widow was accidently left out. That very night the earth of the village started cracking and heavy erosion followed. In panic the villagers began to run in different directions but the abode of the widow remained intact which is presently called Yingnyushang. *Phom Day, Golden Jubilee*, 1952-2002, *Op. cit.*, p. 12.

54. Diary of A. E. Shuttle Worth for the month of October 1895, Secret Department, file no. 439.
55. Interview held with Apisangpa (70), *Op. cit.*
56. Sardeshpande, S.C., *The Patkoi Nagas*, pp. 112-119; Konyak, A. Yanang, *From Darkness to Light*, p. 2.
57. Alemchiba, M., *A Brief Historical Account of Nagaland*, p. 21.
58. Smith, William C., *The Ao-Naga Tribe of Assam*, pp. 52-53.
59. Furer-Haimendrof, Christoph von, *Return to the Naked Nagas*, pp. 44-45.
60. Henshet, B., *Op. cit.*, p. 10. The place Longtrok is situated near Chungliyimti village and occupied by the Sangtam tribe of Tuensang district.
61. 'Slavery in the Unadministered Area between Assam and Burma', 1916, General Department, file no. 324.
62. Mills, J.P., *The Ao Nagas*, p. 6.
63. *Phom Baptist Christian Association, Golden Jubilee,* 1953-2003, *Op. cit.*, p. 11.
64. 'Note on including the Trans-Dikhu tribes within an area of Political Control', 1889-90, Political Department, file no. 14; Hutton, J., *Op. cit.*, p. 8.
65. 'Angpan and Totang VS Phum', 11.6.09, General Department, file no. 269.
66. Furer-Haimendrof, Christoph von, *Op. cit.*, p. 107. The Konyaks called the village Phum or Phom probably because the village was formerly surrounded by banyan trees which are called *Bham* in the Phom language.
67. Interview held with Apisangpa (70), *op. cit.* Apisangpa also stated that sometime after the establishment of Longleng administrative centre, the elders of the Phomching renounced the name given by the Changs and renamed the village as Pongching. *Pong* in Pongching dialect is man and *ching* means village, which can be stated as man's village.
68. 'Raid by the Phum village of Hukpang against Orangkhung', 1910, General Department, file no. 290.
69. 'Raid on Ourangkong', 20.7.1919, General Department, file no. 333.
70. *Ibid.*
71. 'Slavery in the Unadministered Area between Assam and Burma', 1916, *op. cit.*
72. Hutton, J., *Op. cit.*, M.A.S.B., Plate 16.
73. Rahman, Abdur, 'The Place of Female in Phom Society', paper presented in a Seminar entitled 'Socio-Educational Status of Phom Community', held at Yingli College, Longleng on July 9-10, 1997. The Phom people write the word '*Bhum*' to mean cloud but pronounce it as '*Phum*'.
74. Bareh, H.M., *Op. cit.*, p. 93.

75. Ghosh, B.B. (ed.), *Op. cit.*, p. 34.
76. Davis, A.W., *Census of India, 1891*, Assam, Vol. I, quoted in Verrier Elwin, *The Nagas in the Nineteenth Century*, p. 398.
77. Hutton, J.H., *The Angami Nagas,* p. 383. This custom was popular more among the non-Christian people which continued till about the third quarter of the last century.
78. Woodthorpre, R.G., *'General Report of the Topographical Surveys, 1875-76'* quoted in Verrier Elwin, *op. cit.*, p. 385.
79. Bareh, H.M., *Op. cit.*, p. 216.
80. Henshet, B., *Op. cit.*, p. 15.
81. Noklang, C. Amop, *Op. cit.*, p. 29.
82. Bareh, H.M., *Op. cit.*, p. 217.
83. Noklang, C. Amop, *Op. cit.*, p. 22.
84. Mills, J.P., *Op. cit.*, p. 333. There are some groups of villages among the Aos, whose dialects and pronunciation differ. Among the distinct dialects Chongli and Mongsen are remarkable.
85. Noklang, C. Amop, *Op. cit.*
86. *Census 1971, District Census Handbook, Tuensang District*, pp. 26. and 74.
87. Noklang, C. Amop, *Op. cit.*, p. 30.
88. Woodthorpe, R.G., *Op. cit.*, p. 382; Hutton, J., *Op. cit.*, p. 17.
89. Ghosh, B.B., *History of Nagaland*, p. 212.
90. Woodthorpe, R.G., *Op. cit.*, pp. 390-391.
91. Ao, M. Alemchiba, *The Arts and Crafts of Nagaland*, p. 44.
92. Hutton, J., *Op. cit.*, p. 9.
93. Hutton, J.H., *Op. cit.*, pp. 382-383.
94. Davis, A.W., *Op. cit.*, p. 398.
95. Hutton, J., *Op. cit.*, p. 10.
96. *Ibid*, p. 21.
97. Davis, A.W., *Op. cit.*, p. 398.
98. Ao, M. Alemchiba, *Op. cit.*, p. 45.
99. Interview held with L. Shaupang Phom (78), retired government employee, at Longleng on 01-12-2003.
100. Hutton, J., *Op. cit.*, p. 9.
101. *Ibid.*, p. 11.
102. Interview held with Anyak Phom (79), retired *Do-Bhashi*, at Longleng on 11-04-2001.
103. Mills, J.P., *Op. cit.*, p. 47. The custom was probably in vogue in a few villages only.
104. Elwin, Verrier, *The Art of the North-East Frontier of India*, p. 135.
105. *Ibid.*
106. *Ibid.*, p. 139.
107. *Ibid.*, p. 142.
108. Ganguli, Milada, *Op. cit.*, p. 215.
109. *Ibid*, p. 216.

110. Henshet, B., *Op. cit.*, p. 29.
111. *Ibid.*, p. 30.
112. *Ibid.*, p. 25.
113. *Ibid.*, p. 31.
114. Noklang, C. Amop, *Op. cit.*, p. 36.
115. Henshet, B., *Op. cit.*, p. 37.
116. Woodthorpe, R. G., *Op. cit.*, p. 382.
117. Henshet, B., *Op. cit.*, p. 46.
118. Interview held with Kongyan Phom (40), Medical Officer, at Longleng on 05-02-2003.
119. Noklang, C. Amop, *op. cit.*, pp. 35-36; Interview held with Kongyan Phom (40), *op. cit.*
120. *Ibid.*
121. Interview held with Anyak Phom (79), *op. cit.* The interviewee informed that he himself attended many such functions.
122. Henshet, B., *Op. cit.*, p. 50.
123. Hutton, J. H., *Op. cit.*, p. 3.
124. Henshet, B., *Op. cit.*, p. 41.
125. *Ibid*, p. 42. The tribe has four major festivals including *Monyu* which is celebrated in April and the *Pangmo* that falls in November.
126. *Ibid.*, p. 47.
127. Ganguli, Milada, *Op. cit.*, p. 214. Woodthorpe, R.G., *Op. cit.*, p. 384. Woodthorpe stated about the practice referring to the 'Yajim' (Yachem) and 'Chihu' (Yaong) villages.
128. *Ibid*, pp. 384-385.
129. Davis, A.W., *Op. cit.*, pp. 399-400. Davis wrote about the funeral practice of Tamlu and 'Resong' (Bura Namsang) villages.
130. Elwin, Verrier, *The Art of the North-East Frontier of India*, p. 142.
131. *Ibid*, p. 141.
132. *Ibid*, pp. 142-143.
133. *Ibid*, p. 144.
134. Bareh, H.M., *op. cit.*, p. 217.
135. Interview held with Y.B. Angam Phom (47), ex-President of PPC and public leader, at Longleng on 10-04-2003.
136. Hutton, J., *op. cit.*, p. 7.
137. Henshet, B., *op. cit.*, p. 40.
138. Elwin, Verrier, *Nagaland*, p. 10.
139. Woodthorpe, R.G., *op. cit.*
140. 'Slavery in the Unadministered Area between Assam and Burma', 1916, *Op. cit.*
141. 'Angpan and Totang VS Phum', *op. cit.;* Foot note by J.H.H. in J.P. Mills' *The Ao Nagas*, p. 279.
142. Noklang, C. Amop, *Op. cit.*, p. 40; Henshet, B., *Op. cit.*, p. 46.
143. Interview held with L. Shaupang Phom (78), *op. cit.*

2

Historical and Political Evolution till Independence

It has already been stated that the words 'Phum' and 'Phom' were first used by some of the British officers in their official reports and correspondences with the Government. It was perhaps from 1916 onwards, following Hutton's submission of a report on slavery in the un-administered area between Assam and Burma; that the present word 'Phom' gradually replaced 'Phum', which was more frequently used earlier. Writing about this tribe he wrote, "This tribe consists of four villages only, Hukpang, Pongching, Ourangkong, and Mongnyu, and seems closely allied to the Changs."[1] He further noted in his tour diary of 1923, "Pongo is a Konyak village, probably with a strongish Phom admixture permanently at war with Hukpang."[2] In the Annual Administrative Report of 1920-21 it was stated, "As usual the most disturbed area has been that occupied by Konyak and Phom villages between the Yongyu and Dikhu Rivers."[3] The British officials expressed different opinions in regard to two Phom villages – Yaong and Yachem. While camping on the bank of the Dikhu river Hutton noted, "A second deputation came in from Kamahu, and some of the headmen of Yacham, a transfrontier Ao village with probably a good dash of Phom and Konyak blood."[4] J. P. Mills wrote:

> "Yacham and their small neighbour Yong, for instance, speak a dialect resembling Chongli, but follow Phom or Konyak customs to a great extent. Yacham recently told me that they really did not know what they were—Aos would not recognise them as Aos and their trans-Dikhu neighbours would not accept them as kinsmen."[5]

This controversy was finally put to rest when in 1942, S.D.O. (Civil), Mokokchung officially accepted all the villages situated between the Dikhu and the Yungnyu rivers as Phom villages.[6]

The Phom villages of Tamlu and Bura Namsang areas had remained a part of the Naga Hills district for a long time but they had different culture from the Ao[7] and the Konyak tribes in many ways including dress, hair style, language, etc. Christoph von Furer-Haimendrof while visiting the area in 1936-37 referred to Tamlu and Kangching as Konyak villages.[8] L. Kijung Ao, a Naga missionary observed: "Although the Phom have a distinct culture as a separate entity among the Naga tribes, they were mistaken to be grouped with the Konyaks and those who settled closer to the Changs were mistaken with the Chang."[9] The establishment of the Phom Baptist Churches in separation from the Konyak Baptist Churches in the area after 1929 helped the Phom tribe to preserve a distinct Phom identity.[10] The common cultural traits of the Phom villages on either side of the Dikhu river further strengthened their cultural and linguistic identity. The present Tamlu subdivision was a part of the Naga Hills district and the rest of the Phom areas were under the North-East Frontier Tract in 1951.[11] In 1957, Tamlu area was included in Tuensang district.[12] Thus, the territorial integrity of the Phom area was completed which now forms the present Longleng district.

Village Government

Before the formation of modern village councils the Phom villages had two types of village governments, namely the republican government and the other one was republican form of monarchy where the *Angh* (chief) played an important role.

The status of the republican governments which were in existence in most of the Phom villages before coming in contact with the British can be termed as village states where there was total absence of outside interference with the exception of satellite villages. A powerful village used to have subordinate adjoining villages which it used to protect. In return the protected villages had to pay tribute and fighting men to the protecting village. Each Phom village was more or less self-sufficient in needs. The sovereign village assembly determined their internal administration and external policy. Its functions can be divided into administrative, executive, judiciary and legislative. Decision on any matter was taken unanimously.

Each village had a self-governing assembly that was constituted by the members, namely *Shahbupa, Metbupa, Bangba, Manba, Hamba* and the representative of every clan. *Shahbupa* was a skilful orator who had wide knowledge of the customs, culture and history of the tribe. He also acted as judge at the time of emergency.[13] *Metbupa* was the representative of a particular clan whose consent was necessary in taking major decisions by the Village Council. He also caused the war weapons cleaned during war.[14] Most of the meetings of the Council were held in the house of the *Bangba. Manba* was a rich man while *Hamba* was a warrior.[15] Internal disputes of the Phom villages were settled according to the customary laws which were respected by all. External disputes were settled through joint meetings of two or more villages, failing which war became inevitable.

Thus, it can be inferred that the members of the village assembly were elected on the basis of merits. Right person was holding the right portfolio. The requisite qualifications to be a member of the village government were: he should not be the son of an undeclared father, a widower or a handicapped person, and he must be a respectable man of the village.[16] A member could hold office so long it was deemed fit. The members were elected consensually.

However, from 1889-90 the British Government began to appoint *Gaon-Buras* (village headmen) by degrees in the Phom villages. They were helped by village elders who were known as *barricks.*[17] Since then, the *Gaon-Buras* began to play a major role in village administration and in its external policy. With the gradual introduction of the office of *Gaon-Bura* and incorporation of the Phom villages to the British dominion, the sovereign power that was enjoyed by the traditional village assembly for centuries began to decline.

Angh

The *Angh* system of government was also in existence among the lower Konyak villages of Mon district. The Konyak Anghs enjoyed maximum powers, whereas the powers of the Phom *Anghs* were limited and they were assisted by the village headmen (elders). The *Anghs* of the Phom villages usually acted as the heads of warriors, whereas, the village headmen were vested with administrative and judicial powers.[18] The *Anghship* was hereditary based on the principle of primogeniture. On the death of an *Angh* his eldest son assumed his office. A powerful *Angh* exercised his power over the neighbouring villages directly or through his family members. The powerful *Angh* used to collect tributes like paddy, clothes, arms, etc., from their subordinate *Anghs*. Similarly, petty *Anghs* received tributes and free labour service from their own subjects. The power and authority of the puppet *Anghs* confined to their respective villages.

The *Anghship* was in existence in Phom society for a long time in the villages of Yongam, Bhumnyu, Yongshei, Tangha, Kangching, Yongyah and Tamlu.[19] The villages Namsang, Tamlu, Kangching, Tangha, etc., were under the chief of Wanching (Konyak) village.[20] Prior to 1923 the Yongam village was invaded and destroyed by a more powerful neighbouring village Yongyah, which compelled the subdued villagers to accept an *Angh* from the Yungya village. Accordingly, an *Angh* family was sent to Yongam[21] and the successor of the family is still holding the office of the *Angh*. Hutton wrote in 1923, "Yongam was formerly large and powerful village, they told me, which was eventually defeated by Yungya, treacherously of course, and now pays her tribute".[22]

The creation of the office of the *Gaon-Bura* and the help received by him from the *barrick* curtailed the powers of the *Angh* to a great extent.[23] In recent years Village Councils have been created which look after the village administration within their respective jurisdictions. The *Anghs* are, however, enjoying life membership in these Councils, though they are deprived of their original powers.

Gaon-Bura **and *Do-Bhashi***

The British Government created two native administrative agencies, namely *Gaon-Bura* and *Do-Bhashi*. The authorities in Mokokchung appointed *Gaon-Buras* in the Phom villages[24] primarily to stop the practice of headhunting and settle village disputes.[25] They had to abide by the policy of the government in relation to their respective villages. The *Gaon-Buras* of the Tamlu area were appointed earlier than the villages to the east of the Dikhu river. The *Gaon-Buras* of the Tamlu area used to collect house tax annually of Rs. 2 per house and deposit the same in the office of the S.D.O. Mokokchung. In return they received a commission of 12½ per cent on the gross collection. They also received red blankets after every three years.[26] The *barricks* were there to assist the *Gaon-Buras* in the village administration. The European officers intervened only in disputes, which could not be settled by the *Gaon-Buras* and *Do-Bhashis*.[27]

Do-Bhashis were the interpreters who represented the principal villages and tribes. They were the spokesmen of the people they represented and were able to communicate in broken Assamese, the *lingua franca,* with the European officers on all matters concerning the disputes, etc. Piketo Sema wrote, "As mediums of communication, they were entrusted with the responsibility of furnishing district officers with native news thus acting as informants as well as the personnel of the intelligence department."[28] Government orders were communicated to the people through them. They could hear and dispose of the cases which could not be dealt with by the villagers. A dissatisfied party, however, had the right to approach the district officers against the verdict.[29] They received salaries from the government. In 1918, each of the Chang, the Sangtam, the Phom and the Konyak *Do-Bhashis* received Rs. 20 per month from the Mokokchung administration.[30] Kangshi who hailed from Pongching acted as government interpreter at Mokokchung before 1923 for some time. B. Limna of Bhumnyu, N. Nangpong of Tamlu Konyak khel[31], Kaulom of Hukpang and Pongoi of Yongshei[32] were some of the government interpreters during the pre-independence period. Hamyei Phom of Tangha village was appointed grade II interpreter on 1 April, 1942 in place of Ekimo Lotha at Mokokchung Sub-Divisional Office.[33] He was a regular government interpreter from 1942 to the dawn of independence. He played an important role in opening the Longleng administrative headquarters and in the unification of the Phom villages.

The *Bang* and the *Ywo*

Every Phom village had a number of *Khels* (sub-divisions), usually they were from three to five, depending on the size of population and the clan of the village. A *Khel* consisted of one or more clans. In some villages different dialects were spoken by the people of different *Khels*. Villages were divided into *Khels* mainly to strengthen the defence and also to provide shelter to the growing population. However, there was strong unity between the members of the *khels* and in case they were attacked by outside enemies they fought collectively.

Each *khel* had a *morung*, i.e. bachelors' dormitory which was called *Bang* by the Phoms. As regards the functions of the *morung* V.K. Anand wrote, "The *morung* not only acted as a hostel, club, public school and military training centre but also provided the conference hall for the elders and operation room during the active periods of hostilities."[34] The *Bangs* were elaborately carved and ornamented. Not only the people carved various figures of animals, reptiles, human beings, etc., in all parts of the *Bangs* but these were also painted in red, black, and white colours.[35] R.G. Woodthorpe wrote about the *morungs* of this part of the hills in the following words:

> "The *morangs* are divided into three partitions — first, the front verandah, enclosed at the sides; second, the body of the house, containing the sleeping apartments and store-rooms on either side of a central passage: each sleeping-room contains four planked beds, arranged in twos like the berths of a ship, on either side of a small fireplace; third, a large room open to the small back verandah: this contains a fire place, with a few planks as seats round it; this room is floored with immense hollowed beams. In the back verandah, which has a low circular roof, are hung all the trophies of war and the chase."[36]

A peculiar custom prevailing among the Phoms was that the skulls of enemies taken in battle were decorated with a pair of horns attached to the ears. These horns were either of buffalo or *mithun,* and failing these, wooden imitations were attached.[37] This was done presumably to render the skulls deaf.[38] Grass tassels were attached at the ends of the horns.[39] Stones were also used in building the *morungs.*[40] Long trusses of special grass were used for the decoration of the front facades of *morungs.*[41] The following account is found in the Census of India 1891 about the *morungs* of Tamlu and Bura Namsang:

> "These buildings are situated close to the village gate, and at a short distance look like huge thatched bungalows. They consist of a large verandah, generally raised, as at Resong, a considerable distance above the ground, a central hall, and a small back verandah. In the front verandah are collected all the trophies of war and of the chase, from a man's skull down to a monkey's, most of them black with the smoke and dust of years. From the verandah one enters the large central hall. Lengthways along both sides of this are ranged the sleeping berths of the young men, while the centre space, which is

> floored with massive planks, is left quite open, and is used by the braves for their dances. Behind this hall, again, is the small back verandah, which often communicates by a raised footway with the lookout house, situated in some convenient tree just outside the village door."[42]

The Phom boys used to sleep in the *morungs* at night till they got married. Newly admitted batch of boys used to make the fire; collect firewood, water, betel and betel nut for the seniors. They were taught the art of making basket, rope, mat, *dao*, headgear, etc. Here, the Phom youngsters acquired all the necessary knowledge which greatly helped them to guide their society in future. Strict discipline was maintained in the *morung.* It also served as the watch-tower regarding the movements of the foes. *Khel* meetings were held here[43] before the construction of the Village Council hall. On such occasion, people gathered in the *morung* when the meeting was convened.[44]

Shems, i.e. huge log drums were kept in the *morungs*, each of these was made of single gigantic hewn-out log. *Shems* were beaten with wooden hammers to produce various notes with a view to conveying the messages to far-flung areas about various events. B. Henshet writes, "*Shem* is beaten to herald the arrival of festival, to proclaim the feast of merit, to inform the arrival of enemy, victory or defeat in war, to announce community mourning for the death of a rich man, warrior and so on."[45] To denote different events they produced different notes. After all, it was the most popular means of communication in the traditional Phom society.

Most of these age-long creative arts began to disappear and the *morung,* which had remained the chief meeting place of men for long, lost its significance from the mid-twentieth century when the Christian missionaries persuaded the inhabitants of the area to give up the old customs of their forefathers as part of their baptizing mission.[46] Notwithstanding this, the *morungs* are still seen in good conditions in all the Phom villages which remind us of their rich cultural heritage of the bygone days.

During the pre-Christian days, each clan of a village had also a girls' dormitory which was called *Yow* by the Phoms. Unmarried lasses used to sleep in the *Yow.*[47] The young men, especially the lovers of a clan could visit any *yow*, other than their own clan and spent their time in singing love songs and chatting. The boys here received betel leaves from their girlfriends as a gesture of love. The Phoms traditionally follow exogamous principle in the matter of marriage and it is highly shameful to make jokes or use vulgar words before the girls of the same clan. Therefore, the boys were not allowed to visit *yow* of their own clan. In contrast, the girls were not permitted to visit any *morung* except on very special occasions. In case a girl became pregnant her lover had to marry her, failing which a heavy fine, viz. land, house, animals, etc., was imposed on him. For girls, the *yows* were the training grounds. They received various trainings like folk songs, folk dances, ballads, spinning, weaving, etc., which helped them to lead a happy and comfortable life after marriage.

Head-hunting: Its Origin and Growth

The practice of killing, beheading and taking away human head as trophy is commonly known as headhunting. Like other Naga tribes this practice was common among the Phoms and it continued till 1950. There are many stories which are in vogue among the Phoms regarding the origin of this practice. One such story which they claim to have influenced them most runs as follows:

> "Initially, the idea of head-hunting was derived when a spider from one side of a stream went to the other side of the stream hanging over her thread and chopped off the head of a mantis and went back to previous side of the stream."[48]

Whether one believes or not the above story or other stories about the origin of the practice of headhunting, it is an accepted fact that human heads were valued high in Phom society from very early times. The loss of a head, therefore, was immediately retaliated by counter attack. Sometimes, powerful villages also invaded weaker villages with the intention of dominating them and collecting tribute. The boundary dispute was one of the important causes of the conflict between the villages. C. Amop Noklang writes:

> "A man may be poor or from an ordinary family but when he took the head of an enemy, he was given the title *Hamba* meaning hero and was highly revered by the entire community. So, there was a constant competition among the men of the village to obtain the title *Hamba.*"[49]

A man who had collected several heads, enjoyed the privilege of offering a grand feast for the entire community, and as a sign of his bravery he was entitled to tattoo his chest with a particular pattern or design.[50] Human skull was precious for them who held the view that all mental and physical strength of a man was concentrated in the head. It was their common belief that headhunting was also associated with ceremonial cannibalism to increase one's own fertility to get large number of healthy children.[51] Over and above the *morungs,* in some villages war trophies were kept suspended against the front wall of the houses of the senior members of the clan after the completion of the customary ceremonies.[52] The name of some villages reflects the bravery of their inhabitants for which they were known in the days gone by.

As warfare continued ceaselessly among the Phom villages, so every village was compelled to take steps to tighten its defence by planting bamboo *panjis* (spikes), digging ditches, making ladder, planting stumped branch plants and constructing stone and wooden walls. Cross-bow, spear, *dao,* shield and *panji* were some of the weapons used by the Phom warriors while fighting against their enemies. The shield was made of buffalo skin. *Panjis* were planted on the retreating path to resist the movement of the enemies.[53] From the beginning of the twentieth century guns came into use.[54] During raids the warriors used to carry mini baskets ostensibly for carrying heads.[55]

Feuds not only took place among various tribes, villages belonging to the same tribe also occasionally fought each other for mastery. For example, on 15 September, 1921, Yachem village was attacked by about thirty-five villages including Pongching, Mongtikang, Yongphang, etc.[56] Villages like Tamlu and Bura Namsang, with only a valley separating them, were at war for many years in the past.[57] There was even lack of unity among the different *khels* or clans of a village. Hutton wrote in his report that the village of Yongnyah was divided into five clans out of which two were hostile to Yongshei and friendly to the neighbouring village Tangha, the other three being friendly to Yongshei and ill-disposed towards Tangha.[58] Even sometimes one village used to deceive another village in the guise of a friend. Mills reported:

> "A large force of Changs assembled to attack Yacham and reached Yong, a village about a furlong from Yacham, soon after dawn. Yong had promised to help the Changs, but played

> a double game and warned Yacham, who surrounded Yong and left the Changs walk into the trap. Yacham fired a gun, hitting the chief of Litim in the leg, and attacked. The Changs fled in wild confusion and lost fourteen heads.[59]

When the warriors brought heads to their village, they were greeted by the men and women of the village and log drum was beaten with distinct tune which conveyed the messages to the people of far flung areas regarding their victories. The menfolk adorned the formal warrior dress and performed headhunting songs and dances amidst feast and festivity.[60] Their songs reflected the triumph of victories and demoralized the vanquished powers. Today, the practice has become a story of the past. Yet, the songs, dances and stories related to the head hunting are still preserved by the people.

While visiting hostile villages, the Phom people used to wear bits of sword-grass or some other sharp grass as it was the custom usually followed in such cases.[61] Preliminary negotiations between villages at war were carried on by ambassadors appointed for such purposes. Such persons enjoyed immunity as it was believed that killing or harming the negotiators would bring misfortune to the offender and his village.[62] The ambassadors carried with them a branch of a particular tree as a sign of peace-making. In some cases, after peace was restored, belligerent villagers collected water-worn stones and deposited them under their chief trees and took a pledge not to fight again till the stones had rotten. In the event of war being resumed the stones were dug out as 'witnesses'. The perpetrators sought forgiveness for undoing their pledge.[63] Peace was normally restored between the neighbouring villages during agricultural seasons because it was their main stay. When the villages were at peace the competition of head collection ceased for the time being and it created a congenial atmosphere for the boys or girls of one village to visit another village in groups. In this way the unmarried youths of opposite sexes of different villages met one another and spent pleasant moments in singing, dancing and chatting. In the course of such mingling, it was not uncommon that a couple of opposite sexes fell in love and got married.

In those days villagers went to the cultivation field in groups. The armed warriors guarded their children and women while working in the fields. They also provided tight security to them on the way to field and back to the village. The enemies did not even hesitate to chop off the heads of children and women as their war trophies.

From 1888 the British officers sent punitive expeditions to bring the offending Phom villages to book for taking part in headhunting activities, particularly when they committed raids into the areas beyond the Dikhu river. Of the punitive measures taken by them the most serious was the expedition of 16 April, 1888 against Yachem village. The expedition was reportedly sent to punish Yachem and Yaong villages for their raids on Unger and Akhoia villages. Yachem was a large and strongly defended village. It was surrounded by deep ditches with stakes and stout stockades. The armed villagers barred all approaches. They were combating with cross-bow and spears but in the long run the Yachem warriors withdrew their defence amid heavy casualties. On the part of the British, several sepoys were injured.[64] Accompanied by some soldiers, the Deputy Commissioner, Naga Hills district and the Sub-Divisional Officer, Mokokchung, visited the guilty villages and punished them by imposing fine and sentencing the accused to various terms of imprisonment.[65]

Neighbourhood Relations

The Phom villages bordering Assam had a long history of political and trade relations with the plains of Assam since the Ahom period unlike the villages in the remote hills which remained in isolation. Occasionally, however, war broke out between the two. In 1535, hostilities broke out between the Khamjang, Tablung and Namsang Nagas on the one hand and the Ahoms on the other. The Khamjang Nagas soon took to their knees before the Ahoms. The Ahom troops, however, suffered a setback at the hands of the other two and were forced to retreat with the loss of four guns. Shortly after, the Nagas made their submission to the Ahoms and returned the guns.[66]

The fugitive Ahom prince Godapani (afterwards king Gadadhar Singha, 1681-96) sojourned through a few Ao villages from where he proceeded to the Phom and the Konyak areas.[67] It is believed in the Bhumnyu village that once upon a time an Ahom raja (probably Gadapani) made a brief halt in a place near the village. As per another legend of Bura Namsang village, Godapani took shelter for a brief period at Bura Namsang. After ascending the throne the king rewarded the village with various articles, viz. one golden idol, one drum, necklaces, betel plants for plantation, etc., for the hospitality he had received during his short stay at Bura Namsang. Some of these articles are still preserved by the Bura Namsang villagers.[68]

Bura Namsang and other Naga villages near Assam were usually called *Bori*, or dependent by the Assamese people, whereas the Nagas living in the interior hills were called *Abor*, or independent. The *Boris* kept the internal trade in their hands and controlled the access of the *Abors* into Assam.[69] A government report of 1873 stated 'Gelaki' (Geleki), situated on the southern border of Sibsagar district as the *duar* (gate), or gateway to Assam. The Phom people of the villages like Bura Namsang, Tamlu and Kangching entered the plains of Assam through this *duar*. The report further stated that the *duar* was put under the care of four *kotokies* (envoys).[70] The Naga villagers bordering on Assam used to exchange their hill products like cotton, betel, ginger, taro, etc., for the articles in which they were deficient.[71] Yachem and Yaong villages had regular and duty free transaction with the frontier Ao villages since 1888.[72] The people of these two villages went across the Ao villages to buy salt at Amguri and Geleki and this traffic helped them to develop direct communication with Akhoia, Unger, Chuchu and other Ao villages beyond the Dikhu river.[73] The Ao people used to sell salt and cloths to the Phom people for pig, fowl, etc. Some of the Ao villages, i.e. Unger and Chuchuyimlang bought *mithun* from the Phoms.[74]

Trade fair was held once in a year at Bhumnyu village during Monyu festival. People from different Phom villages and also from the Ao, the Konyak and the Chang tribes participated in the trade fair with their products. *Dao,* gun, cotton, etc., were brought by the Konyaks; the Aos living near the Dikhu river brought cloth, tea, etc., and the Phom people received them in exchange of their articles, viz. earthen pot, betel, etc., in the fair. Barter system was the chief means of transaction.[75]

British Policy Towards the Phom Villages

As stated above the Phom villages bordering on Assam had trade relations with the plains of Sibsagar chiefly through the Geleki *duar*. Whenever, outrage was committed by the Nagas the British used to close the *duar* or market, which compelled them to surrender the offenders to the authorities. In April 1861, the Geleki *duar* was closed at the orders of the Commissioner of Assam in consequence of a murder taking place in the *duar*. The *Abor* Nagas surrendered five of their men in connection with the murder under mounting pressure of the *Bori* (or *Boree)* Nagas including Bura Namsang village in the following year of the murder.[76] In 1866, an order was issued which prohibited the Nagas from entering British territory with arms. Following this the Nagas were required to leave all their weapons at the guard-house.[77] In November 1867, the Geleki guard house was once again attacked at night and some of the constables were killed. The *duar* was closed for trade. The closure proved successful. The Tablong, Namsang and other Naga villages, had regular traffic with the tea gardens on the border, jointly traced out the raiders and delivered two of their leaders over to the British authorities for trial. These men, belonged to Yongnyah (*Abor Naga)* village, who in search of human heads stealthily reached there through trackless jungles and attacked the police station under the notion that it was a settlement of rayats.[78]

The district headquarters for the Naga Hills was opened at Samaguting in 1866 but later shifted to Kohima in 1878.[79] The colonial government's desire to extend its administrative control became evident when a new subdivision was set up at Wokha in 1875 to control the powerful Lotha villages of that area.[80] In 1889, the Ao territory was incorporated with the Naga Hills with the concurrence of the tribe who were suffering from the attacks of more warlike tribes across the Dikhu river.[81] The subdivision that was opened at Wokha was shifted to Mokokchung in 1889 with the incorporation of the Ao territories. Phom villages like Tamlu, Bura Namsang, etc., of the present Tamlu subdivision of Longleng district were also annexed along with the Ao areas and added to the Mokokchung subdivision. In order to protect that area from the attack of the villages across the Dikhu river, most notably, Yongnyah and Tangha, a stockade with a guard of thirty militiamen was set up at Tamlu in April 1889.[82] Some of the newly annexed villages to the east of Tamlu were looked after from Tamlu outpost[83] until a post was established at Wakching (Konyak area) in the second decade of the twentieth century.[84]

The Phom villages including Yongshei, Yongnyah and Tangha in the east of the Dikhu river were punished in 1889 for their raids on the Ao villages. These three villages along with Pohum (Bhumnyu) sent an emissary with a small gift to Tamlu outpost expressing their desire to be at peace with the British Government.[85] Since, then the Phom villages abstained themselves from clash with the British. The British administrators were in favour of inclusion of the areas between the Dikhu and the Yungnyu rivers in the politically controlled[86] area in order to stop the village feuds. Even appeals were sought from across the border for assistance on several occasions.[87] In a letter to Maspratt, S.D.O., Mokokchung, dated 20.11.1890 it was stated:

> "The policy to adopt laid down by the C.C. Assam and the Government of India is and always has been one of absolute non-interference with the internal affairs or quarrels of the people across the Dikhu."[88]

At the same time it was made clear to further the villages east of the Dikhu river that any raids on villages on British side of the Dikhu would be followed by prompt and exemplary punishment.[89] Thus, the Government was not in favour of further extension of the political control area to the east of the Dikhu river. In 1893, some villagers of Orangkong killed some people of Yongnyah[90] and again, Yongshei raided Tangha and took several heads along with 16 prisoners in 1910 but the authorities did not take any action ostensibly on the ground that these villages were across the border and did not directly trouble the British.[91]

From 1910 the British set about to extend the area of their political control and in the next three decades expeditions were sent off and on to punish the guilty villages for carrying out headhunting activities.[92] For instance, the Deputy Commissioner of Naga Hills and the S.D.O., Mokokchung, visited Yachem and imposed a fine of two *mithuns* on it for ambushing some Yongshei men while returning from Mokokchung in January 1921.[93] By the end of the third decade of the twentieth century the British brought all the villages extending up to the Yangmun river under their control.[94] Thus, the Phom villages in the east of the Dikhu river remained under political control of the English till independence. Piketo Sema wrote:

> "In the administered areas, the Nagas paid house tax as a recognition of British authority over them and in return received the protection of the Government from the raids of their neighbours living beyond the pale of administration. In the controlled areas, the Government neither realised house tax nor guaranteed protection from the raids of the independent tribes from beyond the controlled areas. Officers were not supposed to interfere much in the internal affairs of villages in a politically controlled area. It was only obligatory to punish

> in murder cases, but, officers might settle disputes if they could. The tribes living beyond the controlled areas were still free from British interference in their affairs."[95]

According to the Indian (Foreign Jurisdiction) Order in Council, 1902, the power over the territories lying between the Naga Hills district and Burma was exercised by the Governor-General in Council or some authority subordinate to him, namely the Governor of Assam.[96] Notwithstanding this, chaotic condition continued in the Phom villages to the east of the Dikhu river. The area came to be known as 'Tribal Area' under Section 311 of the Government India Act, 1935. The area was placed directly under the administrative control of the Governor of Assam and the Deputy Commissioner of Naga Hills district on behalf of the Governor-General of India representing the British Emperor under the provision of section 313 of the Act.[97] However, the administrative responsibility of the controlled areas of the Naga Tribal Area was practically vested in the Sub-Divisional Officer at Mokokchung.[98] The officers of Naga Hills administration were in favour of annexing the territory lying to the east of the Dikhu river but the Government of India did not approve such a line of action.[99] With the gradual annexation of the areas of the Naga Hills district the law and order situation improved quite a lot which facilitated certain development works, whereas the condition of the tribes residing in the areas of the old Tuensang district (Naga Tribal Area) remained practically unchanged. Verrier Elwin wrote:

> "It was populated by martial tribes; there were no communications and no money to build or maintain them; and despite constant urging that it was inconsistent to develop one part of the hills and neglect another, the Supreme Government felt that until there were men and funds available it would be better to leave this territory alone for the time being."[100]

By the Indian Independence Act of 1947 and the Extra-Provincial Jurisdiction Act of the same year, the Government of India took powers similar to those that had been conferred by the Indian (Foreign Jurisdiction) Order in Council of 1902, and carried on its administration[101] in the usual manner.

NOTES AND REFERENCES

1. Hutton, J.H., *The Angami Nagas,* p. 382.
2. Hutton, J., *Report on Naga Hills,* p. 10. In this report his name is written J. Hutton and not J.H. Hutton.
3. Annual Administrative Report of the Mokokchung Subdivision for the year 1920-21, General Department, file no. 342.
4. Hutton, J., *Report on Naga Hills*, p. 2.
5. Mills, J.P., *The Ao Nagas,* p. 2.
6. *Phom Naga Since 1942,* A Tribute to Late Shri M. Hamyei, Rtd. Political Assistant to Deputy Commissioner, p. 3. It is to be noted that Hamyei, from Tangha village, was recruited as an interpreter in Mokokchung S.D.O. office in 1942 by the name of Hamyei Konyak. Therefore, he applied to change his title from Konyak to Phom.
7. Davis, A.W., *Census of India, 1891*, Assam, Vol. I, pp. 245-246 cited in Verrier Elwin, *The Nagas in the Nineteenth Century,* p. 398.
8. Furer-Haimendrof, Christoph von, *Return to the Naked Nagas*, p. 45.
9. Imchen, Panger (ed.), *L. Kijung Ao the Longest Night* (An Outline Biography of the first Naga Missionary), p. 46.
10. *Ibid.*
11. 'Population and Economic Map of Assam, Manipur and Tripura', *Census of India 1951*, Volume XII, Assam, Manipur and Tripura, Part I-A, Shillong, 1954.
12. Interview held with Anyak Phom (79), retired *Do-Bhashi,* at Longleng on 8-12-2003.
13. Henshet, B., *The Phom-Naga Indigenous Religion: A Socio-Philosophical Perspective,* pp. 11-12.
14. *Ibid;* Noklang, C. Amop, *Phom Day: A Basis for Peace in Nagaland,* p. 24.
15. Henshet, B., *op. cit.*, p. 12.
16. *Ibid;* Noklang, C. Amop, *op. cit.*
17. Interview held with four aged *Gaon-Buras,* namely K. Panglem of Sakchi, Phongang of Yongam, Chingshen of Bura Namsang and S. Pangjei of Bhumnyu on 11-01-2004, 08-09-2003, 25-01-2004 and 14-03-2004 respectively.
18. Ao, Tajenyuba, *British Occupation of Naga Country,* pp. 114-117 & 141.
19. Interview held with four aged *Gaon-Buras, op. cit.*
20. Mills, J.P., *op. cit.*, p. 404; Sema, Piketo; *British Policy and Administration in Nagaland 1881-1947*, p. 30.
21. Sema, Piketo, *op. cit.*
22. *Ibid*, p. 35.
23. *Ibid.*
24. Babu, S.V., 'Reorganisation of *Dobashis* in Naga Hills', the *Proceedings of North East India History Association,*21st Session, 2000, p. 231.
25. Interview held with Hepong Phom (83), ex-Interim Body Member and ex-Regional Council Member, at Longleng on 19-11-2003 and 24-04-2005.

26. *Phom Day, Golden Jubilee* 1952-2002, 5-6 June, 2002, *Bushah Laitap,* p. 13.
27. *Phom Naga Since 1942, Op. cit.*, p. 3.
28. Interview held with N. Hamvok Phom (76), *Do-Bhashi,* at Longleng on 15-01-2003.
29. Ao, Tajenyuba, *op. cit.*, p. 151. In official records the names of the villages were mentioned as follows Bura Namsang as Namsang, Tamlu as Nangta or Nengta, Kangching as Kangsang, Tangha as Tangsa and Wanching as Tabloong or Tablungia. 'Modification of the Inner Line of the Sibsagar District', 1901, Foreign – A, Oct., Nos. 2-43. Also see Michell, John, F., *The North East Frontier of India,* p. 223; Hutton, J.H., *The Angami Nagas, op. cit.*, p. 384. As stated by some of the aged Bura Namsang villagers, the village Wanching situated immediately to the east of the Dikhu river was formerly known as Tablung or Tabloong.
30. Interview held with N. Hamvok Phom (76), *Op. cit.*
31. Hutton, J., *Report on Naga Hills*, p. 8
32. Interview held with Anyak Phom (79), *Op.cit.*
33. Interview held with four Village Council Chairmen, viz. S. Pangjei of Bhumnyu, T.C. Nyamnyei Semdok of Sakchi, B. Angshai Phom of Yongam and A. Hamlang Phom of Bura Namsang on 14-03-2004, 22-01-2004, 07-09-2002 and 25-01-2004 respectively.
34. Anand, V.K., *Conflict in Nagaland: A Study of Insurgency and Counter-Insurgency,* p. 44.
35. Woodthorpe, R.G., 'General Report of the Topographical Surveys, 1875-76', in Verrier Elwin, *The Nagas in the Nineteenth Century,* p. 381.
36. Quoted in *ibid,* pp. 381-382.
37. *Ibid,* p. 382.
38. Mills, J.P., *Op. cit.,* p. 205.
39. Hutton, J., *Report on Naga Hills,* p. 5.
40. *Ibid,* p. 4.
41. Ganguli, Milada, *A Pilgrimage to the Nagas*, p. 216.
42. Davis, A.W., *Op. cit.*, pp. 398-399.
43. Noklang, C. Amop, *op. cit.*, p. 25.
44. Interview held with H. Toshi Phom (47), Longleng Ad hoc Town Committee Member and the Treasurer of LTSU, at PPC Colony, Longleng on 12-01-2003.
45. Henshet, B., *Op. cit.,* p. 17.
46. Ganguli, Milada, *Op. cit.,* p. 218.
47. Henshet, B., *Op. cit.,* p. 16.
48. Cited in B. Henshet, *Op. cit.*, p. 22.
49. Noklang, C. Amop, *Op. cit.*, p. 49.
50. *Ibid.*
51. Phom, N. Chingyam, 'Pre and Post Independence Socio-Economic and Historical Background of Nagaland: Especial Reference to Tuensang', printed in the Proceedings of a Seminar entitled "Over-view of Backward Areas of Nagaland Since Independence", Longleng, 2001, p. 68.

52. Tour Diary of S.J. Duncan for May-June 1950, on Column Duty-Phomching Column, Public Records, file no. 61.
53. Interview held with Anyak Phom (79), *Op. cit.*
54. Ghosh, B.B., *History of Nagaland,* p. 137.
55. Tour Diary of S.J. Duncan for May-June 1950, *Op. cit.*
56. Ao, Tajenyuba, *Op. cit.*, p. 116.
57. Mills, J.P., *Op. cit.*, p. 20.
58. Hutton, J., *Report on Naga Hills,* p. 2.
59. Mills, J.P., *Op. cit.*, p. 66.
60. Interview held with Anyank Phom (79), *Op. cit.*
61. Hutton, J., *Report on Naga Hills,* p. 14.
62. Horam, M., *Naga Polity,* p. 116.
63. Mills, J.P., *Op. cit.*, p. 32.
64. Ao, Tajenyuba, *Op. cit.*, pp. 113-114.
65. *Ibid,* pp. 113-121
66. Devi, Lakshmi, *Ahom-Tribal Relations: A Political Study,* p. 34; Gait, Edward, *A History of Assam,* p. 95.
67. Ghosh, B.B. (ed.), *Nagaland District Gazetteers, Mokokchung District,* p. 39. Gadapani, in order to save his life from the hands of Lara Raja (1679-81), an Ahom King, took shelter for some time in the neighbouring hill areas including a few places in the Naga hills.
68. Interview held with P. Oyemth Phom (30), teacher, at Longleng on 15-01-2004.
69. Devi, Lakshmi, *Op. cit.*
70. Ao, Tajenyuba, *Op. cit.*, p. 155.
71. Devi, Lakshmi, *Op. cit.*, p. 22.
72. 'Note on including the Trans-Dikhu tribes within an area of Political Control', 1889-90, Political Department, file no. 14.
73. 'Slavery in the Unadministrered Area between Assam and Burma, 1916', General Department, file no. 324.
74. Mills, J.P., *Op. cit.*, pp. 103-105.
75. Interview held with N. Hamvok Phom (76), *Op. cit.* The trade fair came to an end in the 1950s, when all the Phom villagers began to celebrate the Monyu festival in fixed dates, April 1-6. Prior to this date different groups of villages were following different convenient dates to celebrate the festival.
76. Mackenzie, Alexander, *The North East Frontier of India*, p. 97.
77. Michell, John F., *Op. cit.*, p. 210.
78. Mackenzie, Alexander, *op. cit.*, pp. 97-98. The warriors from Yongnyah village reached Geleki *duar* in search of human heads. Had they known that the British constables were living in the Geleki guard house probably they would not have attacked them.
79. Sema, Piketo, *Op. cit.*, p. 18.
80. *Ibid,* p. 27.
81. Stracey, P.D., *Nagaland Nightmare,* p. 33.
82. Ao, Tajenyuba, *Op. cit.*, pp. 112-113.

83. *Ibid,* p. 162.
84. Elwin, Verrier, *Nagaland*, p. 28.
85. 'Note on including the Trans-Dikhu tribes within an area of Political Control', 1889-90, *Op. cit.*
86. The Naga hills were divided into three areas, viz. administered areas, political control areas and the areas beyond political control. Sema, Piketo, *Op. cit.,* p. 15.
87. 'The Policy to be Adopted in Dealing Trans-Dikhu villages', dated 21.11.91, Political Department, file no. 183.
88. *Ibid.*
89. *Ibid.*
90. Letter from F.C. Daukes, Secretary to the Chief Commissioner of Assam to the Offg. Deputy Commissioner, Naga Hills, 30th May, 1893, Political Department, file no. 43.
91. 'Report of the head taking of a man of Kamahu by a Party of Tangsa man', 7.10.1910, General Department, file no. 276.
92. Alemchiba, M., *A Brief Historical Account of Nagaland*, p. 128.
93. 'Annual Administrative Report of the Mokokchung subdivision for the year 1920-21, *Op. cit.*; Ao, Tajenyuba, *Op. cit.,* p. 115.
94. Sardeshpande, S.C., *The Patkoi Nagas,* p. 114.
95. Sema, Piketo, *Op. cit.,* p. 15. It may be noted here that the present Tamlu subdivision fell under administrative areas, whereas the remaining parts of Longleng district remained as political control areas.
96. Luthra, P.N., *Nagaland from a District to a State*, p. 7.
97. Luthra, P.N., *Op. cit.* The Government of India Act, 1935 defined 'Tribal Areas means the area along the frontiers of India or in Beluchistan which are not part of British India or of Burma or of any Indian State or of any foreign State'.
98. Sema, Hokishe, *Emergence of Nagaland: Socio-Economic and Political Transformation and the Future,* p. 77.
99. Alemchiba, M., *Op. cit.*
100. Elwin, Verrier, *Nagaland,* p. 27.
101. As per the Extra-Provincial Jurisdiction Act, 1947, the Central Government may, by notification in the official gazette, make such orders as may seem to it expedient for the effective exercise of any extra-provincial (any area outside the provinces) jurisdiction of the Central Government, P.N. Luthra, *Op. cit.*, pp. 8 & 69.

3

Social Change

With the annexation of the Phom villages to the west of the Dikhu river by the British in 1889-90, the inter-village feuds practically came to an end and the practice became a story of the past by the time the country became independent.[1] But, in other parts of the Phom inhabited areas, especially to the east of the Dikhu river, the headhunting warfare was still going on in the years following independence. One major cause of the continuation of this cruel practice was the absence of a permanent army base in the area, which could otherwise have taken timely action to avert such clashes and keep a constant vigil in the area.

End of Head-Hunting

In 1948, three Phom villages, namely Yongnyah, Tangha and Yachem raided Yongshei and took about 100 heads. As a measure of punishment, some of the raiders were arrested and after a trial sentenced to various terms of imprisonments.[2] In 1949, while some men of the Orangkong village were fishing in the river lying between the Pongching and Orangkong villages, they were attacked by a group of Pongching people on suspicion of stealing a *mithun*. In this process two heads were severed. Later, the Deputy Commissioner summoned the Pongching chiefs and asked them to produce the offenders. The chiefs yielded; the accused were sentenced to imprisonment.[3] In retaliation, the Orangkong men raided Pongching during March 1950. They killed twelve persons, chopped off eight heads and left the village half burnt. For this the Orangkong chiefs were brought to book and were asked to pay a penalty of 20 *mithuns*.[4] In April 1950, the Pongching village, assisted by the Yongphang, Sakchi, Yangching and several Chang villages, raided Orangkong and cut off the head of a woman and burnt down almost all the houses of the village.[5]

The majority of the Phoms were unhappy with the Pongching village for seeking the help of the Changs to attack Orangkong. They also resented the growing influence of the Changs over the Phom villages.[6] The houses at Pongching were burnt down as a punishment while the other villages involved in the raid against Orangkong were punished by forcing the residents to pay heavy fines and perform several days of mandatory labour. This was the last headhunting incident reported from the Phom villages. In a ceremony organised by the S.D.O. Mokokchung on 17 July, 1950 at Shemong which was attended by all the Phom villages, an oath was taken to the effect that "they would now stop once and for all, all attacks against each other."[7] An administrative centre with some Assam Riflemen was opened at Longleng in 1951 with a view to maintaining law and order throughout the region.

In spite of this, the fear psychosis which had gripped the people for long did not disappear immediately. In order to bring back peace and remove tension once for all, a meeting was held at Longleng on 6 June, 1952 where all the Phom *Do-Bhashis, Gaon-Buras*, public leaders and others took an oath to shun violence for ever.[8] A stone pillar was erected on that occasion at the heart of the Longleng town in memory of the bygone days of headhunting with the following inscription:

> "June sixth, 1952, Phom Day to witness this day wherein all Phoms have pledged themselves to be peaceful and loyal to Government."

In addition, the following decisions were adopted in the meeting[9]:

(i) From today no one will use *dao*, whichever village will repeat the practice, will severely be punished by the other Phom villages jointly.
(ii) All the villages are informed that sixth June will be observed as Phom Peace Day every year.
(iii) Participation in the Phom Day programme is compulsory for all the Phom villages and furthermore, participants may have to carry food and other necessities with them.
(iv) Whichever village will not turn up shall be liable to punishment.

As tension still prevailed in the Phom villages to the east of the Dikhu river, a few powerful villages, viz. Yongnyah, Yachem, Hukpang, Pongo, etc., were entrusted with the responsibility of maintaining peace and harmony and to act as guardians of the adjoining areas.[10] They also adopted a Phom Day flag of red and white colour with the rising sun in the middle.[11] Thus, 6 June remains a red letter day which marks the end of headhunting and the beginning of an era of peace and happiness among the Phoms. The Government of Nagaland has now declared this day as a restricted holiday.

Growth of Christianity and Its Impact

The traditional religious beliefs, which had developed among the Phoms from time immemorial, started declining when the Christian missionaries began to preach Christianity in the area. The mission centre which was opened on 4 October, 1894 at Impur in the Ao area had remained a Christian station for the Ao, the Sema, the Lotha, the Chang, the Phom and the Sangtam churches for many years.[12] A new era had set in among the Phoms when Rev. Wickstrand had baptised, for the first time, three Phoms, namely Imkum, Imrong and Longyi at Impur on 22 September, 1929. Incidentally, all these three persons belonged to Kangching village where the first Phom Baptist Church was established a few months later.[13] That was the beginning of spread of Christianity among the Phom people. In the initial years, Christianity spread in the Phom villages to the west of the Dikhu river and its waves reached the Phom villages to the east of the river when on 17 April, 1941, four persons from Pongching village along with their family members were baptised.[14]

However, the growth rate of Christian converts was at a slow pace during the first half of the twentieth century as it was very difficult to convince them who were rigid and unwilling to abandon their traditional faith. When L. Kijung Ao, a Naga missionary, first tried to spread the gospel among a few Yachem men, the latter vehemently resisted by saying that "Christianity would reduce Yachem people to the status of women."[15] The menfolk of the village Yachem expressed apprehension and observed, "No warfare, no heroic adventures, no headhunting and the village would lose their age-long esteem among the tribes."[16] Notwithstanding this, by 1947 seven Baptist Churches had been set up in the Phom villages with a handful of converts.[17]

By 1952, the number of Phom Baptist Church grew to twelve with

1,166 baptised members. The number of churches increased by leaps and bounds in the following years and in 1960 the total number of Phom Christians rose to 3,906 with twenty churches.[18] The evangelical works gained momentum in the 1960s when more and more people were inclined to Christianity.[19] A strong wave of Christian movement, called the revivalist movement by the Nagas, grew in the Phom areas giving thereby a massive blow to the age-old traditional religious beliefs of the people. By the 1970s, almost all the Phom Nagas were converted to Christianity.[20] For example, out of 17,713 Phom population of Tuensang district, 15,364 were followers of Christianity (86.73%) leaving 2,349 persons only outside the pale of this religion.[21] In 2003, the number of Phom Baptist Church throughout Nagaland grew to thirty-seven of which thirty churches were situated in Longleng district alone.[22]

In 1953, the Phom church had grown as an independent association, viz. Phom Baptist Christian Association, under the Nagaland Baptist Church Council. Initially, the Ao church backed up the Phom Association in terms of training, education, staffing (recruiting church ministries), finance, etc.[23] Rev. Lanumeren, who had served a long time at Longleng, was called back by the Ao church in 1970 and since then the Phom Association had been supervised by Rev. Paushen, a young and energetic man of the tribe.[24] Christianity was brought to the villages of Upper Konyak in the middle of the sixth decade of the twentieth century and a few churches of the area were established under the sponsorship of the Phom Baptist Christian Association.[25] Moreover, some missionaries from the Phom areas were reportedly preaching Christianity among the people of Myanmar (Tiyak Range) since 1997.[26]

The Roman Catholics started preaching their faith in Nagaland from the 1950s. However, they had to face stiff competition from the Baptists in the initial stage.[27] Although the Catholics appeared quite late, they made considerable progress in spreading the gospel by rendering valuable services in the field of education and health. The first Catholic school was established in 1965 at Tuensang where a Catholic Mission was opened officially two years later.[28] Some of the public leaders and students of Yongnyah approached the Catholic Mission of Tuensang to open a school at Yongnyah. A school, namely Christ School was opened there in 1986 but it was not affiliated to the Catholic Church.[29] Encouraged by the rapid success of the Catholic Mission and a school (the New Man School) at Tobu (now in Mon district) some leaders of the Pongo village went there to request the establishment of a similar mission and a school at Pongo. Accordingly, a Catholic Mission and a school, namely the St. Joseph School, were established in 1987 near Longleng town with the approval of the Pongo Village Council.[30] In a short time five Catholic Churches were set up in the Longleng district with 575 Catholic Christians. In addition, the district had 702 Hindu and 53 Muslim populations in 1971.[31] A large number of Hindu and Muslim people are presently residing in the district, the former has a temple while the latter, a mosque at the headquarters town, Longleng.

The impact of Christianity in the social sphere of the Phoms is immense. The converts are forbidden to use the dress that has some association with their traditional habits and practices. The practice of offering something as gift either in cash or kind to church replaced the old practice of offering the same to *thibu* or spirit while performing the rituals. They are debarred from consuming rice beer and a more common beverage, tea has replaced it. They now take tea without sugar and milk. The skulls which were reposed in the *Bangs* were thrown away along with traditional ornaments in 1970s by the Christian Phoms.[32] After conversion to Christianity, they gradually gave up their traditional marriage practices; almost all marriages are now solemnised in church. Curiously enough, in case a girl becomes pregnant before marriage, the couple is debarred from solemnising marriage in the church. To get social recognition, the couple usually arrange a party either in bride's or the groom's house. Only then the couple begins to live together as husband and wife. After passing through the days of warfare and violence Christianity had helped the people to regain peace and happiness. The Christian missionaries played an important role to inculcate the idea of love against enmity in the minds of the Phoms. The medical services rendered by the Christian missionaries in the Phom areas had been remarkable. The people have learnt to live a decent life which has indirectly brought a notable change in the field of health and hygiene. Even the Phom women are no longer confined to their household; they are seen taking a more active part in religious and other social activities alongside the men. The Christian missionaries have done a lot to enrich the Phom language and literature. They have translated several religious books (the Gospel of Mark and the New Testament in 1954 and 1972 respectively) into the Phom language to preach the gospel.[33] As a result of this a large section of the people is now able to read and write in the Phom or the Ao languages despite having no formal schooling. The traditional taboo days are replaced by Sundays. On every Sunday the Christian Phoms take rest without carrying on normal routine works.

Growth of Population

Records of the Phom population prior to 1961 are not available with the exception of a few villages. In 1895, A.E. Shuttle Worth, S.D.O. Mokokchung counted 122 houses at Tamlu and 164 houses at Bura Namsang villages,[34] whereas J. Hutton found 180 houses at Pongo village in 1923.[35] The number of houses increased slowly to 673 at Pongo, 727 at Tamlu and 670 at Bura Namsang villages according to the 1991 census. Only three Phom villages were covered in the census of 1951 with a record of 1,943 populations. According to 1961 census the total number of Phom speaking people of old Tuensang district was 13,361.[36] The sex ratio and the trend of population growth in Longleng district are shown in the following Table 3.1.

Table 3.1: Sex ratio and the trend of population growth of the Phom villages/town under Longleng district

Year	*No. of towns*	*No. of inhabited villages*	*Total population*	*Sex ratio (per 1000 males)*
1971	NIL	25	19,423	910.39
2011	1	49	50,484	905

Source: (i) Census 1971, *District Census Handbook,* Tuensang District.
(ii) *Primary Census Abstract*—Directorate of Census Operations in Nagaland, Kohima.

The Longleng district has the lowest rural (42,871) and urban (7,613) population, which comes to 3.04 per cent and 1.33 per cent respectively of total rural and urban population of the state according to 2011 census. The sex ratio of the district decreased by 5.39 in 2011 compared to that of 1971. It can also be surmised from the above Table 3.1 that the sex ratio, i.e. the number of females per 1000 males in the Phom areas of the district had remained low partly because of the migration of a handful of males from outside. The district of Longleng has the least population in the state with a share of just about 2 per cent as per 2011 census.

The growth of Phom population of Longleng district can be divided into two distinct phases, e.g. near stagnation stage till 1951, growing stage between 1951 and 2011. In the first phase birth rate remained high as a consequence of widespread of illiteracy, lack of knowledge of family planning, economic and defensive advantages of large family, etc. But, death rate was also equally high on account of poor dietary habit, primitive nature of sanitation, absence of modern medical facilities, headhunting, epidemic, etc. Thus, the growth rate of population remained virtually stagnant since high birth rate was balanced by high death rate.

In the second phase from 1951 to 2011, the population increase was rapid. During this period birth rate remained high and death rate declined rapidly. The extension of hospital and medical facilities, economic development including improvement in transport and communication, improvement in nutrition levels, better hygiene and sanitation, etc., have helped the population to grow during this period.

Perhaps the growth of population of Longleng district has begun slowing down in recent years. It further indicates that though many people have become aware of the benefits of small family system, yet the attitude and beliefs of the people have not changed totally. It would perhaps take a much longer time to bring down the growth rate to a more satisfactory level.

The number of the Phom population was slightly fewer than the total population as shown in the above table for the years 1971 and 2011, because a small number of people other than the Phoms are also residing here. A considerable number of Nepalese and a few other non-Phom immigrants, mostly males, have settled down in some of the Phom villages and since then they have mingled with the Phom culture.

The density of population of the district was 89.82 in 2011 per square kilometre. So, it can easily be observed that the per capita cultivable land is gradually on the decline. The rapid growth of population has not only given rise to the problem of unemployment, but has also increased the burden of expenditure of the parents to provide education, housing, medical care, etc., to their children.

Growth and Development of Longleng Town

The growth and extension of urbanization are necessary for the development of economy of a nation. The cities like Harappa and Mohenjodaro existed as early as 2500 BC in India but Longleng, the only town of the district, is of recent origin. The town was first set up as an administrative headquarters in 1951 in an uninhabited land and was named Longleng.[37] A Town Committee, later renamed Town Council, was constituted at Longleng towards the last decades of the twentieth century. Basically, the population of the town increased steadily over the decades due to two reasons: firstly, constant migration of people from the rural areas and secondly, high population growth. Since its creation the Phom people belonging to different villages began to migrate and settle down at Longleng in search of employment, to avail transport and communication, and shopping facilities; schooling, medical and postal services, etc. The trend of population increase of Longleng town is shown in the following Table 3.2.

Table 3.2: Trend of population increase of Longleng town (1951-2011)

1951		*1981*		*2011*	
Total population	*Total house-hold*	*Total population*	*Total house-hold*	*Total population*	*Total household*
195	33	2,509	532	7,613	1,690

Source: (i) Census 1951, Assam, *Naga Hills District Census Hand Book*, p. 3.
(ii) Census of India 1981, *District Census Handbook*, Tuensang District, p. 116.
(iii) *Primary Census Abstract – Nagaland 2011*, Directorate of Census Operations in Nagaland, Kohima.

The rural population of Longleng district constitutes 84.91 per cent, while the urban population, 15.08 per cent as per 2011 census. Longleng is the only place where a large number of people from all the Phom villages co-exist. The opening of Longleng administrative headquarters thus had contributed a lot towards strengthening tribal solidarity. Various voluntary public associations have come into existence, namely the Phom People's Council, Association of Phom Graduates and Officers, *Phomla Hoichem* (Phom Women Organisation), Phom Baptist Christian Association, St. Joseph's Parish (Catholic), Phom Students' Conference, etc. The people of Longleng town are engaged in different occupations besides agriculture. In recent years quite a few inhabitants of the town have started running hotel and restaurants, tea-stalls, hostels for the students, small-scale industries, garment and grocery shops, etc. The status of white-collar Phom workers (*sahib*) and contractors, so-called public leaders of Longleng town and other cities is comparatively high. Undoubtedly, the per capita income of these people is sufficiently enough, thus improving their standard of living. The number of people below poverty line in Longleng town is marginal compared to the rural areas. A major portion of income and savings of the people is spent on house construction, purchasing furniture, electric gadgets, motor bikes and vehicles, etc., and thus lead a contented live.

The growth of the township has also created problems of social nature like unemployment, alcoholism, drug smuggling, etc. The medical department of Nagaland has recently taken certain steps to create general awareness among the residents by organising free medical camps and seminars.[38] The continuous increase of population of the town has led to increase of the value of land.

Education

Before the establishment of the modern schools in the Phom areas the young men of the tribe received informal education at their traditional institutions called *morung*. All young boys of the adolescence stage were admitted to *morung* where they had to undergo long periods of training. As new inmates they had to act according to the instructions of their seniors. Here they learnt handicraft, folk dances and songs, folk tales, martial art, customary law and usages, oral histories, etc. They were also taught to respect their traditional culture and so on and so forth.[39] Thus, the young boys had to undergo a system of value-based education which had been handed down from generation to generation. However, with the spread of Christianity, disappearance of village feuds and the introduction of modern education, the Phom boys gave up the habit of sleeping in the *morungs* compulsorily and the *morung* system of education declined slowly. Like the boys the girls received their informal education in their respective clan dormitories (*Yow).*

The beginning of formal education in the Phom areas can be traced back to the late nineteenth century when a Lower Primary School was opened by the European troops at Tamlu where alphabet and numerals were taught to the pupils in the Assamese language. But, the school did not continue for long and was shut down after some time.[40] It was in 1931 that a Lower Primary School was opened for the second time at Tamlu with the help of a native teacher. Later the school was upgraded to Upper Primary level having classes up to IV with the help of another native teacher of the village.[41] In the subsequent years two more schools were opened – one at Kangching in 1938 and another at Tangha in 1947.[42] Although, the schools were opened at Tamlu and Kangching prior to independence, the attempt to popularise modern education among the Phoms did not succeed due to a variety of reasons, viz. poor response of the people, indifferent attitude of the colonial government and lack of a congenial atmosphere in the area.

Until 1950s the response of the people to such modern education was not at all encouraging as most of the parents regarded the school-going children as "lazy people who do not want to work in the fields."[43] However, the establishment of a Lower Primary School at Longleng in 1950-51 brought about a change in the people's attitude to school education. The school was upgraded to a Middle School in 1957 and again to a high school in 1971. The management of the school was taken over by the Government of Nagaland in 1972.[44]

To meet the growing demand of collegiate education, the Association of Phom Graduates and Officers, in collaboration with the Phom People's Council, established an arts college, namely Yingli College at Longleng in September 1992. Initially, the college started with the Pre-University (PU) class but it was upgraded to Degree level in 1995. The college started with 39 students only in its roll, which rose to 222 in 2012-13 of which 120 is male and 102 is female students. Presently, the college imparts education from Higher Secondary to Degree level. The college was formerly affiliated to the North Eastern Hill University, Shillong, but with the establishment of the Nagaland University, the college came under its jurisdiction. The college is situated in a large plot of land measuring sixty acres at Longongkang, about one kilometre away from the main town Longleng. Till 2012, the college had seventeen teaching faculties and nineteen non-teaching staff. It provides major course in Political Science. The college has also hostel facilities for male and female students. The growth in the number of schools and literacy[45] of the people of the area in the later decades of the twentieth century is shown in Table 3.3.

Table 3.3: Growth of schools and literacy of Scheduled Tribes in the areas of Longleng district (1971-2002)

Year	*No. of primary schools*	*No. of middle schools*	*No. of high schools*	*S.T. literacy percentage*
1	2	3	4	5
1971	23*	3*	1	17.33
1981	33	10	2	31.32
1991	50	13	3	46.08
2002	Govt. : 50 Private : 24	Govt. : 11 Private : 02	Govt. : 05 Private :04	NA

* Number of villages having schooling facilities.

Source: (i) Census 1971, *District Census Handbook,* Tuensang District.
(ii) Census of India 1981, *District Census Handbook,* Tuensang District.
(iii) Census of India 1991, *District Census Handbook,* Tuensang.
(iv) Information for the year 2002 was collected from DIS, Longleng on 22-04-2003 and also from the letter of the Nagaland Board of School Education notification No. 46/2002, dated Kohima, the 17th December, 2002, No. NBSE-21/Ex-RECOG/2002-03.

By 1991, all the thirty-five Phom villages had schooling facilities. In addition to government schools, a number of privately managed schools have come into existence in the district. Interestingly, the private schools of the area have more enrolment than the government schools. It is contended by most parents that they send their children to private schools despite higher expenses because these schools are more disciplined and they impart knowledge more efficiently than the government schools. Even the results of private schools in the High School Leaving Certificate (HSLC) Examinations are much better than the government schools.[46] One reason of the comparatively poor performance of the government schools was the slack administration and management. The authorities in most cases were unable to enforce discipline at all levels and hold classes regularly. Secondly, in most government schools, library buildings, class rooms, sports facilities, infrastructure, science laboratories, auditoriums, etc., were lamentably deficient.[47] In order to improve the condition of government primary and middle schools, the Government of Nagaland has recently communitised the government schools in which the management of schools, payment of salaries to teachers, repair and maintenance of school buildings, purchase of stationery and laboratory equipment, etc., are done by the School Management Committees.[48] The result of this arrangement is yet to be known.

The Phom Baptist Christian Association has also done commendable work of social reconstruction in the Phom areas. The Association is running a hostel with an accommodation of 60 students at Longleng town. In addition to this, it has been extending medical aid and imparting training for self-employment as well as modern techniques of farming.[49]

Till 1950 the medium of instruction in the schools was Assamese. However, the Ao language was introduced in place of Assamese as medium of reading and learning from 1950 to 1953-54 and thereafter English was adopted as the medium of instruction along with Hindi as a subject in the middle schools.[50] The task of preparing text books in the Phom language was undertaken in the divisional headquarters[51] Tuensang, when this area was a part of North-East Frontier Agency (NEFA). In 1955, the Phom language was introduced in the L.P. Schools of the Phom inhabited areas.[52] The Text Book Production Branch of the Directorate of Education, Nagaland, was established in November 1962 with a view to preparing text-books in local languages. Accordingly, text-books in the Phom language were prepared for students up to class IV.[53] In 1977, the Phom Literature Board consisting of 21 members with T. Imdong Phom as Chairman was constituted for the purpose of assisting and advising the Education Department in preparing the school text books in the Phom language. The Board was also entrusted with the task of carrying out such other recommendatory and advisory works as and when sought by the government.[54] The Board is currently functioning from its head office at Longleng. However, the Phom language is taught in the government schools and not in the private schools.

The Phom students were supplied with free text books, rations, blankets, kerosene, etc., since the days of the NEFA administration.[55] The meritorious and needy students still get help from government either in cash or in kind. In comparison with all the Government departments, the Government of Nagaland spends the highest amount in disbursement of salaries of the employees of the education department. The Government of Nagaland has reserved certain number of seats for the backward tribes in institutions of higher education as well as in public employment.[56] In 1977, twenty-five per cent jobs under the State Government was reserved for seven backward tribes and again, in August, 1979, thirty-three per cent of the non-technical and non-gazetted posts were reserved for the backward tribes with the aim of improving their socio-economic condition. The Government of Nagaland has further introduced the roster system since 1986 in case of thirty-three per cent government jobs reserved for the backward tribes in order to have a balanced distribution of the jobs and prevent any tribe from taking undue advantage of reservation.[57]

Among the males, T. Imdong Phom was the first person of the tribe who passed the matriculation examination and later in 1967 graduated in arts. Bukchem became the first post-graduate degree-holder in arts in 1985, whereas Anjo Keikung got doctorate degree in theology in 1988.[58] Among the females, two girl students qualified for the matriculation examination in 1981; one of them, viz. A. Shamthai obtained a bachelor degree in arts in 1986.[59] She is currently working as Headmistress, Govt. High School and also President of *Phomla Hoichem,* a non-government women organisation.

Health and Hygiene

Before coming in contact with modern medical sciences, the Phom people used to depend on their indigenous methods of treatment. The *thibu* treated all types of disease by the application of his so-called super natural or magical powers or by sacrificing animals or by using indigenous plants, herbs, etc. Since, the people had no knowledge of modern medical sciences, they acted under the superstitious beliefs that the malevolent spirits caused all the diseases. People lived in filthy conditions where there was total lack of hygiene and sanitation. The foul odour of dead bodies, which were usually laid hanging on banyan trees or *machan* for several days to let the flesh decompose, often polluted the whole atmosphere beyond imagination. The situation aggravated when famine and epidemic broke out suddenly.[60] E.A. Savi, S.D.O. Mokokchung, while visiting Bura Namsang village on 3 January, 1897 noted, "there was cholera in this village and 16 people had died during last 10 days and several are still ill."[61] Numerous other people also suffered from leprosy[62] which was quite common in the area till the dawn of independence. In the past the people were dirty as they seldom bathed. But they possessed strong body resistance that enabled them to cope with the atrocities of nature. However, the people had some knowledge of treatment of fracture and dislocation of bone joints which were treated by applying herbal substances, a method of treatment which had been practiced for generations through experience and knowledge. In spite of this, a large number of people died every year due to epidemic, septic infection and the like.[63]

Towards the last decade of the nineteenth century a small hospital at Tamlu was opened mainly for the treatment of the troops, although the civil population of the area also availed of the medical facilities available there.[64] With the establishment of a few more hospitals and dispensaries after 1950 the people's attitude towards health and hygiene began to change. The Government of Nagaland is giving top priority to the extension of public health services throughout the state.

Earlier, leprosy being a communicable disease, the lepers were kept in isolation in a colony under regular medical supervision. In 1959, a 50-bedded hospital (colony) for the leprosy patients was opened at Longleng and subsequently its capacity was raised to 100 patients.[65] Over and above the leprosy affected patients from the Phom tribe, lepers from other tribes were also admitted to the Leprosy Colony. Patients here were provided with free medicine, ration, utensils, etc.[66] A Leprosy Mission which was set-up in 1990 under the Phom Baptist Christian Association did commendable work in combating the disease which has reached almost zero level now.[67]

Before the establishment of a hospital in 1958, there was a small dispensary at Longleng run by a pharmacist and a vaccinator.[68] Another health unit was set up at Tamlu in the same year[69] under the supervision of a doctor. In 1982, the area under Longleng Rural Development (RD) Block had one hospital, two dispensaries, one primary health centre and a sub-centre.[70] The number increased to one hospital, two primary health centres and ten dispensaries under Longleng R.D. Block in 1991.

Water, a basic need for daily use for human being, is available in the Phom villages in three ways: rain water, stream or spring well and tap water. All the Phom villages do not have tap or canal water facilities. A number of tanks have been constructed by the individuals or community for collecting and storing rain water. However, most of the people depend on stream or spring well water during dry season since time immemorial. Therefore, certain steps are taken by the villagers to maintain the hygiene of the wells which are not generally shallow. With the onset of monsoon wells are cleaned, repaired and fenced. Before the onset of winter the wells are once again cleaned and repaired. In order to protect the well water from probable pollution, washing clothes, taking bath and rearing cattle near the community wells are prohibited. Violators of the rules may be warned or fined by the Students' Unions or Village Community. Punishment may be inflicted upon the violator up to the extent of restricting the person from fetching water from the common well for a fixed period. In some cases the villagers who do not have running water facilities have to walk long distance down the hill to fetch water from the springs below. Out of thirty-five villages, nineteen villages had running water facilities, seven villages had both canal and well water while nine villages had to depend only on well water till 1991.[71]

Table 3.4: Number of Hospitals/C.H.C./P.H.C./Dispensary under Longleng District 2010-11

Sl. No.	*Hospital/PHC/SHC*	*Total*
01.	District Hospital	01
02.	Primary Health Centre	03
03.	Sub-Centre	08

Source: *Statistical Hand Book of Nagaland* 2011, p.128.

There is a thirty-bedded Community Health Centre (now District Hospital) at Longleng under whose jurisdiction three other Primary Health Centres are providing medical services to the people. The Community Health Centre directly or in collaboration with other centres provides such medical services as mother and child health care, immunization, malaria and leprosy control, blindness control, school health, family welfare, etc. Primary Health Centres and Sub-Centres give free medicine and treatment for minor ailments, emergency treatment and care, and other basic primary health care services at the grassroots level.[72] However, the patients suffering from serious ailments have no other way but to go outside the district for better treatment in good hospitals. Even then, many people are still seen depending on the indigenous medicines or other crude methods of curing the disease. For example, it is not rare to see a sick man consuming the boiled blood of a dog or pig, in the mistaken belief that he would be recovering from illness soon.[73]

Food and Drink

Till about the first half of the twentieth century famine and epidemic broke out almost regularly in the Phom villages. C.R. Pawsey, S.D.O. Mokokchung wrote in 1928 in his tour diary that Tamlu village had no stock of rice at all because the village had three bad harvests in succession and the villagers were holding their *bihu* festival only half-heartedly.[74] S.J. Duncan, D.C. also noted in his tour diary in 1950 about the scarcity of rice in 'Agching' (Auching) and Sakchi village which forced the villagers to spend miserable days.[75] Besides borrowing paddy from the neighbouring villages, people used to take wild roots, wild seeds, *Kochu*, maize, wild green leaves, etc., as substitute of rice when crops failed partially or completely.[76] Since the Phoms were earlier ignorant about the cultivation of potato, cabbage, cauliflower, lady's finger, radish, *dhonia* (coriander), spices, squash, etc., so they were not accustomed to take those vegetables till about the third quarter of the twentieth century. The Phom people are basically rice eater. Most of them take vegetable leaves, *chutneys* (pounding mixture of chilli, dried-fish, soya bean, ginger, tomato, garlic, etc.), boiled curry and fresh bamboo shoot or its liquid substance regularly. They take *roti* (*chapatti*), fried curry, potato, *dal* (pulses) and spices only occasionally. Maize and *kochu* are taken, especially in seasons. Until a few decades back, they did not drink cow milk and a vast majority of them do not consume cow milk at all even today. As a substitute they use milk powder which is available in the shops with tea. Bamboo shoot or its juice is their traditional delicacy.

In course of his fieldwork this researcher interviewed forty persons[77] belonging to the Phom tribe and found all of them non-vegetarian. Further investigations revealed that seventeen of them are used to take elephant meat, fourteen tiger meat and two even snake meat. Again it was found that out of the forty, thirty-nine persons take the meat of bear, buffalo, *mithun*, deer, while all of them take frog besides beef, pork, mutton, fowl, duck and dog meat and fish. Some of them expressed no inhibition in eating the meat of the crow but only for medicinal purposes. None of them, however, has ever taken sheep meat which is not available in their area, though they expressed their desire to taste it whenever an opportunity comes. No wonder, the Phoms are fond of all types of meat as they were in the bygone days. In all social functions meat is served in plenty.

The Phoms were heavy consumers of rice beer. They smoked tobacco by using a home-made smoking pipe. They also chewed *pan* along with a locally-made black tobacco called *kala sada*. A large section of them now smoke *bidi* or cigarette, chew *pan* and drink rice-beer, although there is now a growing aversion for these commodities among the younger generation who prefer branded cigarettes, foreign liquor and in some cases drugs. The sale of alcohol was banned throughout Nagaland after the passing of the Total Prohibition Act of 1989.[78] Consequently, foreign liquor is not openly available, though a few families, mostly of Nepalese origin, are reportedly carrying on an illicit locally-made liquor business in the Longleng district. As mentioned earlier, the Phoms observed food taboo rigidly in the past. The *Angh* and the *thibu* never took the meat of tiger. Some people did not take certain categories of fish, or the meat of snake, elephant, tiger, dog, etc., in the belief that this might cause disaster or they might be attacked by rapacious animals or reptiles if they violated the practice. Many villagers still observe the food taboos though only openly.

Clan

The clan is one oldest entity of the Phom society and it remains practically unchanged over the years. Usually, each *khel* of a village has a *morung* but a *khel* may consist of more than one clan. Different villages have different number of clans and every individual of a village belongs to a particular clan.[79] The Phoms believe that the members of a clan have descended from a common ancestor and they are, therefore, called by that very ancestor's name.[80] Many Phom Nagas use their clan name, viz. Noklang, Keikung, Buchem, Angh, Ngonyean, Namdakli, etc., as surname. The clan system is based on patriarchal system. In some places people belong to the same clans are found among the Phoms and the neighbouring tribes, although they are known by different names in accordance with the local dialects. It is the result of the cross migration of the people of the area in the past.

In the days of headhunting one clan stood by another clan to defend the village against enemies. Thus, it was impossible for a person to live independently outside the clan. The feeling of insecurity made every Naga individual to unite for their survival. It was because of these reasons a village was built by more than one clan. The views of Horam about the Nagas in general are also applicable in the case of the Phoms. He writes:

> The family is a closely knit unit but as it is a small unit it is ineffective, especially in the primitive society, in case of wars, raids and head-hunting. To present an effective front to all external aggression, several families unite on a particular

basis, thus forming a clan. Any clan can be traced back to a single family which has multiplied into numerous families but remain connected to each other. Two or more such clans form a village.[81]

Every clan has a head. The headship is hereditary based on the principle of primogeniture. The members of each clan assemble in the house of their headman to settle disputes arising among them. Here he plays the role of a judge. He is the custodian of the customary laws because the disputes are resolved according to the customary laws. Unsolved cases are referred to the Village Council for arbitration.[82] Important decisions of a clan are taken in the meeting which is usually held in the house of the head. The unanimous decision of a clan is presented by its head in the Village Council meeting. The Village Council members are elected on the basis of clans.

Marriage within the clan (endogamy) is strictly prohibited according to the Phom customary laws. When incest takes place with the result of pregnancy the young couple is not allowed to marry. Violators of the custom are punished by throwing the newly-wed couple out of the village for several years.[83] It is believed that if incest is committed by anybody in a community, it will bring misfortune to the entire community in the form of drought, bad harvest, depredation by wild animals, etc.[84] If a woman is harassed physically, mentally or materially by her husband, her clan men would come forward to rescue her from the sufferings.

Every clan has specific area of land called clan land. The land is cultivated by its members jointly and the paddy yielded from the field is stored in clan granary. If any family goes hungry, especially during festivals, paddy is supplied to the unfortunate family from this granary. In fact, it is a matter of shame for the whole clan in case any of its members goes hungry during festivals. Spare paddy is sold to raise clan fund.

Every clan takes an important part in the society. All the people of a village are loyal to their respective clans. It is mandatory for every clansman, rich or poor, to take part in community works, e.g. construction and repairing the well, approach road, footpath, etc. In case any clan man is found absent from participating clan works without valid reason, the person or even his family is punished with a fine or the family is prevented from enjoying the benefit of the works done by his fellow clan members. Following the death of a person, all the members of the clan join the funeral ceremony voluntarily. When someone constructs a house in the village, all the members of the clan present in the village come forward to assist him. Clan members help one another in turn in the cultivation work.[85]

The unity of the people of various clans, which had remained quite effective throughout the ages, still remains intact in Phom Naga society. However, there is strong unity in the towns among the members of a village rather than clan. Nevertheless, all the members of the clan are very much conscious of their clanship even if they are not living together.

Housing

Over the years a major change has taken place in the selection of sites for building houses as well as the pattern of the houses built. The Phom people had been living in traditional houses till they learnt modern building techniques. They used wooden posts, bamboo mat and thatch or palm leaves in construction. The edge of the roof of a traditional house was low which appeared round in shape rather than a triangle. This was done to prevent the house from being damaged by strong wind. The house had no separate kitchen. The rooms usually remained dark even in daytime and the smoke coming out of the hearths made the walls and roofs pitch black. There was no window for allowing the air to pass through the rooms.[86]

They had neither sanitary or any type of hygienic latrine nor bathroom. They got rid of the call of nature from *machan* (bamboo made platform) or in jungle and the excreta were cleaned by pigs. Most of the villagers used to keep their domesticated animals and birds and the pounding table in the front rooms of their houses. The centre of the house was used as kitchen as well as sleeping and meeting place. The house contained one or two small rooms attached to the kitchen, where the people seldom slept. The floor of the house was mostly half earthen, half *machan*. Bamboo made *machan* was mostly attached to the back of a house and this was used for the purpose of taking rest, holding meetings, washing, handicraft works, etc.[87] The roofs of the houses were allowed to overlap each other. R.G. Woodthorpe while visiting a few Phom villages in 1875-76 observed:

> "The houses in Nian, Kamahu, & C., are very closely packed on each side of long streets, the eaves touching and the

> projecting front gable-ends of opposite houses often overlapping each other: the result is, that even in the middle of the brightest day the streets are wrapped in gloom, so great as to make it difficult to distinguish objects in the front verandahs, the few flecks of sunlight which fall upon the roadway here and there only serving to make darkness greater.[88]

Earlier, the Phom people used to observe a ritual at the time of constructing a house. A person who wanted to build a house for him first collected the building materials. Thereafter, he selected a suitable plot of land and cleaned the site. On an appointed day he invited the village elders to the site to examine the malevolent and benevolent spirits of the site. The elders would then suggest what bird or animal to sacrifice to oust the evil spirits from the site. The blood of the sacrificed bird or animal would be sprinkled in the site and all those who had gathered for construction work would eat the meat of the offering. A little skin and bone of the bird or animal killed would then be wrapped up in a leaf and laid up in the hole of the main pillar. The construction work would then begin and end in the same day. The husband and the wife who were to live in the house would not sleep together for twelve days or so after the kitchen was lighted for the first time. The owner then tied some leaves of a particular tree on the post outside the house as a mark of forbidding the guests from visiting the house for twelve days.[89]

While interviewing four persons (2004)[90], one each from Sakchi, Yongam, Bura Namsang and Bhumnyu, it is found that most of the houses in Sakchi, Yongam and Bura Namsang villages have thatched roof with bamboo wall, whereas majority houses at Bhumnyu village are of corrugated tin roofs with bamboo walls. As per official information there were 522 CGI sheet roofed houses in the twenty-six Phom villages in 1983.[91] As a result of the introduction of the Indira Awas Yojana (IAY), a Centrally Sponsored Scheme for providing housing to BPL households, almost all the villagers have got now CGI sheet roofed houses and moreover, a change has been noticed in the shape of the houses, which have several doors, windows, spacious rooms, etc. Besides these, a number of hill type houses (roof on timber frame with cemented or wooden wall) are seen in the district nowadays. However, RCC (Reinforced Cement Concrete) dwellings are totally absent in the four villages. The floors of the majority of the houses in these villages are earthen, although some houses have wooden or bamboo mat floors. In Longleng town, however, most of the houses are hill type, followed by RCC type.

In the village every Phom house has a *machan*, at the back of the kitchen house. The house has a latrine, invariably *kacha*. Villagers belonging to Sakchi, Bhumnyu and Yongam have separate granaries but most of the villagers of Bura Namsang do not have them.[92] Earlier the cultivators who reaped good harvest used to build large field houses in the shape of buffalo horns which also symbolised fertility,[93] where they took rest, dined and took shelter from rain during the cropping season. However, every cultivator now maintains an ordinary field house. Pigs are reared in a separate shed. Nowadays people prefer to build their houses in open space. Under the impact of Christianity the old method of rituals which were observed at the time of constructing houses disappeared.

Festivals and Musical Instruments

Like other Naga tribes, the Phoms have their own traditional festivals which are observed round the year. Most of the festivals are related to agriculture, the mainstay of their domestic economy. They celebrate their festivals in their colourful attires, wearing indigenous ornaments and taking part in community feasts and singing and dancing. *Monyu, Moha, Bongvum* and *Paangmo* are their main and the most attractive festivals. *Monyu* is celebrated from April 1 to 6 every year following the completion of the sowing season. Earlier, different groups of villages observed this festival either in the months of March or April. However, at the initiative of the Phom Students' Union the dates of the festival are fixed on April 1 to 6 every year for the entire tribe. The Government of Nagaland has declared these days as restricted holidays.

As stated above, the festival marks the end of the dry season and the onset of the rainy season. Log drums are beaten with distinct tunes to herald the commencement of the festival. Before the introduction of Christianity the priests or the village elders performed a ritual to find out whether the coming days would be a blessing or a curse and accordingly, the villagers were put on alert.[94] But, this practice has now been given up by the Phoms. During the festival meat is served in large quantity; the married daughters and sisters are entertained lavishly by a rich meal of meat of domesticated animals.

The Phom people assert that the practice denotes their love and affection for married women. They pray for bumper crops. Each of the six days of the festival has distinct significance. On the first day they collect chiefly two materials, bamboo for *machan* repairing and *morung* decoration and wrapping leaf for distributing meat or cooked food; on the second day rice beer is brewed, though not in large quantity as in the past; on the third day people of different age-groups meet together and feast amidst songs and dances. The fourth day is the day of community festivity. On the fifth day they wear colourful costumes and spend the day by eating, dancing, meeting friends and the near and dear ones. On the sixth day the elderly people exchange food and the younger ones of both sexes eat together on the outskirt of the village.[95]

Moha is a one-day festival which is celebrated usually in May. On this day the people pray for bumper crops. Earlier, a bit from each newly grown sprout was collected and carried to the ritual place seeking blessings for the better growth of the plants.[96] *Bongvum* is another one-day festival which is celebrated in the month of October every year. The day is observed as a thanks-giving day to the almighty for the crops that had yielded during the preceding months. On this day the people take sticky rice and meat mixed with prawns, crabs, bamboo shoots and ginger. In the bygone days, the people killed fowl and its blood was sprinkled on the outer surface of the bamboo pail for storing grains. The cooked food was then tied to the post of the house wrapped in leaves acknowledging the gift of God and soliciting blessings for rich harvests in the years to come. Earlier, the head of the family used to predict the future by looking at the intestine of the bird killed.[97] Nowadays the Christian Phoms offer a small portion of the crop that was reaped in the preceding months to the church on this day. *Paangmo* is another festival of the tribe which falls in the month of November. It is observed to mark the end of the rainy season and the onset of the winter. It is celebrated for three days and during the period of the festival the people clean the village surroundings, wells, etc., and repair their houses. The people kill animals and share the meat and the food with their married daughters and sisters.[98]

With the coming of Christianity, the Phom Nagas start observing Christmas and the New Year's Day with great festivity.

From time immemorial the people have been expressing their joy and sorrow feelings through music. There are very rare people who do not like music. Songs without playing musical instruments are incomplete. The Ao, the Konyak and the Phom music lovers have traditionally been using different musical instruments during festive occasions or in leisure times. Among the different musical instruments used by these tribes mention may be made of bamboo mouth-organ, cup violin, bamboo flute, trumpet, log-drum, etc. Of all the musical instruments the bamboo mouth-organ is the smallest one. Its whole length is about 6 inches long and half an inch in width. The Aos call it *Tepang Kongki* while the Phoms call it *Lipung* and the Konyaks, *Kongki*. This instrument produces four types of melodious sounds. It is played by both the boys and the girls. Through the music of this instrument the youth of opposite sexes exchange their secret messages to each other.

Another popular musical instrument traditionally used by these tribes is cup violin. The instrument is generally made of bamboo; fibrous jungle creeper or hair of a lady is used as string. The instrument produces melodious musical tunes. The Phoms and the Konyaks call it 'Umo'. Another musical instrument used by them is bamboo flute. It produces beautiful sound with different tunes. To make a flute it requires a thin bamboo. A few holes are made in the middle portion. It can be played by both by men and women. It takes quite some time to become an expert to play the flute. It is known *Jemiji* in the Ao dialect, *Vong Lipung* in Phom dialect and '*Wewo*' in Konyak dialect.

For the purpose of making trumpet, traditional materials like thin bamboo, buffalo horns, *mithun* horns, etc., were used. It was blown at the time when the enemies attacked the village, the warriors returned home with the heads of their enemies, the village was on fire, ferocious animals entered the village and also used during festivals and worshipping. Just next to log drum it was a popular musical instrument of various Naga tribes through which they conveyed different informations to the people. The Phoms call it *Amit*, while the Konyaks, *Nyaklong* and the Aos, *Jangzw* or *Tsui*.

The log drum was a popular musical instrument of some Naga tribes including the Aos, the Phoms and the Konyaks. The Konyaks and the Phoms call it *'Shem'* and its Ao name is *Tongten or Sungkong*. The messages of the drum may differ from village to village; therefore, secrecy could be passed on without any difficulty. The log drum was made from the trunk of a huge tree. Several strikers were used to beat the drum to produce different sounds.[99] Except on very special occasions, all these instruments are no longer used by the people. In place of these, youngsters now play the guitar, drum set and other electronic musical instruments.

Dress and Ornaments

A major change had taken place in dress and costumes of the Phom people from the second half of the twentieth century when they came under the influence of the modern world. The traditional dress is nowadays used rarely on very special occasions.

In the past the Phom people were rich in their traditional and ornamental dress, which was used by the people of both sexes. A hornbill feather is generally displayed on the headgear and also in the coronet (an ornament for men).[100] The use of boar tusks, bear's nails and tiger's teeth as necklace was a popular practice at that time,[101] but these are seldom used by the people nowadays. A warrior who had taken a minimum of one head was entitled to wear a head plate.[102] Nowadays, however, any one can wear it without restriction. While performing martial dance, they put on a *dao*-holder and a casket, which was carried by each warrior for carrying the spikes while going on a raid.[103] Bell is tied hanging in the hips while dancing.[104] Earlier, the Phom men used armlet made of different materials like elephant tusk, wood, iron, cane, bamboo, etc.; gauntlet was worn on the wrist glove to make the arms stronger while fighting against the enemy,[105] and leggings made of bear skin were worn during festivals.[106] These armlets, gauntlets and leggings are still used by the people during social gatherings. There are various kinds of spears including headhunting spear, festive spear and common spear. *Daos* of various shapes and for various purposes, e.g. headhunting *dao*, animal hunting *dao*, working *dao,* ceremonial *dao*, etc., were used by them. Among all *daos* and spears, the festive spear and the ceremonial *dao* are the most beautiful and decorative. Among the shields made of buffalo or *mithun* skin, the war shield and the dance shield were the most popular.

Besides using various kinds of traditional hair bands, the Phom women also used to collect fallen hairs for making hair bun.[107] They used crystal ornament earing, which was considered as the most valued wealth for them.[108] During festival and also at other times the women wore cornelian bead necklaces.[109] Those jewellery are today used only occasionally and on very special occasions. The women are fond of bangles which are used during festivals, while performing a dance.[110]

Among the shawls worn by the women, the Phom *Lakshong* is the most gorgeous.[111] The border of this shawl is red; the white middle part is embellished with a variety of designs woven with different coloured thread. Black colour segment is used on both sides in between the red segments on the border and the middle part. They had, earlier, two types of shawls, i.e. the rich woman's shawl and the shawl for the warrior's wife and daughter. But, these shawls are no longer in use and are replaced by a common shawl as mentioned above. It is noticeable that no woman would wear a man's shawl and *vice versa*. In the olden days, the women of the tribe used to wear narrow and short *mekhalas*. From about the mid twentieth century, they began to weave and use long *mekhalas*, i.e. Phom *mekhalas*.[112] Of all the *mekhalas*, the *Mongsum Ashak* is the most common and popular.[113] There are two or three types of the common *mekhalas* which vary in design and colour.

Man's shawls are of three types, e.g. ordinary man's shawl, rich man's shawl and warrior's shawl. In recent past, the rich man's shawl was selected as national attire for the Phoms and it can be worn by any men without restriction.[114] The colour of this shawl is red with parallel white band in the middle in which arrow marks are found. The Phoms now sport hand-made waist coat. As a result of their contact with the outside world, the young men have now taken to half pants and trousers, shirts, hats, vests, foot wears, jackets, sweaters, coat and the neckties. They have discarded the old style of haircutting and tattooing their bodies. Likewise, the Phom women have started using *salwar kameez*, petticoats, trousers and tops besides cosmetic and ready-made jewellery.

Status of Women

Like all Naga women the Phom women take an important part in indoor and outdoor activities. They fetch water from the hill streams, collect firewood from forest, pound rice, cook food, look after the children and weave garments in their looms. Daughters help the mothers in all household works and thus making themselves fit for all domestic works before marriage. Men and women work side by side in the fields. Regretfully, when they are employed as hired labour in cultivation work women are paid less than men. A few enterprising women sell their handloom products to support their families. Women of the adjoining villages of Longleng town bring fruits, firewood, vegetables, etc., for sale at the Longleng market. One would often see in the Longleng town a number of shops being run by the women.

With the spread of modern education in the Phom inhibited areas the society began to change, which immensely helped to raise the status of the Phom women. It has already been mentioned that a Lower Primary School was opened at Tamlu in 1931, which unsealed the gate of formal education to the Phom children. Unfortunately, till the third quarter of the twentieth century the women were far lagging behind in education as compared to males. The Phom parents were mainly responsible for retarding their progress. They used to send their sons to school to receive education, whereas the daughters were confined to domestic or field works and to look after the children. Many of the parents even thought that it was useless to impart education to their daughters because after marriage they would go to the house of their husbands leaving them behind. However, this negative notion of the parents began to wane slowly.

The progress of education among the Phom women can be estimated from the following examples. Among the females, two girl students for the first time qualified the matriculation examination in 1981. A lady ought to be mentioned here is Ms A. Shamthai Phom who was the first lady obtained Bachelor of Arts degree in 1986. The name of Ms Konjai is noteworthy because she was the first Phom lady passed M.A. Another illustrious Phom woman is Dr (Ms) Anungla Imdong who is the first person from the tribe obtained Ph.D. degree in 2009. In 2008, Ms Nyeie Leinak, a higher secondary student of Yingli College won the first runner-up prestige in the state level beauty contest.

Nowadays the girls are performing better than the boys in schools. Thus, the Phom-Naga women in Longleng district are rising up faster than men and becoming equally competent as men in many fields. Today, quite a few Phom women are working as missionaries. They have got the right to participate in public meeting and give public speech, which were impractical in the traditional society. With the spread of education the female literacy has also gone up rapidly. The percentage of female literacy of the district was 69.63 against that of 74.48 male as per 2011 census.[115] Undoubtedly, the Phom women living in the towns or cities to some extent have made progress in higher education. The parents of those areas are well off and hence they can afford the money to impart higher education to their daughters. Many Phom women are employed in government service.

The Phom society is both patriarchal and patrilineal. Daughters are debarred from inheriting immovable properties such as land and house, although these can be used by them throughout their life.[116] In the absence of male child, property of the deceased can be claimed by the nearest male relatives.[117] A woman can purchase land or house but after her death these cannot be claimed by her daughters and such properties are shared by her husband's close male relatives.[118] Thus, the customary law deprives the women of inheriting immovable properties on the one hand, but on the other, it helps to check transferring out land from one village to another as marriage between villages or between different tribes and also with non-Nagas have become a common practice in recent years. However, a woman can enjoy the property of her husband after marriage but she cannot sell it.

As inter-village feud was a regular practice in the olden days, so marriage within the village was a necessity. Things have, however, changed now. Today, the Nagas are free to choose their life partners. Among the Phoms, payment of bride-price was in practice earlier and the same was paid in the form of brass plates, animals, etc. Sometimes feuds broke out between the families on the question of bride-price following the break-up of marriage.[119] The practice, however, disappeared because of the impact of Christianity. A young man who made an offer of marriage had to help his would-be father-in-law in cultivation and in domestic works.[120] R. G. Woodthorpe wrote, "Here, as very generally, I think, in these hills, a youth having taken a fancy to a girl, either of his own or a neighbouring village, has to serve in her parents' house for a certain time, varying from one to two or more years, according to agreement, before he can marry her, as was Jacob's case."[121] Both courtship and arranged marriages are prevalent among the Phoms. Different age groups of the Phom people and their marital status as per 1971 census are given in the following Table 3.5.

Table 3.5: Age and marital status of the Phom tribe, 1971

		Age 0 – 14	*Age 15 – 44*	*Age 45+*
Male	(M)	3,685	3,359	2,184
Female	(F)	3,372	3,367	1,746
Never married	(M)	3,685	2,027	57
	(F)	3,372	1,378	58
Married	(M)	0	1,281	1,985
	(F)	0	1,931	1,351
Widow	(M)	0	35	110
	(F)	0	51	296
Divorced or	(M)	0	1	17
separated	(F)	0	7	41

Source: Census 1971, *District Census Handbook*, Tuensang District, pp. 92-94.

No hard and fast rule is followed as to the upper age limit for marriage. Monogamy is a common practice. Divorce is rare and widow remarriage is allowed. If a widow is married outside the clan of the deceased husband she cannot claim the property or even children of her dead husband. In case she gets married to any member of the clan of deceased husband she cannot claim the property of her expired husband unless the children come to stay with her. Interestingly, if an unmarried woman deposits lakhs of rupees in her bank account, no one can claim the money even after her marriage. In case of divorce without mutual understanding, the guilty person is punished heavily according to the customary law.[122] In a Christian society like the Phoms a man cannot go for second marriage without divorcing his first wife. Demented or disabled persons generally remain unmarried. In Phom society neither the husband nor the wife calls each other by name. A woman is neither allowed to use the title nor surname of her husband after marriage. Obviously, a woman cannot change her title drawn from her father's title even after the marriage.

The Phom Village Councils are dominated by men. A woman can neither be the chief nor a member of the Village Council.[123] They cannot enjoy the headship right of a clan. From the time of the third Assembly Election (first for Old Tuensang district) in 1974, the Phom women got the right of exercising franchise. Since 1980, they were, however, included in the Village Development Boards, a process which empowered them to formulate and implement various development schemes. Today they are seen taking active part in various social functions. Yet, there was no Phom female representative in the Nagaland Legislative Assembly as well as in the Longleng Town Council in the past as it is today. Until 2011, no fewer than nine times State Assembly Elections were held for the Tamlu-49 and the Longleng-50 constituencies but surprisingly, no woman came forward to fight an election.

In the days of head-hunting certain prejudices were prevalent among the people of Phom society. The women were considered as weaker section. It was, therefore, they were forbidden from doing or taking part in certain social activities or functions. They were forbidden to touch male weapons like spear, shield and *dao*. They were deprived of becoming the members of the Village Council most probably because the council also functioned as war council. Today, the society has undergone a change. The women, who were treated as weaker section, are now seen working in the security service.

The spread of Christianity, extension of so-called modern education, the amalgamation of alien and indigenous administration, etc., enhanced the social status of the Phom women quite a lot barring a few respects. Hopefully, the position of women will improved to the satisfactory level as the society will keep changing in future as well.

NOTES AND REFERENCES

1. Furer-Haimendrof, Christoph von, *Return to the Naked Nagas*, p. 164.
2. Ao, Tajenyuba, *British Occupation of Naga Country*, p. 117.
3. *Ibid*, p. 118.
4. *Ibid*.
5. *Ibid*, p. 119.
6. Tour Diary of S. J. Duncan for May-June 1950, on Column Duty – Phomching Column, Public Records, file no. 61.
7. Tour Diary of S.J. Duncan for February-March 1951, Public Records, file no. 61; *Phom Naga Since 1942*, A Tribute to Late Shri M. Hamyei, Rtd. Political Assistant to Deputy Commissioner, p. 8.
8. *Ibid*.
9. Phom Day, Golden Jubilee 1952-2002, June 5-6, 2002, *Bushah Leitap*, p. 19.
10. Interview held with Anyak Phom (79), retired *Do-Bhashi*, at Longleng on 11-04-2001.
11. Noklang, C. Amop, *Phom Day: A Basis for Peace in Nagaland*, pp. 59-60. The red colour signifies blood, white colour indicates peace and the rising sun symbolises disappearance of darkness.
12. Alemchiba, M., *A Brief Historical Account of Nagaland*, p. 157.
13. Imchen, Panger (ed.), *L. Kijung Ao The Longest Night* (An Outline Biography of the first Naga Missionary), p. 46.
14. Noklang, C. Amop, *Op. cit.*, p. 47.
15. Imchen, Panger (ed.), *Op. cit.*
16. *Ibid*.
17. Phom Baptist Christian Association, Golden Jubilee 1953-2003, *Bushah Laitap*, p. 21.
18. Philip, P.T., *The Growth of Baptist Churches in Nagaland*, p. 156.
19. *Ibid*, p. 157.
20. Henshet, B., *The Phom-Naga Indigenous Religion: A Socio-Philosophical Perspective*, p. 59.
21. Census 1971, *District Census Handbook*, Tuensang District, p. 99.
22. Golden Jubilee, Phom Baptist Christian Association, *Op. cit.*, p. 21.
23. Imchen, Panger (ed.), *Op. cit.*, p. 156.
24. Philip, P.T., *Op. cit.*
25. Konyak, A. Yangang, *From Darkness to Light*, p. 46; Sardeshpande, S.C., *The Patkoi Nagas*, p. 122.

26. Phom Baptist Christian Association, Golden Jubilee, *Op. cit.*, p. 30.
27. Singh, Prakash, *Nagaland*, p. 173.
28. Oottukalathil, Joseph, 'Education, the Means to Development and the Contribution of the Catholic Church in Tuensang District', printed in the Proceedings of a Seminar entitled "Over-view of Backward Areas of Nagaland Since Independence", Longleng, 2001, p. 65.
29. *Ibid.*
30. *Ibid.*
31. Census 1971, *Op. cit.*, pp. 76-77.
32. Noklang, C. Amop, *Op. cit.*, p. 26; Interview held with H. Toshi Phom (47), Member of Longleng Ad hoc Town Committee and Treasurer of Longleng Town Students' Union (LTSU), at PPC Colony, Longleng on 12-01-2003.
33. Ghosh, B.B. (ed.), *Nagaland District Gazetteers,* Tuensang District, p. 189.
34. Diary of A.E. Shuttle Worth for the month of October 1895, Secret Department, file no. 439.
35. Hutton, J., *Report on Naga Hills,* p. 10.
36. *Census 1951 Assam*, Naga Hills District Census Handbook; *Census of India 1961*, Vol. XXIII, Nagaland, Part II-C; *Census of India 1991*, District Census Handbook, Tuensang (pp.154 & 163).
37. The literal meaning of Longleng is sloping flat stones. Stone is called *long* and *leng* means sloping flat in Hukpang and Pongching dialect. When the administrative headquarters was opened at Longleng, flat and sloping stones were found available in the site. Three villages, viz. Bhumnyu, Hukpang and Orangkong jointly adopted the word Longleng and the administrative headquarters was named so. Interview held with Anyak Phom (81), *Op. cit.,* on 08-12-2003.
38. Phom, O. Kongyan, 'Health and Hygienic Problems of the Backward Areas of Nagaland—An Observation', printed in the *Proceedings of a Seminar* entitled "Over-view of Backward Areas of Nagaland Since Independence", Longleng, 2001, p. 43.
39. Noklang, C. Amop, *Op. cit.*, p. 25.
40. Phom, S. Chaidok, 'Growth and Development of Modern Education in Phom Community', paper presented in a Seminar entitled "Socio-Educational Status of Phom Community", held at Yingli College, Longleng on 9-10 July, 1997.
41. *Ibid.*
42. *Ibid.*
43. Chungpang, Namchei L., 'Over-view of Backward Community of Nagaland—Phom', printed in the *Proceedings of a Seminar* entitled "Over-view of Backward Areas of Nagaland Since Independence", Longleng, 2001, p. 79.
44. Borooah, N., 'The School Report', in the *Souvenir*, The Silver Jubilee 1972-97, Government High School, Longleng, pp. 35-36.
45. A person who can both read and write with understanding in any language

is taken as literate. All the children of the age of six years and below were treated as illiterate in 1991 census, whereas in the 1971 census children upto four years were treated as illiterate.

46. A total number of 228 students appeared in HSLC Examinations from Government High School, Longleng during 1999-2001 of whom 72 got through (31.57), whereas during the same period 259 students appeared in the Examinations from the Phom Lempong and M.T. Carmel Schools (private) of whom 181 students passed (69.88). Islam, Nurul, 'Over-view of Backward Areas of Nagaland since Independence with Special Reference to Educational Status of Phom Area', printed in the *Proceedings of a Seminar* entitled "Over-view of Backward Areas of Nagaland Since Independence", Longleng, 2001, p. 40.
47. *Ibid.*
48. *Nagaland, 2002*, p. 113.
49. *Annual Report 1995*, Holistic Child Development India, pp. 8-9.
50. Interview held with L. Shaupang Phom (78), retired government employee, at Longleng on 01-12-2003. He was admitted to a school in 1945 at Tamlu and later served in various capacities in the government of Nagaland.
51. 10 Years' *Progress in NEFA: A Brief Account of Administrative and Development Activities in North East Frontier Agency Since Independence*, p. 32.
52. Interview held with L. Shaupang Phom (78), *op. cit.*
53. Aier, Yajen, *A Brief History of Education in Nagaland During the Last 25 years: From 1947 to 1972*, p. 9.
54. *Nagaland Gazette*, No. 23, 15 March, 1978.
55. Ghosh, B. B. (ed.), *Op. cit.*, p. 187.
56. Speeches of S.C. Jamir, Chief Minister, Nagaland, 2000, 'Inaugural Address at the Seminar on Development of Mon District on 12th April, 2000', p. 36.
57. *Naga Assembly News*, No. 20, January-June 1996, p. 10.
58. Phom, S. Chaidok, *Op. cit.* T. Imdong Phom of Kangching village is a retired Deputy Director of the Directorate of School Education, Bukchem of Orangkong village was a former Minister of the Nagaland Council of Ministry and Anjo Keikung was the Acting Chairman of the Nagaland Public Service Commission.
59. Rahman, Abdur, 'The Place of Female in Phom Society', paper presented in a Seminar entitled "Socio-Educational Status of Phom Community", held at Yingli College, Longleng on 9-10 July, 1997.
60. Interview held with Hepong Phom (83), Ex-Interim Body Member and Ex-Regional Council Member, at Longleng on 19-11-2003.
61. *Tour Diary* of E.D. Savi for the month of January 1897, Secret Department, file no. 44.
62. *Tour Diary* of C.R. Pawsey for the month of December 1929, Secret Department, file no. 452.
63. Phom, O. Kongyan, *Op. cit.*, p. 42.
64. *Diary* of A. E. Shuttle Worth for the month of October 1895, *Op. cit.*

65. Elwin, Verrier, *Nagaland*, p. 95.
66. *Babu Oukshokching Baptist Attoi, Silver Jubilee Bushah Lai,* (Silver Jubilee History Book) 1959-1983, p. 3. In 1978, the medical staff for the Leprosy Colony, Longleng were as follows: Leprosy Medical Officer: 01, Stuff Nurse: 02, Physiotherapist: 01, Laboratory Technician: 01, Non-Medical Supervisors: 01 and Para Medical Workers: 06. Ghosh, B. B. (ed.), *Op. cit.*, pp. 205-206.
67. Phom, N. Chingyam, 'Pre and Post Independence Socio-Economic and Historical Background of Nagaland: Especial Reference to Tuensang', printed in the *Proceedings of a Seminar* entitled "Over-view of Backward Areas of Nagaland Since Independence", Longleng, 2001, p. 74.
68. Interview held with Kongyan Phom (40), Medical Officer, at Longleng on 05-02-2003.
69. *List of Health/Medical Units in Nagaland*, Department of Health and Family Welfare, 2000, p.5.
70. *Village-wise Index of Development* (as on 1st April, 1983), p. 30. It may be noted that till the opening of another Rural Development Block at Tamlu in 1995-96, the lone Rural Development Block, Longleng was covering the Phom villages of the present Longleng district.
71. *Census of India 1991*, *Op. cit.*, pp. 50-54.
72. *Citizens' Charter*, Health and Family Welfare Department, Kohima, 2002, p. 18.
73. Interview held with Kongyan Phom (40), *Op. cit.*
74. Tour Diary of C.R. Pawsey for the months of April and May 1928, Secret Department, file no. 452.
75. Tour Diary of S. J. Duncan for the months of May-June 1950, *Op. cit.*
76. Interview held with Y. Heong Phom (56), ex-Vice-Chairman, Longleng Area Council, and the Vice-Chairman, Longleng Ad-hoc Town Committee, at Block Colony, Longleng on 27-11-2001.
77. The researcher interviewed (2003-05) forty Phom people, eight persons each belonging to Sakchi, Bhumnyu, Yongam, Bura Namsang villages and Longleng town. The interviewees were of different social status and age, roughly from thirteen to seventy years.
78. Ao, A. Lanunungsang, *Rural Development in Nagaland*, p. 153.
79. Interview held with Lima Hamyei (56), Head Assistant to Deputy Commissioner, Longleng and N. Hamvok Phom (76), *Do-Bhashi*, at Longleng on 14-09-2003 and 15-01-2003 respectively.
80. Horam, M., *Naga Old Ways and New Trends*, p. 68.
81. Horam, M., *Social and Cultural Life of Nagas* (the Tangkhul Nagas), p. 62.
82. Interview held with Lima Hamyei (56) and N. Hamvok (76), *Op. cit.*
83. *Ibid.*
84. Henshet, B., *Op. cit.*, p. 39.
85. Interview held with Lima Hamyei (56) and N. Hamvok (76), *Op. cit.*
86. Four senior persons belonging to Sakchi (2004) Bhumnyu (2004), Yongam (2003) and Bura Namsang (2004) were interviewed regarding housing system by the researcher.

87. *Ibid.*
88. Woodthorpe, R. G., 'General Report of the Topographical Surveys, 1875-76', quoted in Verrier Elwin's *The Nagas in the Nineteenth Century*, p. 382.
89. Interview held with Y. Heong Phom (56), *Op. cit.*
90. Four senior persons belonging to Sakchi (2004), *Op. cit.*
91. Village-wise Index of Development (As on 1st April, 1983), p. 290.
92. Four senior persons belonging to Sakchi (2004), *op. cit.*
93. Hutton, J., *Op. cit.* p. 8.
94. *Festivals of Nagaland*, p. 26.
95. *Ibid.*, p. 27.
96. *Ibid.*
97. *Ibid.*, p. 28.
98. *Ibid.*
99. Ao, A. Lanu (ed), *Naga Cultural Attires and Musical Instruments*, pp. 113-126.
100. *Ibid.*, p. 20.
101. *Ibid.*, pp. 22-25.
102. *Ibid.*, p. 37.
103. *Ibid.*, p. 47.
104. *Ibid.*, p. 52.
105. *Ibid.*, pp. 52-57.
106. *Ibid.*, p. 68.
107. *Ibid.*, p. 81.
108. *Ibid.*, p. 82.
109. *Ibid.*, p. 90.
110. *Ibid.*, p. 101.
111. *Ibid.*, p. 107.
112. Interview held with L. Shaupang Phom (78), *Op. cit.*
113. Ao. A. Lanu (ed), *Op. cit.*, p. 95.
114. Ao, M. Alemchiba, *The Arts and Crafts of Nagaland*, p. 44.
115. *Primary Census Abstract–Nagaland 2011, Directorate of Census Operations in Nagaland, Kohima.*
116. Interview held with L. Shaupang Phom (78), *Op. cit.*
117. Bareh, H.M., *Encyclopaedia of North-East India*, Vol. VI, *Nagaland*, p. 215.
118. Interview held with L. Shaupang Phom (78), *op. cit.*
119. *Ibid.*
120. Henshet, B., *Op. cit.*, p. 14.
121. Woodthorpe, R.G., 'General Report of the Topographical Surveys, 1875-76', *Op. cit.*, p. 382. R. G. Woodthorpe wrote this while visiting Yongshei village. A Naga youth named Jacob accompanied Woodthorpe in this survey.
122. Henshet, B., *Op. cit.*, p. 14.
123. Interview held with L. Shaupang Phom (78), *Op. cit.*

Phom Traditional House

A morung (Bang) for boys

Mother Church, Longleng Town

Jhum field (Yongphang) under preparation

Aerial View of the Longleng Town

Phom women returning from field

A Phom girl in her traditional loom

A Phom young man playing cup violin (traditional instrument)

A long-drum (Sakshi)

An old Phom woman spinning thread from raw cotton

A folk dance of the Phom women

A man playing trumpet

Phom women pounding rice in their traditional pounding table made of wood

A village gate in Bhumnyu village

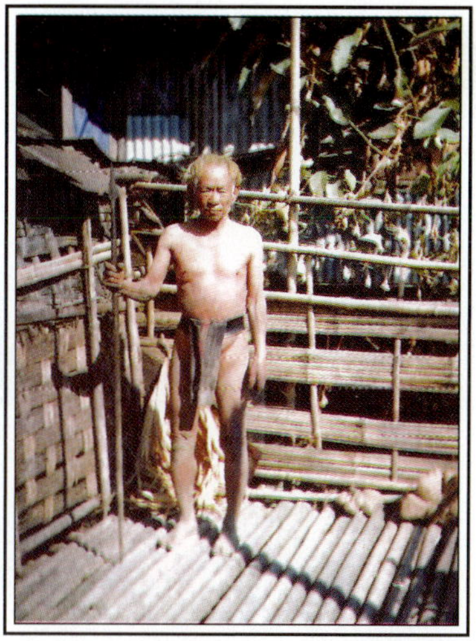

An elderly Phom Naga in his traditional attire

A Phom man in his martial attire

A Phom *Do-bhashi* (interpreter)

A Phom young man in his warrior shawl which is distinguishable from other shawls by white arrow marks woven in the centre of the shawl

Two Yingli college students

4
Economic Transformation

The structure of the economy of an area, as suggested by S. I. Saleh, can broadly be classified into three sectors, Primary, Secondary and Tertiary.[1] People are generally engaged in these three sectors, though occupational structure and mode of production may vary from sector to sector. The sector "which engages itself mainly in the production of commodities, whose production process involves considerable utilisation of natural forces or resources may be termed as the 'Primary Sector' while the sector which mainly concentrates on the production of commodities whose creation involves manipulation of materials or non-human factors to create from utility, may be called the 'Secondary Sector', and the sector which produces services, that is something that does not contain physical element in them, may be christened as the 'Tertiary Sector'."[2] Based on the above mentioned definition we can include agriculture, animal husbandry, forestry and fishery, mining and quarries, etc., in primary occupation. These provide basic need for human existence, i.e. food and raw materials. Secondary occupation comprises manufacturing and small enterprises. It includes cottage, small-scale, medium-scale and large-scale industries. The main activity is to transform the nature of production into finished products. Tertiary occupation covers transport and communication, trade and commerce, organised banking, professional arts, government and allied services, etc. On the basis of the three sectorial occupations, a few aspects of the economy of the Phom people of Longleng district are analysed in the following pages.

Livelihood Pattern

Till about the first half of the twentieth century the livelihood pattern of the Phom people was primitive. Although they chiefly depended on agriculture, they had no knowledge of sustainable method of production. Some people were engaged in traditional industries and business, but none of these was their mainstay. However, from the beginning of the second half of the twentieth century the livelihood pattern of these people began to change. With the spread of modern education, business, growth of new administrative set-up, etc., the structure of the economy of the area showed signs of change. In course of time some people have taken up various professions as their principal livelihood other than agriculture. The livelihood pattern of the Scheduled Tribe population of Longleng District can be seen from Table 4.1 given below.[3]

Table 4.1: Livelihood pattern of the Scheduled Tribe population under Longleng District (1971 & 2011)

	1971			*2011*		
	P	*M*	*F*	*P*	*M*	*F*
1. Scheduled tribe population	18,637	9,684	8,953	48,615	25,268	23,347
2. Total number of main workers	8,314	4,760	3,554	20,944	11,547	9,397
3. (a) Cultivators	7,919	4,418	3,501	16,837	8,415	8,422
(b) Agricultural labourers	52	35	17	278	164	114
4. Livestock, forestry, fishing, hunting and plantation, orchards & allied activities	13	13	—	—	—	—
5. Manufacturing, processing, servicing and repairings						
Household industry	3	3		199	118	81
Non-household industry	1	1	—	—	—	—
6. Construction	17	17	—	—	—	—
7. Trade & commerce	1	1	—	—	—	—
8. Transport, storage & communications	4	4	—	—	—	—
9. Other services	304	268	36	—	—	—
10. Marginal Workers	—	—	—	9,624	4,726	4,898
11. Main Other workers	—	—	—	3,630	2,850	780
11. Non-workers	10,323	4,924	5,399	19,916	10,229	9,687

Source: (i) Census 1971, *District Census Handbook,* Tuensang District, pp. 78-79.

(ii) Census of India 1991, *District Census Handbook,* Tuensang, pp. 391-393.

Table 4.1 clearly shows that with the rise in population a small number of people began to take up professions other than agriculture for their livelihood. The table also reveals that less than half of the total Scheduled Tribe people of Longleng district constitute the main workers. And again, out of 20,944 main workers, 16,837 were cultivators according to 2011 census. It indicates that cultivation is their main occupation and all the cultivators possess more or less good cultivating lands where they work. In the time of need they extend their helping hands to one another rather than hired labour. This is the reason why the number of agricultural labourers is negligible in the Phom society. The number of persons taking part in household industry had increased in 2011 as compared to 1971. A small number of people were engaged in construction work like building houses and roads, laying telegraph lines and water ways, constructing water reservoirs, industrial plants and such other allied activities which fall under this category of work. The Phoms are now in the early stage of learning the basics of trade and commerce. No doubt, a good number of them are in government service. All Naga women play an important role in productive activity and the Phoms in particular have started to involve themselves in non-agricultural activities only gradually.

Agriculture

Agriculture remains the mainstay of the Phom people for centuries. Undoubtedly, certain sustainable changes have taken place in the method of cultivation of varieties of crops and fruits, commercialisation of agricultural products, etc. The Phom people practise *jhum* cultivation traditionally, while the other form of cultivation is terrace (wet rice cultivation). It is worth mentioning here that they had no knowledge of terrace cultivation earlier. It was introduced in the area in the second half of the twentieth century by the government. The Angamis of the Kohima district and Chakesang of Phek district, on the other hand are traditionally accustomed to the terrace cultivation.

Shifting cultivation, better known as *jhum* cultivation, is the most ancient system of cultivation which is still practised by the Phoms in a big way.[4] In the *jhum* system of cultivation a hilly plot of land is used for two to three years successively and thereafter the land is allowed to lie fallow for some years till the soil regains its fertility. When a plot of land is left fallow another plot is taken up for cultivation. In this way after a gap of a few years they come back to the same plot of land which was left fallow a few years earlier. The cycle of rotation varies from village to village depending on the availability of land and population. The rapid growth of population has reduced the cycling period. A cultivator at the same time tills one or two plots of land usually, one being new and the other, old. Seeds are sown in March or April and the ripened paddy is harvested in July or August. Weeding and harvesting are done usually by the people of different age groups. The members of every group offer their labour to one another in turn. Terrace cultivation is done usually in a gentle slope of land by means of artificial irrigation system. Growing paddy plants are transplanted in the field in June or July and the paddy is harvested in October or November.

Jhum cultivation has several demerits. It needs intensive human labour. It is prone to land erosion; it causes deforestation and rapid loss of fertility, etc., whereas in the terrace field manure is not washed away, cow dung and other manures can be used to restore the fertility of soil. Again shifting cultivation is affected by inadequate rainfall but there is less chance of this in wet rice cultivation because water is controlled and supplied generally from natural water sources as and when required. The slash-and-burn agriculture also causes air pollution. People of the district receive black rain water in the beginning of the rainy season.

The Government of Nagaland has been encouraging terrace cultivation by offering 50 per cent subsidy to the farmers for making the terrace fields.[5] Most of the minor irrigation channels have been laid through government assistance in the form of cash subsidy. Despite all this, the majority of the Phom cultivators still practise *jhum* cultivation because they can produce a large variety of crops, i.e. millet, maize, taro (colocasia), pumpkin, beans, cucumber, varieties of chillies, ginger, garlic, brinjal, sweet potato, gourd, etc., alongside paddy in the *jhum* fields, whereas in terrace fields nothing else can be grown except paddy. Several factors, i.e. steepy terrains, scarcity of water, lack of capital, etc., discourage the villagers to give up *jhuming* altogether and take up terrace cultivation. In the villages where *jhum* cultivation is practised extensively, farmers in general are not inclined to take up terrace cultivation for fear of damage to the paddy by wild birds. There are many cultivators who had practised terrace at one time but abandoned it later as they found it difficult to maintain the canals which are washed away by rainwater every year. This researcher met thirty-eight cultivators belonging to four villages and the Longleng town but found nonc who practises only terrace. Majority of the people of Longleng town are engaged in various activities other than agriculture. Naturally, they practise neither terrace nor *jhum*. The three villages, each under Longleng and Tamlu administration tilling the largest irrigated area are shown in the Table 4.2.

Table 4.2: Area under cultivation of the three villages each under Longleng and Tamlu (1981)

Name of villages	*Wet rice cultivation (in hectares)*	*Jhum cultivation (in hectares)*
Longleng circle		
1. Pongo	28.33	2,889
2. Sakchi	28.33	1,631
3. Yangching	24.28	801.28
Tamlu circle		
1. Ladaigarh	105.22	0
2. Bura Namsang	84.98	360.17
3. Kangching	48.56	194.25

Source: Census of India 1981, *District Census Handbook,* Tuensang District, pp. 117-137.
(*Note*: The figures given here appear to be an over estimate of the actual area under wet rice cultivation. From my field study I have found the number of such cultivation to be much below the figures shown here.)

As per 1991 census, Ngetchungching, Shamnyuching, Ladaigarh, Tamlu H.Q., Kangching and Bura Namsang were the six villages practising the highest tracts of terrace cultivation.[6] Thus, the villages of Tamlu sub-division have larger area of terrace fields than the villages of the upper hill ranges. The Phom cultivators generally do not practise double cropping. According to a government report, out of twenty-five villages under Longleng Rural Development Block, twenty-four villages had terrace fields, two villages had high-yielding varieties of paddy, nineteen villages had minor irrigation facilities and only two villages practised double cropping.[7] The number of villages having minor irrigation facilities under Longleng Rural Development Block is mentioned in Table 4.3.

Table 4.3: Minor Irrigation Commissioned in 27 Phom villages

	Total no. of villages	*No. of villages having M.I. schemes*	*Total area under irrigation (ha.)*			*Surface flow irrigation scheme (completed)*	
			Surface irrigation	*Lift irrigation*	*Total area (ha.)*	*No. of schemes commissioned with year*	
1987-88	25	25	1086.8	0.00	1086.8	46 (Before 1982-83)	492 (1982-1987)
1994-95	—	25	470.51	0.00	470.51	91 (Before 1989-90)	109 (1989-1994)
2000-01	25	25	524.79	0.00	524.79	243 (1994-2001)	—

Source: (i) *Report on Census of Minor Irrigation Schemes in Nagaland 1987-88*, pp. 16, 34-35.
(ii) *Report on Census of Minor Irrigation Schemes in Nagaland 1994-95*, pp. 16, 210-211.
(iii) *Report on Census of Minor Irrigation Schemes in Nagaland 2000-01*, pp. 15 & 88.

In addition to the minor irrigation schemes, two major irrigation projects were completed in 2002, one at Pongo and another at Yaong village. Work of four other major irrigation projects was in progress in 2003.[8]

In course of his field study the researcher met 32 cultivators belonging to four villages of Sakchi, Bhumnyu, Yongam and Bura Namsang. Of these thirty-two peasants, twenty-six cultivated their own land while six others besides tilling their own land, took others' land on lease on the condition to pay a fixed amount of money or rendering physical labour or supplying a fixed quantity of crops for one or two years. It is also observed that all the Phom cultivators did not possess sufficient cultivable land. Of the thirty-two cultivators mentioned here, sixteen were capable of producing paddy which was enough for consumption throughout the year. On the other hand the rest sixteen produced paddy which met their requirement for eight to eleven months in the year. This shortage, however, does not occur every year but once or twice in several years. This shortfall in production is generally attributed to the *jhum* system of cultivation under which a cultivator tills a particular plot of land for two to three years consecutively without trying to retain its fertility. In case, the newly selected plot happens to be infertile, it also leads to crop shortage. In the event of crop failure, many cultivators take paddy on loan on the condition that the loan shall be repaid as soon as the next harvest is over with fifty per cent interest. Nowadays the Phom cultivators, instead of taking paddy on loan, prefer to purchase it either from the fellow villagers who have a surplus or buy rice from markets to tide over the scarcity.

The Phom cultivators do not use chemical fertilisers at all but depend on natural fertility of the soil.[9] A few use improved seeds and pesticides. They do not use modern agricultural machineries like power tiller, tractor, pump set, seed drill, maize sheller, etc. The cultivators of Sakchi, Bhumnyu and Yongam do not use bull for ploughing their fields which is however not the case with the people of Bura Namsang. Ploughing was unknown till it was introduced as a scheme by the government in the foothills in the third quarter of the twentieth century.[10] Moreover, the villages bordering Assam have large plateau. The sides of the cultivated fields are demarcated by planting stones or lily flower plants.

Horticulture

The Phom Nagas were unaccustomed to the cultivation of potato, squash, mustard, cabbage, cauliflower, coriander, lady's finger, pea, onion, long bean, radish, papaya, plum, pear, litchi, different varieties of tomato and brinjals, etc., till the second quarter of the twentieth century. The following two Tables 4.4 and 4.5 would explain the number of fruit and vegetable orchards and the marketing of the commodities under Longleng Rural Development Block during 1985-86 (Table 4.4).

The tables further suggest that in addition various types of fruits, vegetables like potato, sweet potato, ginger, onion, brinjal, tomato, *topioca, kochu*, etc., are grown in large quantity nowadays. A part of the produce is sold which enables the orchard holders to earn something. The farmers living nearby Longleng town sell their produce at Longleng. Women and girls are seen carrying the loads of agricultural products to the markets. Villagers bordering Assam sell their products, especially betel at the Naga bazaar, near Geleki (Assam-Nagaland border) and make handsome profit. Of late a section of the Phom people in the border has begun to grow tea, a nontraditional plantation crop. Six small tea growers of Longleng district have already been registered with the Tea Board of India.[11]

Table 4.4: Total no. of fruit orchards and marketing of fruits in Longleng Rural Development Block, 1985-86

Total no. of fruit orchards						Marketing of fruits		
Sl. No.	Fruits	No. of villages growing fruits	No. of orchards	Area under orchards (in ha.)	Total production of fruits (Qtls)	Quantity sold (retail sale Qtls)	Total cash returns (Rs.)	Average returns per quintal (Rs.)
1	2	3	4	5	6	7	8	9
1.	Pear	20	104	38.9	372	271	22985	85
2.	Plum	9	24	8.9	59	41	4350	106
3.	Peach	9	38	13.3	82	48	3065	64
4.	Orange	25	345	131.9	1872	1662	242345	146
5.	Banana	24	281	112.4	1505	1224	178670	146
6.	Guava	21	193	74.9	532	393	33790	86
7.	Pineapple	20	160	65.5	472	406	75200	185
Total			**1145**	**445.8**	**4894**	**4045**	**560405**	**—**

Source: Survey of Area and Production of Horticulture Crops in Nagaland 1985-86, pp. 274 & 277.

Table 4.5: Total no. of vegetable orchards and marketing of vegetables in Longleng Rural Development Block, 1985-86

Total no. of vegetable orchards						Marketing of vegetables		
Sl. No.	Vegetables	No. of villages growing vegetables	No. of orchards	Area under orchards (in ha.)	Total production of vegetables (Qtls)	Quantity sold (retail sale Qtls)	Total cash returns (Rs.)	Average returns per quintal (Rs.)
1	2	3	4	5	6	7	8	9
1	Potato	8	30	11.2	785	100	19860	199
2	Sweet potato	13	43	15.4	335	35	6900	197
3	Ginger	7	25	10.0	865	185	71000	384
4	Onion	5	28	11.2	875	170	33500	197
5	Brinjal	1	1	0.4	68	—	—	—
6	Tomato	1	1	0.4	228	—	—	—
7	Topioca	1	1	0.4	117	—	—	—
8	Kachu (colocasia)	16	64	25.6	1638	500	123500	247
Total			**193**	**74.6**	**4811**	**990**	**254760**	—

Source: *Survey of Area and Production of Horticulture Crops in Nagaland 1985-86*, pp. 274 & 278.

Animal Husbandry

Domesticated birds and animals, viz. pigs, cattle, fowls, *mithuns*, etc., occupy an important place in the economy of the Phom people. They reared animals for meat and also as a medium of exchange in the past. These practices are still in vogue. The Phoms reared livestock and poultry birds but the method of breeding and fostering was unsustainable. Cross-bred cattle, pig, improved species of fowls, etc., were introduced in the area in the later decades of the last century. The number of livestock and fowls available under Longleng Rural Development Block during the period 1982-2003 is given in the following Table 4.6.

Table 4.6: Livestock of the Phom villages for the year 1982, 1987 and 2003

Species	*No. of households covered : 4245 1982*	*All villages were covered 1987*	*No. of households covered : 15554 2003*
1. (a) Cross-bred cattle	90	788	3975
(b) Indigenous cattle	2217	4316	7063
2. Buffaloes	121	06	Nil
3. Mithuns	34	47	1539
4. Goats	537	3285	1182
5. Horse, ponies, mules, donkeys, camels	30	Nil	Nil
6. (a) Cross-bred pigs	356	985	5269
(b) Indigenous pigs	7239	5375	10950
7. Dogs	1235	2625	5640
8. Sheep	Nil	04	Nil
9. Rabbits	Nil	Nil	93
10. Fowls (cock, hens, chick)	17875	Desi: 8652	43845
11. Duck (drake, duck, ducklings)		Improved: 5918	6216
(a) Desi	144	951	878
(b) Improved	101	965	2930

Source: (i) *Report on Thirteenth Quinquennial Livestock Census 1982*, pp. 6-15.
(ii) *Report on Fourteenth Quinquennial Livestock Census 1987*, pp. 34-47.
(iii) *Report on Seventeenth Quinquennial Livestock Census 2003*, pp. 181-191.

Table 4.6 shows that the buffalo population decreased drastically over a period of five years and by 2003 the animal was no longer domesticated in the Phom villages. On the other hand, the table reveals that in addition to indigenous animals and birds, the Phom people began to rear a considerable number of cross-bred livestock and improved fowls. In the olden days, *mithun* was considered as the symbol of prosperity, but no *mithun* is found now in Yongam and Bura Namsang villages. Most of the owners keep the animals for sale and also for meat. While interviewing forty persons belonging to four villages and Longleng town, it was found that out of the forty interviewees, three persons do not sell their domestic animals or birds while the rest thirty-seven sell them in part. An approximate gross annual income of the thirty-seven persons interviewed comes to Rs. 2,31,900.00 from the sale of livestock and fowls, the annual average income per head being Rs. 6,267.56 approximately.

Until recently, the Phom people had no knowledge of rearing elephant, horse, pigeon, duck, sheep, rabbit, etc. Except Bura Namsang, the villagers of Sakchi, Bhumnyu and Yongam do not have cowsheds. Pigs were kept freely earlier by the rural Phoms. Some villagers used to keep them in pens under the platform at the back of the *morung* used generally as latrine.[12] Of late, they have ceased to rear pigs freely but started to confine them in separate sheds. However, except pig they still rear other animals freely. Villagers keep off the animals from their cultivation fields by erecting bamboo fencing. In Phom areas indigenous cows are not reared by their owners at home but these are allowed to stray in the jungle. This animal is generally used for meat and not for its milk.

The number of fowls reared by the Phom villagers is the highest as compared to other domesticated birds. The meat and egg of these are in great demand among the people. Table 4.7 given below gives an idea of the number of hens and eggs for the year 1987-88.

Table 4.7: Availability of hens and eggs at the end of 1987-88

Name of circle	*No. of hen maintained for egg*		*Average egg yield per hen per year*		*No. of eggs produced during 1987-88*		*Total no. of eggs produced*
	Desi	*Improved*	*Desi*	*Improved*	*Desi*	*Improved*	
Longleng	2005	2927	60	144	120300	421488	
Tamlu	1028	408	60	144	61680	58752	
					181900	480240	662140

Source: Singh, R.D.N. and Zeliang, T. (ed), *Development Profile of Animal Husbandry in Nagaland*, p. 135.

Interestingly however, there has always been a shortage of meat of cattle and buffaloes for consumption. To overcome the shortage, these animals are now imported in large number from Haluating area in Assam. Dog is another common domestic animal of the area, which is reared for guarding house as well for its meat. The Government of Nagaland is giving a lot of attention to combat animal disease by establishing veterinary units in the area. In 2010-11, there were one Veterinary Hospital, one Dispensary, one Stockman Centre and two Veterinary Outposts under Longleng district.[13]

Forest

A large part of Longleng district is covered by green forests. The district receives high degree of rainfall and the climate is suitable for luxurious growth of various species of flora. Barring a small area of forest near the Bura Namsang village, the rest of the forest lands of the district are under the control and management of private owners. There is no Reserved Forest, Wild Life Sanctuary or Protected Forest in the district. Since, there was no government forest in this area, the Forest Department had taken steps to purchase some forest lands from private owners to start new plantations. In 1977-78, 437.47 hectares of land were purchased by the Government of Nagaland from the Bura Namsang village. Except this small plot of purchased forest, the rest of the forest can be termed as Village Forests or Forest under Private Control.[14]

Trees like *koroi*, *poma*, *sopa*, *gomari*, *gogra*, *khokon*, *hollock*, *sam*, *am*, *badam*, *betula*, pine, *mekahi*, *neem*, *kadam*, *lali*, etc., are found in abundance in the district. Pine forests are seen in the hills at an elevation of 1000 to 1500 metres, although the tree is found mixed with *betula*, *prunus*, *schima*, etc.[15] Broadleaved species like *koroi*, *poma*, *sopa*, *gomari*, *gogra*, etc., are generally found in the hilly area below 1800 metres and above 500 metres.[16] In addition to the above mentioned trees, some other forest wealth such as sand, stone, bamboo, cane, *agor*, thatch, etc., are found in abundance.

Till the middle of the twentieth century, the Phom people did not purchase any building materials for purpose of house construction. They used to collect all kinds of building materials such as thatch and leaves, timber, cane, bamboo, etc., from the forests. They also collected firewood and other forest produce for making basket, mat, etc. They still depend on the forest for all such materials. A few saw mills had been set up in some of the Phom villages but these were closed down by 1995. One of the major disadvantages of productive exploitation of forest resources of this hilly district is poor transport facilities. The villages situated in the south-east of the district like Auching and Sakchi supply a small quantity of timber to Marioni (Assam) *via* Tuensang and Mokokchung. Bura Namsang and other four villages bordering on Assam supply timber to Naginimora saw mill. Other Phom villages send timber to Tuli (Mokokchung) saw mill and it is sold at the rate of Rs. 150 to 200 per CFT for class I wood. Some contractors buy plank or timber from villagers directly after paying necessary revenue and obtaining a permit from the Forest Department. Timber is collected from the forests mostly during the dry season for commercial purpose. Some farmers have started tree plantations since the last two decades of the last century.[17]

Wild animals like boar, black bear, tiger, deer, monkey, porcupine, wild goat, jackal, jungle cat, wolf, fox, flying squirrel, hare and various species of birds were abundant in the jungles in the past. But, as a consequence of indiscriminate killing of these animals and birds in the years gone by, the number of wild animals and birds has decreased considerably. Many of the precious birds and animals such as peacock, hornbill, vulture, kingfisher, skylark, swan, crow, lion, tiger, elephant rabbit, rhinoceros, monkey, chimpanzee, mongoose, etc., have already become extinct from the vicinity of the Phom areas. With the growth of population as well as extension of the cultivable lands during the last few decades the forest area has also decreased to a large extent.

Since 1973 the Government of Nagaland had imposed a ban on killing of wild animals throughout the state from 1st March to 31st October[18] and the same is respected by the Village Councils. If anyone is found damaging the forest resources by any means or stealing them from the forests of others or belonging to the community, a fine is imposed upon the guilty person either in cash or kind.

Industry

There is no large or medium-scale industry in Longleng district. However, some indigenous small-scale cottage industries are seen at several places. These industries require intensive manual labour and can provide subsidiary or part-time employment to several unskilled labourers and artisans. The art of working these industries is crude and the same is handed down from generation to generation. On the other hand, modern small-scale units which are few in number in the district depend on sophisticated machinery and equipment and are capable of providing full time employment to skilled workers. In the following few pages a brief account of these industries such as weaving, basket-making, decorative work, woodwork, pottery, blacksmithy, etc., is given.

Weaving

Weaving is an art in which the Phom women are highly skilled. They weave *mekhalas*, shawls, bags, etc., in their looms with distinct designs and colour combinations. They used to weave man's loin cloth and woman's waist wrapper at home before the introduction of modern dress.[19] They weaved cloths with hand-spinning thread of cotton. Cotton was grown more or less in every village. With the arrival of mill-made yarn in the market at a cheaper price, the women have started purchasing ready-made yarn from market for the purpose of weaving. This has indirectly affected cotton cultivation in the district. Simultaneously, the easy availability of coloured thread in the market no longer encouraged the production of indigenous dye.[20] Villagers rarely spin yarn at home nowadays. In recent years they have started weaving waistcoat, necktie, bed sheet and other clothes required in their day-to-day life. Weavers also earn a little by selling their products.[21] Interestingly, the Phom weavers do not use Flying Shuttle, Dobby, Jacquard looms, etc.

Bamboo and Cane Handicrafts

Baskets of various shapes and sizes are in use among the Phoms. They carry grains, household articles, firewood, water containers, etc., in the baskets. Basket-making is usually a pastime of the old men. The baskets are carried hanging from the head on the back with the help of a strap. Among other cane and bamboo-made traditional handicrafts mention may be made of the winnowing fan, mat, *chunga*, cup, hat, etc. These articles are made at home or purchased from the artisans directly by the customers.[22]

Decorative Works

Some decorative works have remained in use and are quite popular among the Phom people from time immemorial. These decorative works include headgear, decorated spear, decorated *dao* handle, *dao* holder, parts of ceremonial dresses, war shield, casket, etc. These are produced by the artisans skilled in this art. Unfortunately, like many other indigenous art this art is fast dying out in Phom Naga society.

Woodcarving

The Phom men were expert in woodcarving work in the past. They carved the figures of animals, birds, reptiles in the pillers and beams of the *morung* and in places of dwelling. They also made wooden platter, log drum, rice pounding table, smoking pipe, cup, *dao*-case, etc. This art, though waning, is still practised by a few people. The Phom woodcarvers do not use modern tools and machineries in their work. Thus, their products are generally crude and unpolished which cannot compete with the superior machine-made articles.

Pottery

The making of earthen pots has remained exclusively a vocation of the womenfolk in Phom society. In some villages the women produce various types of earthen pots by hand with the help of a stick but without a wheel.[23] The manufacturing process is simple. After collecting the clay they grind it in a stone plate. Thereafter, with the help of a round stone and shaping sticks made of bamboo, earthen pots are made. The pots are then dried in the sun for several days before burning them in fire. The pots produced are of different shapes and sizes.[24] Pot-making clay is available in Pongo and Yongphang villages; hence maximum number of pots was manufactured in these two villages alone. People from the neighbouring areas come and buy pots directly from these villages. The pot-making industry, no doubt, has suffered a setback with the arrival of steel and enamel pottery in the market. Yet, cooking pots made of earth are still in great demand among the people. One reason of this perhaps is that the Phom people believe that the food cooked in the earthen pot is more tasty and hygienic than the one cooked in aluminium or steel pots.[25]

Carpentry

Before the formation of Naga Hills-Tuensang Area (1957), carpentry was a compulsory subject in all M.E. Schools. So, all the students receiving education in these schools had to learn carpentry work.[26] Pupils are still imparted training in carpentry in the government schools. Some self-trained people in recent years have taken up this work as means of livelihood. The implements used are rude and unsophisticated.

Blacksmithy

In some villages, viz. Pongo, Auching, Yongphang, Bhumnyu, etc., black-smithy work is carried on extensively. Besides using imported iron from Assam, the Phom blacksmiths also depend on iron parts of motor vehicles. They make various iron implements such as muzzle loading gun, *dao*, sickle, hoe, axe, spear head, etc. However, these are not sold in markets but are purchased directly by the people from the blacksmiths.[27] Since, they use outdated hand tools (forge) for manufacturing iron implements, the quality of production is poor.

Motor Repairing

With the introduction of motor vehicles, e.g. jeep, truck and bus, mostly for transporting goods and carrying passengers, a few motor repairing garages or workshops have been set up at Longleng town.

Tailoring

Earlier, the art of tailoring was totally unknown to the Phom people. The increasing demand of western dress has helped the setting up of a few tailoring shops at Longleng town and also elsewhere. We give below a list of small-scale industry units under Longleng Sub-District Industries Centre.

List of Small-Scale Industry Units

1.	Weaving and Knitting	: 35
2.	Rice-mill	: 24
3.	Blacksmithy	: 21
4.	Bakery	: 06
5.	Handicrafts	: 14
6.	Carpentry	: 07

(*Contd.*)

List (*Contd.*)

7.	Cane and Bamboo	: 03
8.	Furniture	: 07
9.	Bee keeping Unit	: 02
10.	Pottery	: 01
11.	Motor Workshop	: 03
12.	Printing Press Unit	: 01
13.	Sawmill	: 04
14.	Ready-made Garment	: 04

Source: Sub-District Industries Centre, Longleng. The figures are of 1984-85.

It is to be noted here that the hand-loom and handicraft products of the district are rarely sent out for sale. It is due to several reasons. Firstly, business acumen has not yet developed among the Phoms. Secondly, inadequate transport facilities in the area and the high cost of raw materials lead to the rise of price of the finished products. The quality of these products being poor and crude, they cannot compete with the superior mill-made products coming from the plains. Nevertheless, a few small-scale industries, i.e. rice mill, bakery, carpentry, pottery, motor repairing workshop, etc., are running fairly well in the district.[28]

Since the establishment of the Sub-District Industries Centre (now District Industries Centre) at Longleng in 1984, it has been playing a vital role in the development of small-scale industries. The district has a Rural Artisan Programme (RAP) Training Centre. Prior to 1989-90, the Government of Nagaland provided loan with subsidy to the youths to set up small-scale industries. Nowadays subsidies are given to the applicants who have already purchased machineries for such purposes or have opened industrial units at their own cost.[29] Under a Centrally Sponsored Scheme, twelve industrial sheds were constructed at Longleng. The District Industries Centre has been trying to motivate the local entrepreneurs or artisans to set up units in these industrial sheds. However, acute scarcity of electricity and water supply always act as a deterrent in this respect.[30] In Nagaland, all entrepreneurs wishing to open small industrial units have to obtain licences from the State Government. But, such licences are not as a rule given to anybody other than a Naga as a result of which no outsider can apply for a licence.[31] This has no doubt provided an opportunity to the local youths to take to this vocation more seriously, though it has also hampered the industrial growth of the province by restricting competition.

Transport and Communication

If agriculture and industry are regarded as the body and the bones of the economy of a region, transport and communication system can be termed as their nerves, which helps the uninterrupted movement of men and materials. Improved transport facilities not only contribute to expansion of market for goods, but also encourage setting up of industries for production of quality materials. In other words expansion and better transport facility always determine the pace of development of a region.

Longleng district is completely dependent on road transport. The only road that the colonial government constructed in the last decade of the nineteenth century was a bridle path that connected Tamlu with Geleki (Assam) and Mokokchung.[32] Except this, there was no road worth the name barring the narrow footpaths linking the villages. These footpaths were highly steep and covered by jungles during monsoon. After independence a few motorable roads were constructed throughout the region. The first such road from Longleng to Changtongya (Mokokchung district) was constructed in 1954. Prior to the construction of this road government officers used to come to Longleng on foot. The same road was widened in 1958-59. In 1975-76, the suspension bridge over the Dikhu river was replaced by a concrete bridge which enabled heavy vehicles to cross the river. A jeepable road between Tuensang and Longleng was built in 1958.[33] The construction work of a gravel road from Tamlu to Wakching (Mon district) was started in 1964.[34] Two suspension bridges, one over the Dikhu river on Tamlu-Wakching road and the other over the Yangmun river on Champang (Mon district)-Longleng road were built later.[35] Till the end of the twentieth century all the roads and bridges, were in poor shape due mainly to heavy rainfall, which occasionally disrupted road communications, especially during the rainy season. There was no blacktopped road in the entire area.[36] Road distance from Longleng and Tamlu to other important places of Nagaland is shown below:

Road Distance from Longleng and Tamlu to other Important Places of Nagaland

1.	Tuensang to Longleng via Sakchi	:	75 kms.
2.	Champang to Longleng	:	47 kms.
3.	Changtongya to Longleng	:	34 kms.
4.	Dimapur to Longleng	:	266 kms.

(*Contd.*)

(*Contd.*)

5.	Dimapur to Tamlu	:	239 kms.
6.	Mokokchung to Longleng	:	80 kms.
7.	Kohima to Longleng via Mokokchung	:	232 kms.
8.	Mon to Tamlu	:	80 kms.
9.	Longleng to Amguri (Assam)	:	91 kms.

Source: (i) *Basic Facts 1997, Nagaland*, pp. 35-36.
(ii) *Statistical Hand Book of Nagaland* 2001, pp. 28-34.
(iii) *Statistical Hand Book of Nagaland* 1996, p. 40.

The Government of Nagaland has classified the following roads as State Highways in 2000: (i) Tuensang-Changtongya road via Auching and Longleng, (ii) Merangkong-Wakching road via Tamlu and (iii) Aboi (Mon district)-Longleng road.[37] However, the thirty-four kilometres State Highway connecting Longleng with the National Highway No. 61 at Changtongya and the road covering fourteen kilometres from Tamlu to the National Highway No. 61 at Merangkong (Mokokchung district) were the only tarmac surfaced roads till 2001-02.[38] However, all these roads are narrow, without proper drainage and prone to accident.

According to 1991 census, out of thirty-five Phom villages, four villages had footpath links while the rest thirty-one villages were connected by rural *cutcha* roads.[39] Some villages have agricultural link roads,[40] i.e. road that connects the main village with the cultivation fields or plantations.

There is no railway, shipping and civil aviation facilities in Longleng district. A few kilometres of the Dikhu river within the district are of course navigable, though no passenger or cargo service is available. The nearest railway station is Amguri, situated at a distance of 91 kilometres from Longleng town.

Before the establishment of a few shops and markets at Longleng town in 1961, rations and other essential commodities were dropped from the air for the use of the government employees. After 1961 all such articles were carried to Longleng in jeeps.[41] Public goods carrier (truck) started plying from 1979. Regular private night bus service between Longleng and Dimapur started in 1995. A Sub-Station of the Nagaland State Transport (NST) was set up at Longleng in 1985. In the same year NST bus started plying between Longleng and Amguri.[42] This service was subsequently extended to Dimapur. Another NST bus service operating from Tamlu to Amguri in 1986[43] was later extended to Dimapur.[44] Now NST bus is regularly plying between Longleng and Mokokchung. Tamlu has regular private bus service to Amguri. In addition mini taxis run in all these roads during daytime. Until recently Sakshi and Yongnyah, the two EAC headquarters, did not have bus service.

Development of modern postal communication system in the north-east has been a story of colonial period, and for Longleng district, it is of recent origin. In 1981, only three villages of Longleng district had postal service,[45] which developed marginally in the last twenty-five years. A list of postal network with locations in Longleng district is given in Table 4.8.

Table 4.8: Classified list of post offices as on 1st April, 2003

Longleng SO	*Class C/798625*
1. Hukpang	: E
2. Nian	: E
3. Pongching	: E
4. Sakchi	: E
5. Yachem	: E
6. Yongnyah	: E
Naginimora SO (Mon)	Class C/PCO/798622
7. Bura Namsang	: E
Tuli SO (Mokokchung)	Class C/CSO/PCO/798618
8. Tamlu	: E

Note: Class C : Single Handed Office
PCO : Public Call Office
E : Experimental Branch Office
SO : Sub-Office

Source: *Classified List of Post Offices in North Eastern Circle* (corrected as on 1st April, 2003), pp. 43-45.

There is no telegraph facility at Longleng. Efforts were made to install a manual telephone exchange at Longleng as early as 1982,[46] but without success. The administrative headquarters of Longleng was, therefore, deprived of telephone service till 2003. The place was finally brought under telecommunication network when a microwave exchange centre was inaugurated by A. Sangtam, M.P. on 23 January, 2004. During the last four decades of the twentieth century, the radio (transistor) set had remained as the only means of receiving information and entertainment for the rural Phoms. News and other programmes are regularly broadcast in the Phom language from the All India Radio, Kohima. There were 53 radio sets in the eighteen surveyed Phom villages in 1977[47] and its number multiplied in the subsequent years. Today almost every household owns a radio. From the last decade of the twentieth century television has become the most popular medium of entertainment for these people. Both Longleng and Tamlu Rural Development Blocks have Community Information Centres (CICs). These CICs provide internet facility having access to World Wide Web.[48]

Electricity

There was no electricity in the Naga Hills-Tuensang Area before 1960. Kohima was the first place in Nagaland to be electrified in the same year.[49] Electricity was introduced at Longleng in 1964-65.[50] Till 1977 out of twenty-five Phom villages, only three were electrified with only ten houses receiving electric connection.[51] In the following years the demand for electricity had grown considerably and by 1997 all the Phom villages were electrified.[52] In spite of this, the overall power situation continued to be unsatisfactory and erratic.[53] There were two power sub-stations, one at Tamlu with 250 KVA (33/0.433 KVA) power capacity and another at Longleng with a capacity of 150 KVA (11/0.4 KVA). Power has been supplied to Longleng from the power station of Changtongya town. There was no bulk consumer till June 2003. It indicates that the electric power was not used for commercial purpose by the people. It was used by them for domestic consumption, or for non-commercial purpose.[54]

Trade and Commerce

The Phom villages bordering on Assam had commercial relations with the people of the plains through the Geleki *duar* since the days of the Ahom rule. These villages used to exchange their hilly products for dried fish, salt, molasses, tobacco, iron, etc.[55] The villages in the remote hills used to obtain their requirements from the bordering villages. But, due to the prevalence of ceaseless inter-village feuds, the transaction among the villages of the inner hills remained very much limited.

Before the introduction of money economy, brass plates of different shapes and sizes were in use as currency among the Phoms. These plates were called *nyamnyu,* or *laya*, *langnyu*, *langha* and *langla* by them. The *nyamnyu* had the highest value while the *langla*, the lowest. A *nyamnyu* was valued equivalent to a bison or a large quantity of paddy. It was used ordinarily by the rich people. The rest three were more prevalent than the *nyamnyu*. These brass plates were also used while paying bride-price or fines and also as medium of exchange for buying animals, chickens, crops, etc.[56] The *laya* was used as medium of exchange by the Aos while trading with the Phoms.[57] The Phom people of the interior villages virtually had no knowledge of the modern coinage before independence. R.G. Woodthorpe while visiting the Phom villages in 1875-76 wrote, "They did not understand money, except as an ornament to be affixed to the waist-belt; so we gave them some salt, a commodity highly prized by them."[58] However, when the Phom villages were brought under British control, they began to learn the use of modern currency. It was only after independence the circulation of money became more widespread among them. Consequently, the traditional currency system and the system of barter became obsolete.

Till about 1960 salt, dried fish, tea leaves, etc., were purchased from Amguri and Geleki in Assam by the villagers of the upper hills of the district.[59] The shopkeepers of Longleng town now depend on goods coming from Jorhat, Dimapur and Guwahati. Citronella oil was sent out from the area earlier.[60] Locally produced vegetables and seasonal fruits like mustard leaf, squash, sweet potato, bean, pumpkin, *kochu*, ginger, mushroom, banana, orange, pear, papaya, plum, etc., are however sold at Longleng town by the people of the nearby areas. In trade, the villagers generally do not use the metric weights; rather they follow their traditional weighing procedure. In Longleng town the majority of the shopkeepers are non-local.[61]

The people of Tamlu sub-division buy grocery, cosmetics, hardware, cattle, etc., at Geleki, Simaluguri and Naginimora because these places are nearer and bigger weekly markets are held here. They sell their agricultural and forest products, e.g. millet, *kochu,* ginger, chilli, papaya, orange, betel, jack fruit, banana, sugarcane, timber, bamboo, cane, etc., in these markets. The land owners of the area have been selling a large quantity of coal and stone to the contractors of Assam. The forest produce is sent out in trucks hired for the purpose, whereas the agricultural products are generally carried by the people to the markets in baskets on their back. The logs and bamboos are transported floating in the downstream of the Dikhu river. Elephants are usually used to transport the logs from dense forests to the roadside or the river bank. There is no daily or weekly market at Tamlu and Kongshong with the exception of a few small shops.

There are no market as such at the EAC headquarters of Sakshi and Yongnyah barring twelve to fifteen small shops each at these two places. In the olden days, the people of Yongnyah went to Geleki bazaar *via* Tamlu to purchase iron. The shopkeepers of Yongnyah buy goods from Longleng. As there is lack of marketing facility, so the cultivators of the area cannot sale their agricultural products except a small quantity of betel, ginger and timber, which are sold to the petty merchants of Assam. The log is supplied to Assam floating on the water of the Dikhu river.

Sakshi is situated in the middle of Longleng and Tuensang towns and there, the people purchase their day-to-day requirements from both these towns. Before setting up of grocery shops in this place many a people from Sakshi used to go to Marioni on foot in search of salt. Now the people of both Sakshi and Yongnyah buy cattle at Longleng and Haluating. The artisans of Sakchi village sell their products, i.e. basket, handmade gun, *dao*, etc., to the neighbouring tribes. The people of Yachem and Yoang sell vegetables and other seasonal crops at Changtongya.

Banking

There was no bank at Longleng till 1979. A branch of the State Bank of India (SBI) was opened at this place in that year. But, the bank had only a few customers as most people were unaccustomed with the modern banking system. Now, partly due to the rise in literacy and partly due to necessity, the Phom people have started to take advantage of the banking facilities available in their land. The majority of the account holders are, however, government servants. Amount of deposit in personal segment is higher than other segments, i.e. commercial and industrial (C&I), Small Industrial Business (SIB) and agriculture. The number of persons seeking loan has remained extremely small. Although the Village Development Boards' (VDB) office bearers and government officials usually take the responsibility of recovering the loan, yet the bank has been experiencing very low recovery percentage.[62]

Moneylending business is carried on by a section of the people throughout the district. There are some professional money-lenders and women societies, which lend money at an interest ranging from ten to fifteen per cent per month. The Phom Baptist Churches also give loan to the needy people from their own funds at nominal interest.[63] When the people suffer from affliction, they borrow money from the local money-lenders. Some people of the Tamlu sub-division have opened bank accounts at the SBI or Vijaya Bank Branch at Naginimora.[64] The post offices functioning in the area also provide money transaction facilities to the people.

Rural Development

Nearly 84.91 per cent population of Longleng district lives in the rural areas according to 2011 census. The infrastructure of rural areas such as the road and transport, education, banking, communication, health, power supply, cottage and small scale industries, etc., are poor as compared to the urban areas. A vast majority people depend on agriculture. Therefore, both the Central and the State Governments have implemented and executed a number of sustainable development programmes and schemes since independence with the aim of improving the socio-economic conditions of the people living in the rural areas, thereby improving the quality of life.

Prior to independence no developmental activities as such took place in the Phom inhabited areas of Nagaland. There was no road and bridge, school building, hospital, market places, etc., in the eastern side of the Dikhu river. After independence, particularly following the opening of an administrative centre at Longleng in 1951, some development works were taken up half-heartedly. In consequence, the pace of development from 1951 to 1962 remained extremely slow. It was only in October 1962 when a Community Development Block was set-up at Longleng, a few development programmes were initiated under the supervision of the Block. The Block covered an area of approximately 480 sq. miles extending up to Tuensang town with a population of 33,620 spreading over 58 villages.[65] With the creation of a few more such blocks in 1965-66 the jurisdiction of the Longleng C.D. Block was curtailed to twenty-four villages with a population of 14,285.[66] The Block had a Block Development Committee with the EAC, Longleng, as Chairman, Block Development Officer (BDO), Longleng, as Secretary and several other officials as well as non-official members.[67] The nomenclature of the C.D. Block was thereafter changed to Tribal Development Block and again to Rural Development Block.

During the period 1963-69 a number of developmental schemes were taken up. Carpentry tools, black-smithy sets, paddy husking machines, sewing machines, etc., were distributed among the people on subsidy basis.[68] Among other schemes taken mention may be made of setting up of minor irrigation projects, construction of jeepable and village approach roads, suspension log bridges, supply of drinking water, establishment of maternity and child welfare units, construction of adult literacy centres and community halls, supply of CGI sheets to private L.P. and M.E. Schools, etc.[69]

Up to 1979 all the rural development programmes were implemented directly by the block level staff without involving the villagers at the grassroots. A. Lanunungsang Ao wrote, "The government subsidies were simply distributed under various schemes either in cash or in kind in the form of giving piece meal without bearing such fruits."[70] With this experience in mind the Village Development Board (VDB) was constituted in each government recognised village to enable the villagers to actively participate in preparing village development schemes and implementing them. Another objective of the creation of the VDB was to remove the role of intermediaries and stamp out corruption.

The Government of Nagaland framed Model Rules in this connection in March 1980, known as the Village Development Model Rules, 1980 which were further revised in 1989. The members of the Village Development Board are chosen by the Village Council. The tenure of members is three years unless decided otherwise by the Village Council by a resolution. The Deputy Commissioner is the ex-officio Chairman of the Village Development Board.[71] The members of VDB Management Committee select one among themselves as the Secretary whose educational qualification should be matriculation and above.

According to the Revised Model Rules, "The minimum strength of members of the Management Committee of the VDBs shall not be less than 5 (five) members and the maximum number not to exceed 25 (twenty-five) members."[72] The Revised Model Rules further provided that "the number of women members to be included in the Management Committee of the VDBs should not be less than one-fourth of the total number of members of the Management of the VDBs."[73] The actual position is as follows during 2002-2004.

Table 4.9: Strength of male and female VDB mambers of four villages

Year	*Name of villages*	*Total members*	*No. of female members*	*Qualification of VDBMC secretaries*
2002	Yongam	09	02	B.A.
2004	Bhumnyu	12	01	Matriculate
2004	Bura Namsang	06	01	Class X
2004	Sakchi	25	01	HSSLC

Source: Statement given by the four VDBMC Secretaries belonging to Yongam (2002), Bhumnyu (2004), Bura Namsang (2004) and Sakchi (2004) villages.

Table 4.9 shows that the strength of female members in Sakchi and Bhumnyu villages was less than what was stipulated in the Rules. It is further seen that of the four secretaries of the VDB Management Committees three were matriculate, the minimum qualification which is laid down in the rules and the fourth, not. The Secretary receives Rs. 12,000 per annum as honorarium. Sakchi, Bhumnyu and Bura Namsang VDB female members are women social workers, i.e. pastress who are educated but the two female members of Yongam village have no formal school education.

Sources of Fund

All the Central and State Governments sponsored village development programmes and schemes are implemented through the VDBs. One important source of income of the VDB is the Matching Grant. The Government of Nagaland contributes annually an amount equivalent to the village fund, raised voluntarily by the villagers and invested in fixed deposit account in a bank. In order to have a balanced distribution of resources among the villages, an upper limit of Rs. 75,000 was fixed by the government initially. The amount has been raised to Rs. 2.50 lakhs for each VDB since 1995-96.[74]

In addition, every village was given Grant-in-aid at a specified rate for carrying out schemes of community development. Originally, the allocation under this head was made at the rate of Rs. 100 per tax-paying household with a minimum of Rs. 5,000 for a village.[75] The amount was raised to Rs. 750 per household with a minimum of Rs. 50,000 for a village having less than 66 households from 1995-96.[76] Both Grant-in-aid and Matching Grants are state sponsored schemes.

According to the Naga customary laws any outsiders or outside agencies cannot buy or mortgage the lands of the Nagas. Hence, the individuals desire to borrow money from the government, bank or any other financial institution can avail the benefit through the VDB because it also acts as a security for the repayment of loan.

Table 4.10: Grant-in-aid released under Village Development Board Programme during 1980 to 2009-10

Year	*No. of Block*	*No. of V.D.B.*	*Grant-in-aid*	*VDB Secretary Honorarium*	*Total Fund Credited to VDBs*
1980-85	01	25	Rs. 34,61,800	NA	NA
1986-87	01	24	Rs. 9,86,600	NA	NA
2009-10	02	30	Rs. 13,137,000	Rs.360,000	Rs. 13,497,000

Source: (i) Maithani, B.P. & Rizwana, A., *op. cit.*, pp. 25-27.
(ii) *Statistical Handbook of Nagaland 2011*, p. 210.

Integrated Rural Development Programme (IRDP), a major self-employment scheme, was started in 1980-81 but it was restructured as *Swarnjayanti Gram Swarojgar Yojana* (SGSY) in 1999.[77] Another scheme, namely *Jawahar Rozgar Yojana* (JRY) was introduced in 1989 but later modified into *Indira Awas Yojana* (IAY) and Million Well Schemes (MWS) in 1993-94.[78] Among the other Centrally Sponsored Schemes in operation, mention may be made of the *Jawahar Gram Samriddhi Yojana* (JGSY), Employment Assurance Scheme (EAS), Basic Minimum Services (BMS) including Rural Housing, Road Connectivity and Grant-in-aid and the Integrated Rural Energy Programme (IREP).[79] The EAS aimed at providing 100 days manual works in a year to the rural poor. A person who is above 18 years and below 60 years can seek and avail this scheme.

Following the creation of Longleng district, the District Rural Development Agency (DRDA) was created. There are three Rural Development Blocks in Longleng district, namely Longleng Block, Tamlu Block and Sakshi Block each headed by a Block Development Officer (BDO). The VDB schemes are identified and selected on the basis of priority with technical support from the BDOs. The schemes approved by the BDOs are then submitted to the Chairman (DC) of VDBs through the Project Director, DRDA for approval. On receipt of the necessary approval, the schemes are taken up for implementation and after submission of satisfactory report of completion the fund is released.[80]

Table 4.11: Schemes implemented and target achievements up to 1982-83 under various Rural Development Programmes under Longleng Block

Sl. No.	*Schemes*	*Numbers*
1.	Community halls	6
2.	Panchayat halls	31
3.	Libraries	7
4.	Village gates	3
5.	Play ground	36
6.	Public latrine	10
7.	Public urine shed	11
8.	Resting shed on kheti road	17
9.	Wire, rope suspension bridge	10
10.	Stone steps	24
11.	Villages having pine apple farms	39
12.	Villages having orange farms	20
13.	Villages having other cash crops	6
14.	Community fishery ponds	5
15.	Individual fishery ponds	20
16.	Villages having social forestry	24

Source: Nagaland Rural Development in Action, pp. 40-45.

Table 4.12: Target achievement during 1983 till February 84 under IRDP under Longleng Block

Schemes	*Subsidy Rs. in lakhs*	*Beneficiary*	*Target*
Land Development	1.63	108	81 (in acre)
Minor Irrigation	1.85	72	115 (c.a. in acre)
Horticulture	0.16	11	8 (in acre)
Animal Power	0.04	2	2 (in pairs)
Forestry	0.54	10	33 (in hect)
Poultry	0.05	2	2 (in unit)
Dairy	0.50	1	1 (in unit)
Tailoring	0.02	5	5 (in no.)

Source: Nagaland Rural Development in Action, pp. 52-58.

The more important subdivisions headed by the Additional Deputy Commissioners (ADCs) have Sub-Divisional Planning Boards (SDPBs) consisting of heads of offices and other important persons.[81] The SDPB no longer exists at Longleng since Longleng sub-division was upgraded to a district in 2004. Thereafter, a District Planning and Development Board (DPDB) was constituted with one local MLA as the Chairman in July 2004.[82] The meeting of the DPDB is held once in every month to discuss various subjects relating to development activities.

Following the identification of some parts of Nagaland including the Longleng district as socio-economically backward, the Government of Nagaland has launched a special programme known as 'Development of Backward Area Programme' to accelerate the pace of economic development of these areas with a view to bringing them at par with the more advanced areas of the state.[83] A new department called the 'Department of Underdeveloped Area' (DUDA) was set up in Kohima recently with the aim of coordinating and implementing speedily various government development schemes so as to remove intra-state disparities.[84] The Department supervises implementation of reservation quota for the backward tribes in government services.

NOTES AND REFERENCES

1. Saleh, Swabera Islam, *Nagaland's Economy in Transition Since 1964*, pp. 69-70.
2. *Ibid.*
3. As data for the Phom population are not shown in the 2011 census separately, so the scheduled tribe population as a whole has been taken into account here in order to get a general idea about their occupational pattern considering the fact that a very small number of the Scheduled Tribe people other than the Phoms live in Longleng district. Non-workers are those who do not take part in any economic productive activity.
4. The researcher interviewed eight cultivators each from Sakchi (2004), Longleng (2004), Bhumnyu (2004), Yongam (2002) and Bura Namsang (2004). Over and above the information gathered from them, the researcher has used other official records to substantiate his views.
5. *Census of India 1991, District Census Handbook*, Tuensang, p. 17.
6. *Ibid*, pp. 51-55.
7. *Statistical Hand Book of Nagaland 1981*, p. 176.
8. Letter of E.R. Huskha Yeptho, SDO, Irrigation and Flood Control, Longleng, No. I & FC/LLG/ACT-19/2002-03/68, 9 April, 2003. E.R. Huskha Yeptho gave this information through a letter to the researcher in response to his querries.
9. It is to be observed that cow dung, the most commonly used manure in the plains, is not available in large quantity as the Phom people do not generally rear cow in their sheds.
10. Bhattacharya, P. K., 'Economic Evolution of the Naga Society – A Glimpse', the *Highlander*, Vol. III, No. 2, September 1975.

11. Islam, Swabera, "An Overview of the Backward Areas of Nagaland – Suggestions for Economic Development", printed in the Proceedings of a Seminar entitled "Over-view of Backward Areas of Nagaland Since Independence", Longleng, 2001, p. 7.
12. Hutton, J., *Report on Naga Hills*, p. 14.
13. *Statistical Handbook of Nagaland 2011*, p.258.
14. *Annual Administrative Report 1992-93*, Department of Forest, pp. 9-10.
15. *Annual Administrative Report 1998-99*, Department of Forest, Ecology and Environment and Wild Life, p. 4.
16. *Ibid*, p. 3.
17. Interview held with T. Ngecham, FGD at Longleng on 30-05-2004.
18. *Annual Administrative Report 1981-82*, Nagaland Forest Department, pp. 17-18.
19. Interview held with Y. Pangong (49), UDA, Sub-DIC, Longleng, at Longleng on 30-01-2003.
20. Ao, M. Alemchiba, *The Arts and Crafts of Nagaland*, pp. 7-8.
21. Interview held with Y. Pangong (49), *Op. cit.*
22. *Ibid.*
23. Ao, M. Alemchiba, *Op. cit.*, p. 81.
24. *Ibid*, pp. 81-82.
25. Interview held with Y. Pangong (49), *Op. cit.*
26. Ghosh, B.B. (ed), *Nagaland District Gazetteers, Tuensang District*, p. 93.
27. Interview held with Y. Pangong (49), *Op. cit.*
28. *Ibid.*
29. *Ibid.*
30. *Nagaland 1998*, p. 65.
31. Saleh, Swabera Islam, *Op. cit.*, p. 190.
32. Shakespear, L.W., *History of the Assam Rifles*, p. 170.
33. The information was collected from H. Lakphak, SO (PWD) R/B, Longleng on 10-03-2003.
34. Resolution passed in the 2nd Session of the Tuensang District Regional Council held on 28th and 30th April, 1964. A copy of the Resolution was supplied to the researcher by Hepong Phom, ex-Interim Body Member and ex-Tuensang District Regional Council Member.
35. *Nagaland Gazette*, No. 21, 15 February, 1966, p. 216.
36. Bareh, H.M., *Encyclopaedia of North-East India*, Vol. VI, *Nagaland*, p. 220.
37. *The Warrior*, Vol. 29, April 2000, No. 4, p. 40.
38. The information was collected from H. Lakphak, *Op. cit.*
39. *Census of India 1991*, *Op. cit.*, pp. 51-55.
40. *The Warrior*, Vol. 30, November 2001, No. 11, p. 24.
41. Interview held with Apisangpa (70), retired *Do-Bhashi*, at Bahok Colony, Longleng on 20-05-2004. He also informed this scholar that prior to 1961 there was only one grocery shop opened in 1957.
42. The information was collected from M. Imti, In-charge NST, Longleng on 15-02-2003.

43. *Nagaland 1986*, p. 66.
44. *Nagaland (1993-2002) A Decade of Stability, Progress and Development*, p. 47.
45. *Census of India 1991*, *Op. cit.*, p. 17.
46. Saleh, Swabera Islam, *Op. cit.*, p. 41.
47. *Statistical Hand Book of Nagaland 1981*, p. 180.
48. *Nagaland 2002*, p. 120.
49. Rao, V. Venkata, 'Modernization of the Naga Society', in B.B. Kun[illegible].) *Modernization in Naga Society*, p. 49.
50. A copy of the Resolution passed in the Second Session of the Tuensang District Regional Council held on 28th and 30th April, 1964 was supplied to the researcher by Hepong Phom, ex-Interim Body Member and Tuensang District Regional Council Member.
51. *Statistical Hand Book of Nagaland 1981*, pp. 175 & 180.
52. *Village Level Development Indicators* as on 31.3.97, p. 131.
53. Bareh, H.M., *Op. cit.*
54. Abenthung, Junior Engineer (Power), Longleng Sub-Station in reply to the questions of the researcher, dated 17th June, 2003.
55. Interview held with P. Oyemth Phom (30), teacher, at Longleng on 15-01-2004.
56. Interview held with N. Hamvok Phom (76), *Do-Bhashi*, at Longleng on 15-01-2003.
57. Mills, J. P., *The Ao Nagas*, p. 102.
58. Woodthorpe, R. G., 'General Report of the Topographical Surveys, 1875-76 in Verrier Elwin *The Nagas in the Nineteenth Century*, p. 391.
59. Interview held with T. Ponglong Phom (52), Chairman of Subdivisional Chamber of Commerce Unit Longleng, at Longleng on 12-10-2003.
60. *Ibid.*
61. Bareh, H.M., *Op. cit.*, p. 216.
62. Information given by Karuna Kanta Deka, Assistant Manager, SBI, Longleng Branch, on 25-03-2002.
63. Interview held with T. Ponglong Phom (52), *Op. cit.*
64. Interview held with P. Oyemth Phom (30), *Op. cit.*
65. *Statistical Hand Book of Nagaland 1965*, pp. 90-91; A copy of the Abstract of Proceedings of the Tuensang District Regional Council, Fourth Session (3rd to 8th June, 1965, p. 13) was collected from Hepong Phom, ex-Interim Body Member and the ex-Tuensang District Regional Council Member.
66. *Statistical Hand Book of Nagaland 1968*, pp. 194-195.
67. *Nagaland Gazette*, No. 8, 31 July, 1967, Part-I, pp. 36-37.
68. *Nagaland*, 1963-1969, pp. 41-44.
69. *Ibid*, pp. 16-17.
70. Ao, A. Lanunungsang, *Rural Development in Nagaland*, p. 209.
71. 'The Village Development Boards Model Rules 1980' cited in B.P. Maithani

and A. Rizwana's *Decentralised Development: A Study of Village Development Boards in Nagaland*, pp. 95-101.

72. *Village Development Boards Model Rules 1980* (Revised), dated Kohima, the 21st November, 1989, p. 2.
73. *Ibid.*
74. *Annual Administrative Report 1995-96,* Department of Rural Development, p. 4.
75. Maithani, B.P. & Rizwana, A., *Op. cit.*, p. 24.
76. *Annual Administrative Report 1995-96, Op. cit.*, p. 3.
77. Datt, Ruddar & Sundharam, K.P.M., *Indian Economy,* p. 405.
78. *Ibid,* p. 408
79. *Annual Administrative Report 1999-2000*, Department of Rural Development, p.1.
80. *Souvenir 1980-2005*, Commemorating 25 Years of Village Development Boards, Department of Rural Development, pp. 7-8.
81. Roy Burman, B.K., *Towards Poverty Alleviation Programmes in Nagaland and Manipur,* p. 77; *The Warrior*, Vol. 32, August 2003, No. 8, p. 53.
82. *The Warrior,* Vol. 33, September 2004, No. 9, p. 44.
83. *Annual Administrative Report 1985-86,* Planning and Coordination Department including Department of Economics and Statistics, Town Planning Organisation and Evaluation Unit, Kohima, p.6.
84. *The Warrior,* Vol. 33, April 2004, No. 4, p. 5.

5

Administrative and Political Development

It has already been stated that at the time of independence the Phom area to the east of the Dikhu river remained in the category of political control as a part of 'Tribal Area' while the Phom villages to the west of the river constituted parts of the Naga Hills district, a frontier district of the province of Assam. The power over the 'Tribal Area' (later known as the Tuensang Area) was exercised by the Governor-General through his Agent, the Governor of Assam. The Indian Independence Act of 1947 made no immediate change in its status and the Extra-Provincial Jurisdiction Act of the same year authorised the Government of India to carry out its administration as before.[1] The first administrative centre was opened on 27 January, 1948 at Tuensang[2] as an outpost of the Mokokchung subdivision.[3] The course of political development of the region took a new turn following the establishment of an administrative centre at Longleng in 1951.

In the Constitution of India the 'Tribal Area' was designated as the 'Naga Tribal Area'[4] and included in Part B of the Sixth Schedule along with the Balipara Frontier Tract, the Tirap Frontier Tract, the Abor Hills District and the Mishmi Hills District of the North-East Frontier Tract.[5] The entire area was to be administered by the Governor of Assam, now as the Agent of the President of India.[6]

The North-East Frontier Agency (1951-57)

Prior to the establishment of an administrative centre at Longleng, the Phom villages remained under the following administrative circles; the villages Yongphang, Yangching, Sakchi, Pongo, Pongching, Orangkong, Bhumnyu, Hukpang and Auching were under Tuensang circle; Yachem and Yaong under Ongpangkong; and the rest of the

Phom villages under Wakching circle. As soon as the Longleng administrative headquarters was set up, almost all the Phom villages were brought under its jurisdiction.[7]

The Naga Tribal Area which was originally administered by the Deputy Commissioner of the Naga Hills on behalf of the Governor of Assam was separated from the Naga Hills and included in the North-East Frontier Tract in 1951.[8] Tuensang was upgraded to a district on 10 November, 1951[9] when the first Political Officer was appointed.[10] The Naga Tribal Area was re-designated as 'Tuensang Frontier Division' and the North-East Frontier Tract came to be known as 'North-East Frontier Agency' (NEFA) from 1954.[11]

By 1957 the political situation of the Naga Hills District and Tuensang Frontier division took an alarming turn. From the time of joining the Naga National Council (NNC)[12] by Angami Zapu Phizo, an eminent radical Naga leader, the demand for an independent state for the Nagas gradually began to gain momentum. Initially, he, with support of other members of the NNC, resorted to a non-violent method of agitation to achieve the goal.[13] But, soon it was replaced by an armed struggle. Indian security forces were deployed in the Naga hills to meet the situation. The Indian security forces and a section of the Nagas were thereafter locked in an unending war. A warrant of arrest was issued against Phizo; but he managed to escape to England *via* erstwhile East Pakistan (now Bangladesh) in 1956.[14] Realising the futility of the armed struggle the moderate Naga political leaders and also the church leaders put their heads together to end violence in Naga hills. A section of these leaders met Prime Minister Pandit Jawaharlal Nehru in September, 1956 and requested him to stop army operations as a first step towards restoration of peace and normalcy. They also extracted from him an assurance that the Naga people would be granted maximum autonomy with a special administrative and political status as soon as peace returned to the hills.[15]

In these prevailing political conditions the first Naga People's Convention (NPC) was held at Kohima from 22 to 26 August, 1957 to initiate moves for a peaceful settlement of the Naga problem.[16] The Convention was attended by large number of delegates from all the tribes of the Naga Hills district and the Tuensang division. One of the important resolutions adopted in the Convention was to reunite the 'Naga Hills District' of Assam and the 'Tuensang Frontier Division' of NEFA with a single administrative unit under the External

Affairs Ministry. After the convention, a nine member delegation of the Naga People's Convention met the Governor of Assam in Shillong on 23 September, 1957 and then the Prime Minister of India in New Delhi on 25-26 September, 1957.[17] In response to their proposal an Act, called the Naga Hills-Tuensang Area Act, 1957, was passed by the Indian Parliament creating a new administrative unit by the name Naga Hills-Tuensang Area (NHTA).[18] The new administrative unit was brought into being on 1 December, 1957 under the Ministry of External Affairs and administered through the Governor of Assam acting as the Agent of the President of India.[19] The NHTA was divided in the same year into three districts, viz. Kohima, Mokokchung and the Tuensang districts.[20]

As noted above, before the formation of NHTA, Naga Hills was a district of Assam headed by a Deputy Commissioner with headquarters at Kohima while Mokokchung was a subdivision administered by a Sub-Divisional Officer. The district was allotted three seats in the Assam State Legislative Assembly. But in response to the boycott call given by Phizo through the NNC, the Nagas boycotted the First General Election held in 1952. Three Nagas were elected uncontested to the Assam State Legislative Assembly in the Second General Election of 1957; but after six months they quit the seats after the Naga Hills district was separated from Assam and formed into NHTA in December 1957.[21] There was no legislative assembly for the Tuensang division during the NEFA period. It was the Union Government which framed laws and regulations for this area.[22] The Agency was administered by the Governor of Assam acting as the Agent to the President of India. The Governor was assisted by an adviser. The Agency Secretariat was situated in Shillong.[23]

Till 1957 the present Tamlu subdivision remained a part of the Naga Hills district. But, the Ao, the Konyak and the Phom tribes had been vigorously claiming for long that the Tamlu area was always a part of their territories. The government finally accepted the demand and ultimately united the Tamlu area with the Tuensang district in the same year.[24]

Formation of Statehood

After the first Naga People's Convention, the moderate Naga leaders, who wished to resolve the Naga problem within the framework of the Constitution of India, organised the second Naga People's

Convention at Ungma village from 21 to 23 May, 1958. It was attended by a large number of delegates representing various Naga tribes. The Convention constituted a Liaison Committee of eight members. The Committee was formed with the purpose of finding out a permanent solution to the Naga problem, the outcome of which was to be placed for consideration by a Select Committee.[25] The Select Committee in its meeting at Kohima on 11 December, 1958 studied the report submitted by the Liaison Committee and resolved to appoint a Drafting Committee, which included among others Hamno (Hamyei) a member of the Phom tribe.[26] The Committee drafted a sixteen-point proposal which, *inter alia,* suggested the following:

(i) the creation of a new state within the Indian Union to be known as 'Nagaland',

(ii) no Act or Law passed by the Union Parliament would have legal force in this state unless specifically approved to it by a majority vote of the Nagaland Legislative Assembly regarding:
  (a) the religious or social practices of the Nagas,
  (b) Naga customary laws and procedure,
  (c) civil and criminal justice so far as these concern decisions according to Naga customary laws, and
  (d) the ownership and transfer of land and its resources,

(iii) a Regional Council would be formed for Tuensang district by the elected representatives from all the tribes in Tuensang district,

(iv) to supplement the revenues of the province, there would be a need for the Government of India to pay out of its consolidated fund as grant-in-aid, and

(v) the Rules embodied in the Bengal Eastern Frontier Regulation, 1873, would remain in force in Nagaland.[27]

The third session of the Naga People's Convention was held from 22 to 26 October, 1959 at Mokokchung, where the pros and cons of the sixteen-point proposal were discussed.[28] The Convention approved the draft as the basis of future negotiation with the Government of India for the settlement of the Naga problem. A fifteen-man delegation with Dr. Imkongliba as the leader was formed to negotiate with the Government of India.[29] The delegation went to New Delhi in July 1960 and after discussing with Prime Minister Pt. Nehru and senior officials of the Ministry of External Affairs, agreed to a partially modified draft as suggested by them.[30] Meanwhile, the Government of India promulgated on 24 January, 1961, the Nagaland Transitional Regulation for the administration of the Naga territory during the transitional period pending creation of a Nagaland state.[31] The Naga Hills-Tuensang Area thus came to be known by the name 'Nagaland' as per the Regulation. It was also provided that an Interim Body and an Executive Council would be constituted for a period of three years from the date of its first meeting. The Regulation further stated that "the Interim Body shall not discuss any matter exclusively affecting or relating to the Tuensang District except with the consent of all the members from the District."[32]

His Excellency the Governor of Assam, General Shrinagesh inaugurated the Interim Body on 18 February, 1961 and administered the oath of office to the members. The Body consisted of 42 members of whom two belonged to the Phom tribe, namely Hepong Phom and Pauting Phom.[33] The members of the Body were selected on the basis of consensus depending on their knowledge and experience and not on the basis of adult franchise.[34] Unfortunately, however, Dr. Imkongliba Ao, Chairman of the Interim Body, was shot dead by an assailant on 22 August, 1961 while returning home from his pharmacy at Mokokchung. A few days later Pauting Phom, another member of the Interim Body, was killed (29 August) by an underground activist[35] at his residence at Longleng. Thus, an eminent Phom public leader laid down his life for participating in the formation of statehood. Following these two assassinations Tekasosang and Anyak Phom were elected to the Interim Body.[36] The Thirteenth Constitution Amendment Bill and the Nagaland State Bill were passed by the Parliament and the President of India assented to these bills on 4 September, 1962. The tenure of the Interim Body expired on 30 November, 1963 whereupon a new state 'Nagaland' came into existence as the sixteenth state of the Indian Union.[37] The new state was formally inaugurated by the President of India Dr. S. Radhakrishnan on 1 December, 1963.

Following the creation of the state of Nagaland steps were taken to reorganise the administration with a view to making it more accessible to the people at the grassroots. Some of the innovations are discussed below.

The Village Council

The traditional village government, called the *Pangshan* by the Phoms, had remained in existence in the Phom villages from the days of yore. The *Gaon-Buras* took an active part in the village administration along with the *Barricks,* i.e. village elders. In fact, this system of village government has been in force till today[38], though new laws regarding formation, powers and functions of the *Pangshan* have been enacted from time to time. In the past, the *Pangshan* also performed the duties of a war council, but with the disappearance of the village feuds, these duties ceased automatically.

After independence certain measures were taken to make the Village Councils act more democratically and effectively. For example, the Nagaland (Transitional Provisions) Regulation, 1961 made it mandatory for each village to have a Village Council and several villages taken together formed a Range Council, also called Area Council.[39] The Nagaland Village and Area Councils Act, 1978, also stated that each government recognised village should have a Village Council.[40]

The Village Council consists of members, chosen by the villagers themselves in accordance with the prevailing customary practices and usages, and approved by the Government. The hereditary village chiefs, *Gaon-Buras* and *Anghs* are ex-officio members of such Council who have voting right. A person is not eligible to be a member of the Village Council who is not a citizen of India and is below twenty-five years of age.[41] The total number of the members of the Council is decided by the villagers in accordance with the need and size of the population. As per the statements of the Village Council Chairmen of Sakchi, Bhumnyu, Yongam and Bura Namsang villages[42], the members of the four Village Councils are elected on the basis of consensus of the members of the *khels* and there is complete absence of party affiliation. Of the four Village Councils, Sakchi had the highest number of members, viz. 52 in 2004 of whom twenty-two were *Gaon-Buras* and the rest elected by the people. On the other hand Bhumnyu had 41 and Bura Namsang 41 and Yongam 15 members in 2002.

The term of the Village Council is five years unless dissolved or extended by the State Government.[43] The elections for the Village Councils in Nagaland were held regularly.[44] The members of the Council select an experienced person as their Chairman. The term of office of the Chairman is five years. He receives a lump sum amount as honorarium. Every Village Council has also a Secretary. The names of the selected/elected members are submitted to the government through the Extra Assistant Commissioner or the Sub-Divisional Officer (Civil) for formal government approval.[45] Senior government officers such as Extra Assistant Commissioner, Sub-Divisional Officer, Additional Deputy Commissioner and the Deputy Commissioner exercise control over the Councils falling under their jurisdictions.[46]

The Village Councils settle all disputes, both civil and criminal, in accordance with the customary laws and practices. The customary laws are the unwritten and socially accepted laws, which may even vary from village to village. These laws had been followed by the Phom ancestors, generation after generation. All are bound to follow and respect the customary laws. Fine is imposed in most cases on the offenders. Some aspects of Phom-Naga customary laws are stated below:

1. ***Ordeal***: When there is absence of evidence, the Phoms follow the traditional method of ordeal to settle the disputes. While performing such methods the supposed super natural objects like the sun, the moon, the stars, etc., are used as witnesses and the parties involved in a dispute claim their innocence by swearing in their name. This primitive method is used mostly in land disputes. C. Amop Noklang wrote:

    > "In such a case, the elders or the party eat or bite the earth saying, "I am eating or biting this earth in the name of the god or the sun, moon, stars, and heaven and earth. If I am guilty, let this earth make me die or sick". The one who gets sick or die earlier is declared as guilty."[47]

2. ***Citizenship***: As reported by the four Village Council Chairmen mentioned above, the Council in the past, granted residency right to outsiders. A person desirous of enjoying such right had to select and adopt a guardian who was willing to act as a guarantor. He then submitted his request through his guardian to the Village Council which held its general meeting (called citizenship meeting) generally in the month of January every year. All the residents of the village were invited to the meeting. After a few years (the period varies from village to village) since the request was taken for consideration, the person was granted citizenship right. During this interim period, the villagers carefully observed

the conduct of the person. This practice of granting residency right is no longer exercised by the Phom villages nowadays since the educated villagers have now become more apprehensive of the probable adverse consequences of opening their villages to outsiders.

3. ***Homicide***: In case of accidental homicide, the murderer is expelled from the village for a certain period of time. For culpable homicide a heavy fine is imposed along with expulsion from the village for ever.
4. ***Theft***: Habitual thefts are punished by beating them black and white with cane and itchy plants with their hands and feet tied to the *morung* pillar. Sometimes, their ears are pierced forcibly.
5. ***Fire Incident***: If a person burns others property intentionally or unintentionally, the case is solved considering its nature. In the case of extreme punishment the guilty person is banished from the village. In the case of burning the jungle, a fine is imposed with a pig on the culprit. If a person burns a village he is fined with a dog for ceremonial cleaning of the village. In case a *morung* is also burnt, the offender is punished by a fine of land and a dog.
6. ***Sexual Assaults***: Sexual assaults on womenfolk are considered as serious offence and the offenders are usually penalised by taking away their lands as fine. Rape case is very rare here. The crime is viewed seriously. If a rapist is found on the spot he may be killed. The rapist is also punished heavily by confiscating his land, animal and money.
7. ***Marriage***: A negotiator who is usually a close relative of the groom plays the necessary role for the engagement of a couple. On the breach of engagement without any valid reason, defaulter may be fined in double the number of the articles exchanged during the engagement. If a boy elopes with a girl without the knowledge of the girl's parents, the family members of both the families get together and legitimise the marriage. If a couple run away despite the objection of the girl's parents, the boy may be fined with a plot of land or landed property or any other article.
8. ***Divorce***: Both husband and wife have the right to divorce one another on the grounds of adultery, violation of marriage vows and conflict of views and opinion in the family. If a

husband divorces his wife without any valid reason, he is penalized to payment of land, pig or any other movable or immovable properties. However, in the case of women divorcing her husband without any valid reason, she is sent back with empty-hand. If the children stay with their divorced mother, then the divorcee can claim maintenance fee from her former husband.

9. ***Succession***: Father is the head and ruler of the family. On the death of a father, his eldest son becomes the next head.
10. ***Adoption***: The practice of adoption is prevalent among the people of the Phom-Naga tribe since time immemorial. The Phom parents adopt son or daughter for different reasons. The parents without natural issue opted to adopt a child and bring it up as their own child. The orphans are generally adopted and brought up by their close male relatives. Many well-to-do families are seen adopting poor children, although they have their own children. As soon as a child is adopted his relation with the natural parents is ceased automatically. The adopted father may have immense love and affection for the adopted child, but, in any case he cannot enjoy the same rights as usually enjoyed by the eldest son or daughter. He cannot enter into matrimonial alliance with any clan members of his natural parents. If the adopted son or daughter commits any crime in the society the adopted parents are to take the responsibility. He has no right over clan as well as natural father's properties.
11. ***Transfer of Land***: An individual has the right to transfer or sell his land to his fellow villager. However, collective lands such as clan land, *khel* land and village land cannot be transferred without the consent of their members. Village land whether individual or collective cannot be sold to outsiders. Land may be transferred to government or to private agencies for development purposes by an agreement signed between the parties.
12. ***Inheritance***: Property inheritance rights of women have already been explained in the earlier chapter. However, the son who takes care of aged parents or bears their funeral expenses is entitled to inherit the ancestral house. And if the same duties are done by a person other than their own clan members, he is given a suitable piece of land or a portion of the property.

13. ***Debt*:** Lending or borrowing loan with or without interest is a common practice in every society. It is the duty of the person who takes loan to pay off his debt. Here among the Phoms the burden to clear the family debt may fall upon the father or the eldest son of the family. If the debt is not repaid the case may be referred to the Village Council. In the case of failure to clear the debt the clan members of the incurring family are to clear the debt. If the clan members are to share the burden of debt, then the ancestral property of the family would be shared by the clan-men.

Clan disputes are settled by the clan members themselves. The Village Councils ordinarily do not take up such cases unless referred to them for opinion. A party dissatisfied with the decision of the Council can appeal to the nearest administrative officer (civil) for retrial in his customary (law) court. Unsolved village disputes are referred to the nearest administrative officer (civil) by the Village Councils themselves. Of the aforesaid four Village Councils, the Sakchi Council once had referred one case to the Additional Deputy Commissioner, Longleng. The case was afterwards solved by the Village Council after it was referred back to it. The Phom Nagas have full faith in their age-long customary laws and always abide by the decisions of their elders. It has now, more or less become a practice to appoint some persons in each Phom village to keep watch on their village when the villagers are busy in the fields or in other activities during day time.[48]

After the formation of the Village Development Boards (VDBs) in 1980-81, the Village Councils have started implementing various development schemes through the VDB Management Committees. The Nagaland Village and Area Councils Act, 1978 entrusted the Village Councils a number of other duties, namely maintenance of law and order; keeping civil administration and the police informed about the presence of strangers, vagabonds or suspects, etc.; enforce orders passed by the competent authority on the village as a whole; report the outbreak of epidemics to the nearest administrative or medical officer; stoppage of transfer of immovable property without the consent of the Village Council, etc.[49]

The Area Council

The Area Councils, which were earlier known as Range Councils[50], were constituted on attaining the statehood of Nagaland. These Councils were usually constituted at the administrative centres representing all the Village Councils of the specified areas.[51] There were two Area Councils in the Phom areas—the Longleng Area Council and the Tamlu Area Council. The administrative heads like the Extra Assistant Commissioner, the Sub-Divisional Officer (Civil) or the Additional Deputy Commissioner of Longleng acted as the ex officio Chairman of the Longleng Area Council. The members of the Councils were elected by the members of the Village Councils. Initially, one village used to send one representative to the Area Council. After five years of attaining statehood, each large village sent two representatives, whereas smaller village only one each.[52] The State Government nominated two persons, one of them a woman, to the Council.[53] Each Council had a Vice-Chairman elected by the members from among themselves. The term of the Council was five years.[54] The Vice-Chairman received a daily allowance when he was on tour in connection with his assigned duties.[55] Each member was paid a lump sum salary by the government.[56] When a seat fell vacant the concerned Village Council elected another member in his place.[57] The Council met at least twice but not more than four times in a year.[58] The Area Council members elected the members of the Tuensang District Regional Council on the basis of one representative for a population of about five thousand.[59]

The Area Council scrutinised the development schemes formulated by the different Village Councils and after coordinating and consolidating all such schemes into one for the entire area, submitted it to the appropriate authority indicating the priorities.[60] Until 1973 all such schemes were sent to the Regional Council, Tuensang through its representatives as well as administrative (civil) heads of the concerned areas. The proposals were discussed elaborately in the Regional Council. The final resolutions were submitted to the Nagaland Legislative Assembly through its representatives and the Deputy Commissioner, Tuensang. From 1974, the resolutions of the Councils were sent to the government through the respective administrative heads of the concerned areas, a copy of which was sent to the local MLA for information.[61] The Council had the power to settle disputes provided that such cases were referred to it voluntarily by the villages. In the event of epidemic or infectious diseases breaking out the Council had to initiate all preventive measures to combat the disease.[62] By the Nagaland Village and Area

Council (Second Amendment) Act, 1990, the Government of Nagaland abolished the Area Councils with immediate effect. Subsequent to the abolition of the Area Council, all assets and liabilities of the Area Council were taken over by the State Government.[63]

Tuensang District Regional Council

The Sixteen-Point Agreement which was agreed by the Naga People's Convention and the Government of India in July 1960 clearly stated, "The Governor shall carry on the administration of the Tuensang District for a period of 10 (ten) years or until such time when the tribes in the Tuensang District are capable of shouldering more responsibilities of the advanced system of administration."[64] The Agreement further added: "And at the end of ten years the situation will be reviewed and if the people so desire the period will be further extended."[65] The Tuensang District Regional Council consisting of thirty-five members representing various tribes of this district was constituted on creation of the State of Nagaland in December 1963.[66] It is noteworthy that some of the members of the Regional Council from the Phom Areas were surrendered underground leaders. The Deputy Commissioner of the district acted as the ex-officio Chairman of the Regional Council, whereas, the Vice-Chairman of the Council was elected by the members from amongst themselves. The Constitution (Thirteenth Amendment) Act, 1962, also provided that no Act of the Legislature of Nagaland should apply to the Tuensang district unless approved by the Regional Council.[67] One of the members representing the district in the Legislative Assembly of Nagaland was appointed Minister for Tuensang Affairs by the Governor.

During the First and the Second General Elections (1964 and 1969) the members of the Longleng and the Tamlu Area Councils elected their representatives to the Tuensang District Regional Council from among themselves. The Longleng Area Council and the Tamlu Area Council elected three and one member respectively, while the other one was a Governor nominated member.

The members of the Regional Council received monthly salaries besides daily allowances for attending meetings. In addition the Vice-Chairman and the members of the Council were eligible to draw travelling allowances for the journey undertaken by them in connection with their official duties.[68]

The Village Councils, Area Councils and the Tuensang District Regional Council prepared various schemes pertaining to development of their respective areas. Greater emphasis, however, was laid on construction and repairing of roads, building of irrigation projects, extension of water supply, setting up of dispensaries, expansion of forest land and plantation of valuable trees like *hollock,* pine, *mekahi, gomari* and *khokon,* construction of school buildings, etc. But, since these bodies were not given any real financial power their duties were confined to preparation and submission of schemes to the government. Thus, in the absence of financial powers for implementing the schemes, these bodies remained essentially recommendatory bodies. Happily, many of these schemes were carried into effect by the Government of Nagaland.[69]

The ten-year period of Tuensang District Regional Council was coming to an end in 1973 whereupon in an emergency session held in March 1973 it was resolved to dissolve the Regional Council and place Tuensang district at par with other districts of the state of Nagaland.[70]

The Tuensang District Regional Council was set-up in consideration of the socio-economic backwardness of the tribes of the Tuensang district. It was a well-planned step which benefited the people who were given an opportunity to take part in the democratic process of the government and make them fit for shouldering the responsibility in the years to come.

Elections to the Nagaland Legislative Assembly

The State of Nagaland Act, 1962 provided for a unicameral Legislative Assembly with sixty seats for the state.[71] The first election to the Nagaland Legislative Assembly was held in 1964. As per the provisions of the above Act, forty Members of the Legislative Assembly (MLAs) were elected by the people of Kohima and Mokokchung districts, whereas six MLAs were chosen from Tuensang district by the Tuensang District Regional Council. Of these six members, none was from the Phom community.[72] As in 1964, elections were held only in Kohima and Mokokchung districts during the second State Legislative Assembly Election of 1969, when forty MLAs were elected from these two districts. This time the number of seats for Tuensang district was fixed at twelve and the Tuensang District Regional Council sent by consensus all the twelve members to the

State Legislative Assembly. There was complete absence of party politics. Of the twelve members, two hailed from the Phom areas, viz. Oditemba Phom of Yachem village and Thanglong Konyak of Tamlu village.[73] Soon after becoming MLAs, both Oditemba and Thanglong joined the Naga Nationalist Organisation (NNO), a political party which came to power in Nagaland.

The third Nagaland Legislative Assembly Election was held in 1974. Unlike the earlier elections the election of 1974 was held in the entire state of Nagaland including the old Tuensang area. Thus, after a period of ten years since the first General Election in the state in 1964, the old Tuensang area, was brought under the electoral map of Nagaland. The Delimitation Act, 1972 (76 of 1972), fixed sixty territorial assembly constituencies for the purpose of holding election, including two seats for the Phom areas – 49 Tamlu Assembly Constituency and 50 Longleng Assembly Constituency.[74] Both the Constituencies are reserved for the Scheduled Tribes.[75] Since then these two assembly constituencies were held by the Phom Nagas in all subsequent elections. The results of the assembly elections in these two constituencies during 1974-2013 are shown in Table 5.1.

Some of the MLAs from the Tamlu and the Longleng Assembly Constituencies, namely N. Metpong Phom, Bangjak Phom, Chenlom Phom, Bukchem Phom and B. Phongshak Phom held important portfolios in the ministries formed in the state from time to time. Chenlom Phom was appointed Deputy Speaker and thereafter the Speaker of Nagaland Legislative Assembly in 1987.

S.C. Jamir led Congress (I) political party won both the general elections held in 1994 and 1998. But the election of 1998 was exception in the history of Naga politics because only the Congress (I) and some independent candidates took part in this election. This situation arose due to the refusal of the opposition parties to field their candidates on the call of the NGOs and the Naga *Hoho* to boycott the election. Their slogan was 'Nagas want solution, not election'. Thus, elections were held in only seventeen Legislative Assembly Constituencies of the state including the Tamlu and the Longleng Constituencies, whereas in the remaining forty-three seats the candidates returned uncontested.[76] The overall percentage of vote cast in the seventeen constituencies was 46.95; the highest percentage of vote recorded was at Tamlu, i.e. 99.80. Longleng came third with 98.00 per cent.[77]

The tenth, eleventh and the twelfth general elections for the

Table 5.1: Result of Assembly Elections in Tamlu and Longleng Constituencies, 1974-2013

Year	Name of constituency with its number	Name of elected candidate	Party to which affiliated	Votes polled
1974	49 Tamlu	Wokshing	UDF	1687
	50 Longleng	N. Metpong Phom	IND	1618
1977	49 Tamlu	Banjak Phom	IND	3441
	50 Longleng	Chenlom	UDF	2213
1982	49 Tamlu	Bangjak	Cong	4618
	50 Longleng	Chenlom	NNDP	4462
1987	49 Tamlu	Banjak Phom	Cong-I	3434
	50 Longleng	Chenlom	Cong-I	2736
1989	49 Tamlu	Bangjak Phom	NPC	3501
	50 Longleng	Bukchem Phom	NPC	5003
1993	49 Tamlu	Phongshak B. Phom	INC	14000
	50 Longleng	Chenlom M. Phom	NPC	11840
1998	49 Tamlu	B. Phongshak Phom	INC	15120
	50 Longleng	Shami Angh	IND	11843
2003	49 Tamlu	Nyemli Phom	INC	9427
	50 Longleng	Chenlom Phom	JD (U)	8595
2008	49 Tamlu	P.Dako Phom	Independent	NA
	50 Longleng	S.Pangnyu Phom	NCP	
2013	49 Tamlu	B.S.Nganlang	JD(U)	7276
	50 Longleng	S.Pangnyu	NPF	13171

N.B. : UDF : United Democratic Front, INC : Indian National Congress, IND : Independent, JD(U) : Janata Dal (United), NPC : Nagaland People's Council, Cong-I : Congress(I), NNDP : Naga National Democratic Party, NCP: Nationalist Congress Party and NPF: Naga People's Front.

Source: (i) *Results of the General Assembly Elections of Nagaland* (Fourth Edition), pp. 19-73.
(ii) *Report on the General Elections to 10*th *Nagaland Legislative Assembly 2003*, p. 68.
(iii) *The Nagaland Post*, March 1, 2013.

Nagaland Legislative Assembly were held in 2003, 2008 and 2013 respectively. The S.C. Jamir led Congress Government got major setback in the election of 2003. This time a new coalition government called the Democratic Alliance of Nagaland (DAN) came to power headed by Neiphiu Rio, the leader of the Naga People's Front (NPF), which was earlier known as the Nationalist Naga Democratic Party (NNDP). The two MLAs elected from Tamlu and Longleng constituencies joined the DAN Government and one of them Chenlom Phom was given the portfolio of the ministry of Fisheries, Printing and Stationary. The DAN Government came back to power in the

2008 assembly election and Neiphiu Rio once again became the Chief Minister of the state. The two elected Phom MLAs joined the DAN Government and both of them were made as the Parliamentary Secretaries of different departments.

In the twelfth Nagaland Legislative Assembly election held on 23 February, 2013 the Neiphiu Rio led Naga People's Front political party got a landslide victory. The election was overall peaceful. However, the polling party which reached Ladigarh on 23 February to conduct poll there was cordoned off by the Assam police. So, no voter dared to turn up to the polling station to cast their vote. Following this incident re-poll was conducted there under tight security. There was a breath-taking contest between JD (U) and NPF candidates of 49 Tamlu Assembly Constituency. The NPF candidate S. Pangnyu of 50 Longleng Assembly Constituency defeated his nearest rival NCP candidate by a margin of 4235 votes. Neiphiu Rio was sworn in for a third straight term as chief minister of Nagaland on 5 March along with eleven ministers by the governor. S. Pangnyu was elevated from being parliamentary secretary for rural development and REPA to minister of industries and commerce. B.S. Nganlang had to be satisfied with the post of parliamentary secretary of land resources. The result of the election brought no significant change to the Naga women as they repeatedly failed to enter the assembly since statehood.

A remarkable feature of the election process in the Phom areas is that the people have been giving more importance to the candidates than the parties to which they were affiliated. Defection has always been a practice; a candidate winning the election as an independent or on the ticket of one party has no inhibition to switch his loyalty in favour of another party whenever an opportunity arrives. This is done either in the interest of the community he represents or for personal gain. No wonder, the Phom MLAs in the legislature have shown a tendency to be on the side of the party in power. Consequently, no political party succeeded to have a foothold in the Phom areas in the last forty years.[78] Sporadic violence takes place among the supporters on the eve of elections. It also creates a rift between the villages for the time being.

When the Assembly election approaches a festive atmosphere is witnessed among the people. During election the villagers get themselves into several groups in support of their candidates and each group enjoys feasts thrown by their candidates. The candidates fielded in the election fray are seen holding meetings to woo the voters. In some cases camps were opened at all important villages where supporters of the candidates are entertained with food and drink for several days.

From the very beginning the Village Councils of the Phom areas have been taking an important part in elections. On the eve of an election the members of the Village Council hold meeting with a view to taking opinions of the people and also study the situations and to take decision to whom to support or how to divide votes among different candidates. Likewise, when an eminent Phom leader decides to contest an election, the Village Council to which he originally belongs, canvasses for him in the election.[79]

Longleng Ad Hoc Town Committee and the Town Council

The Longleng Ad hoc Town Committee, a non-Government body, was first constituted in 1984. The committee was formed with the aim of assisting the administration for better management of the town. A. Oditemba Phom, ex-MLA was its first Vice-Chairman. The Committee was, however, dissolved in 1989 by the Additional Deputy Commissioner, Longleng, allegedly on charge of mismanagement and inefficiency.[80] After a gap of several years, on 24 September, 1998, a second Ad hoc Town Committee was formed. The Committee consisted of thirteen members including four members nominated by the ADC, Longleng. The other members were elected by the people of each *khel* of the town. Initially, the Committee was constituted for three years. Subsequently, on the expiry of its term, its tenure was extended for another year. The members of the Committee elected Y. Heong Phom as its Vice-Chairman. The ADC, Longleng acted as the ex-officio Chairman.[81]

The Longleng Ad hoc Town Committee performed a number of public welfare activities among which the most important were: maintenance of health and hygiene in the town, stoppage of free movement of animals, fixation of prices of various articles of sale, supervision of dispensaries for detecting spurious and outdated medicines, selection of sites for shops selling animal meat, providing dustbins in public places and regular clearance of garbage, prevention of illegal construction of houses and business premises, etc.[82] The term of the Longleng Ad hoc Town Committee came to an end in 2003.

In the same year, the Government of Nagaland by a notification decided to constitute Town Councils in various towns of Nagaland including one at Longleng.[83] The number of members of the Longleng Town Council was fixed at fourteen including three government nominated members. The term of the Council is five years. The first election to the Council was held on 8 December, 2004. The result of the Longleng Town Council Election 2004 is shown in Table 5.2:

Table 5.2: Longleng Town Council Election 2004

Sl. No.	*Municipal/Town*	*Ward No.*	*Name of elected candidate*	*Party affiliation*
1.	Longleng	1	Imliakum	NPF
2.	Longleng	2	Lepdang	NPF
3.	Longleng	3	Leisha Leinak	NPF
4.	Longleng	4	Ngapten	NPF
5.	Longleng	5	L. Chingai	INDP
6.	Longleng	6	Ponglong	NPF
7.	Longleng	7	Longphe	NPF
8.	Longleng	8	H. Ozuk	NPF
9.	Longleng	9	H. Aniam	BJP
10.	Longleng	10	A. Angai	BJP
11.	Longleng	11	M. Nokham	NPF

N.B.: NPF: Naga People's Front, BJP: Bharatiya Janata Party and INDP: Independent.

Source: *The Warrior*, Vol. 34, January 2005, No. 1, p. 12.

The Council elected Leisha Leinak as Chairman and Longphe as Vice-Chairman. The members of the Council were not paid any regular salary but were entitled to draw a sum of Rs. 150 a day as sitting allowance for attending meetings. The Council receives government funds for implementing various development schemes relating to the town which include repairing and expansion of old roads and opening of new ones. It is also running a government recognised computer training institute at Longleng town. The Council has also been assisting the district administration to maintain law and order in the town area. It fixes the prices of various articles of sale and issues licences to the traders.

The elections of Municipal and the Town Councils including the Longleng Town Council of Nagaland have remained due since 2009.

This political deadlock arose due to lack of general consensus among the Nagas about 33 per cent reservation of seats for women, although the Government of Nagaland had already promulgated one-third reservation of all elected seats for women in the Municipal and the Town Councils in 2006 by an amendment of the Nagaland Municipal Act, 2001. The Guwahati High Court had already given ruling on 21st October, 2011 in favour of 33 per cent women reservation and directed the State Government to hold the election to various Municipal and the Town Councils within a stipulated time frame.[84]

The Longleng District: Its Administrative Development

The process of evolution of Longleng from an administrative centre to a district started in November 1951 when an Assistant Political Officer was placed in charge of this place.[85] But, the centre was soon shifted to Mon leaving only a *Do-Bhashi* outpost with a battalion of the Assam Rifles and a school in the former place.[86] Thereafter, in deference to the people's wish, a Base Superintendent was appointed to look after the administration;[87] but the post was soon replaced by an Area Superintendent and again, in 1956 it was upgraded to an Assistant Political Officer.[88] During the NEFA period each division was under the control of a Political Officer who was assisted by officers of all technical departments, Divisional Medical Officer, Divisional Agricultural Officer and so on. The subdivisions were in charge of either Political Officers or the Assistant Political Officers, who had under them Base Superintendents and Area Superintendents.[89] The Naga Hills-Tuensang Area (Administration) Regulation, December 1957 changed the designation of Political Officer, Additional Political Officer and Assistant Political Officer to Deputy Commissioner (DC), Additional Deputy Commissioner (ADC) and Assistant Commissioner (AC) respectively.[90] Longleng, which was then a subdivision headed by an Assistant Commissioner was upgraded to a subdivision under a Subdivisional Officer (Civil) on 26 January, 1978 and thereafter made an ADC's headquarters on 15 August, 1987.[91]

Demands, however, were voiced from time to time to grant Longleng the status of a district. From the beginning of the present century the aspiration of the people found expression through a number of memorandums submitted on behalf of some Non-Governmental Organizations (NGOs) to the Chief Minister, Nagaland and His Excellency the Governor of Nagaland, urging them to seriously consider the question of upgradation of the Longleng subdivision. Moreover, some of the political parties of the area were seen making this an election issue in the general election of 2003. Two MLAs belonging to the Phom community, having won the election of 2003, joined the Democratic Alliance of Nagaland Government on the condition that it would fulfil this demand. Neiphiu Rio, the C.M. of the state, expressed full support for this demand. In a speech delivered on the occasion of the Phom Day celebration on 6 June, 2003, he assured the people that "the DAN Government would look into all possibilities of upgrading Longleng Sub-Division to a District status."[92] He followed up his promise when he himself formally declared the inauguration of the Longleng district at an impressive function held at Longleng town public ground on 26 January, 2004.[93] Thus, the long cherished dream of the Phom people was finally realised. With the creation of this district Longleng became the eleventh district of Nagaland.

There are at present five administrative centres of the district, namely the Yongnyah, the Sakchi, the Namsang (Kongshang) and the Yachem headquarters, in charge of Extra Assistant Commissioners and the Tamlu subdivision headed by an Additional Deputy Commissioner. The Tamlu subdivision was first opened as an administrative circle in 1958[94] and later upgraded and inaugurated to ADC Headquaters on 2 May, 2012 by Chief Minister Neihiu Rio. The headquarters of the Extra Assistant Commissioner of Yongnyah was first opened on 8 November, 1983 as a circle office by the then Chief Minister, S.C. Jamir. The EAC headquarters at Sakshi was also inaugurated by the Chief Minister Jamir on 21 June, 1999.[95] The two other EAC headquarters, one at Namsang (Kongshang) and the other one at Yachem were opened in 2011 and 2012 respectively.

The *Do-Bhashi* (DB) and the *Gaon-Bura* (GB)

Do-Bhashi, a government agency has been playing an important role in the field of administration of justice and maintenance of law and order since the days of the colonial rule. Prior to independence, the Phom tribe had only one or two *Do-Bhashis* attached to the Mokokchung Sub-Divisional Office. The number has risen considerably since then. Today, each government recognised village has more than one *Do-Bhashi*. With the opening of new administrative centres in the Phom areas, the *Do-Bhashis* got their customary (law) court attached to each centre. They are recruited from different villages and towns. The *Do-Bhashis,* attached to the offices of the Extra Assistant Commissioners and the Sub-Divisional Officer (Civil), are recruited from the villages within their respective jurisdictions while the *Do-Bhashis* of the Deputy Commissioner's Court at Longleng are from different villages and towns of the district. Though each administrator has a *Do-Bhashi* Customary Court, the number of *Do-Bhashi* varies according to the rank of the administrator. The court of the Deputy Commissioner has the highest number whereas the court of the Extra Assistant Commissioner has the lowest. Earlier, the Area Superintendent and the Circle Officer had *Do-Bhashi* Customary Courts.[96]

The *Do-Bhashis* are vested with the powers of trying cases according to the customary law.[97] Before the formation of the police department in the state (1963), it was the duty of the *Do-Bhashis* and the *Gaon-Buras* to apprehend the offenders and produce them before the nearest administrative officer.[98] The cases in which a non-Naga is involved and which cannot be settled according to the customary law are decided by a magistrate of class II or class I rank.[99] They also help the officers in maintaining law and order in their territories.[100]

Inter-village disputes, especially land disputes, are referred to the administrative officers, who settle them amicably with the help of the *Do-Bhashis*. A case which cannot be settled in the E.A.C.'s court is referred to the Additional Deputy Commissioner or the Deputy Commissioner of the district. From the beginning the *Do-Bhashis* have been recruited from among the menfolk only.[101]

The *Gaon-Bura* is another government agency in Nagaland, which was created by the British. The number of *Gaon-Bura*s of the Phom villages vary from village to village according to seize of the population. After receiving requests from the Village Councils, the *Gaon-Bura*s are appointed by the Deputy Commissioner or the Additional Deputy Commissioner.[102] There is no fixed term of their appointment. They collect the house tax and deposit the same in the treasury. Unlike the *Do-Bhashis*, they do not receive salary. They are given red blankets for their work.

Non-Governmental Organisations

During the second half of the twentieth century quite a few non-governmental organisations were established in the Phom areas with various aims and objectives. Currently, some of these organisations are very active in the district.

The Phom People's Council (PPC)

The Phom People's Council, which was established in 1990, is the apex body of all non-governmental organisations working in the Phom areas. The organisation consists of the Village Council Chairmen, Village Council members, prominent Phom leaders, retired government servants, church leaders, etc. The general meeting of the Council is held once a year when its office bearers are selected. It takes decision on almost all the problems faced by the community from time to time. It also acts as a peace keeping body. One notable work of the Council is the establishment of a community college in collaboration with the Association of the Phom Graduates and Officers, thereby bringing higher education to the doorsteps of the Phom students. The Council mediated in a dispute over the Tobu issue (Konyak-Chang land dispute) and settled the boundary disputes of the Phom villages.[103] The Eastern Nagaland People's Organisation (ENPO) is the apex body of the backward tribes of Tuensang, Mon, Longleng and Kiphre districts and the PPC has its representatives in the ENPO. The ENPO instead of accepting the autonomous council as proposed by the state cabinet has been demanding a separate state, to be called Frontier Nagaland, comprising the aforesaid four districts more vigorously since 2010. The organization even submitted its memorandums to the Government of India in this connection.

The Association of Phom Graduates and Officers (APGO)

The Association of Phom Graduates and Officers was formed in January 1990. The main objectives of the Association are: to foster unity and harmony among the Phom people; to advise and coordinate the activities of all such organisations of the area, and to encourage and promote all socially useful and productive activities.[104] The Association can be called an intellectual body of the tribe because all the members of the Association are university graduates. Moreover, it consists of a number of experienced technical and non-technical Phom officers. It holds its general meeting once a year in which its office bearers are selected, although other meetings are held from time to time whenever required. The APGO has its representatives in the Eastern Nagaland Gazetted Officers Association.

Phom Students' Conference

The Phom Students' Conference (PSC), the apex body of all the Phom Students' Unions, was established in 1958. Every Phom village has a Students' Union. The Phom students studying in different places, especially outside Longleng, meet once a year, usually during winter vacation when they come home. The Phom Students' Conference discusses and decides all important issues concerning the welfare of the villages or the tribe as a whole. The resolutions adopted in the meetings are given great importance by all concerned. Over the years the Phom Students' Conference has performed a number of commendable works through the Village Students' Unions at the grass-roots levels. They have succeeded in stopping free movement of pigs, cows and dogs in public places. They also stopped free rearing of *mithuns* in most of the villages. They have helped the villagers to construct hygienic sanitary latrines. They are helping the villagers to build houses keeping a minimum distance from each other to prevent houses catching accidental fire. The Village Students' Unions exercise the power of imposing fines on the students discontinuing studies in the middle of the academic session, for gambling, for sexual abuse, for not attending church service and showing disrespect to elders and for smuggling and trafficking in drugs, etc. They occasionally render physical service to raise funds for their unions.[105] Before the division of Tuensang district in 2004 there was a student body called the Tuensang-Mon Students' Federation, which was renamed the Eastern Naga Students' Federation in 2006. The PSC has its representatives in this Federation.

The Phomla Hoichem

The *Phomla Hoichem* (Phom Women's Union), a Phom woman organisation was formed on 9 May, 1992 at the initiative of Mrs. Asangla Sangtam, the wife of Mr. T.C. Sangtam, the then ADC of Longleng. The organization has its headquarters at Longleng. It holds its meetings from time to time. It has the office bearers like the president, the vice president, the secretary, the joint secretary and treasurer. Membership is open to all Phom women. The organization was formed with the following objectives: to develop and promote the bond of unity among the Phom women, to fight social evils, to offer financial assistance to orphans and the destitute, to encourage women to participate in all corporate activities, to provide relief and other forms of assistance during natural calamities, to fight for women's rights and to revive and preserve the cultural heritage of the Phom Nagas. The organisation has performed a number of commendable works since its establishment. It carried on house to house search to detect alcohol and other narcotic substances (drugs). It also held seminars and discourses in collaboration with the medical department to create awareness among women regarding family planning measures, etc. The organisation extended financial assistance to the sufferers whose houses burnt accidentally.[106]

Besides the *Phomla Hoichem* every Phom Baptist church has women organization. This organization is trying to educate the women by organizing seminars, workshops and trainings.

Christian Organisations

There are mainly three Christian organisations, viz. Phom Baptist Christian Association (PBCA), Revival Church and St. Joseph's Parish (Catholic) in Longleng district. Although the main aim of these organisations is evangelical, they have been rendering humanitarian services to the people, especially in the fields of health service, education, etc.

Militancy

To many scholars the root of militancy in Nagaland can be traced back to the last days of the colonial rule when the Nagas began to express great fear of being exploited economically and politically by the people of the plains. In a memorandum submitted to the Simon Commission in January 1929 by the Naga Club, established in 1918, urged upon the Commission to exclude the Nagas from the proposed reforms and keep them under direct administrative control of the centre so as to save them from being completely overwhelmed by the people of the plains.[107] Later, the Naga National Council went a step further and in a memorandum submitted on 19 June, 1946, it suggested that, "the Naga hills should be constitutionally included in an autonomous Assam, in a free India, with local autonomy and due safeguards for the interests of the Nagas".[108] But, within a year the NNC changed its stand and started clamouring for independence by submitting another memorandum to the Government on 20 February, 1947.[109]

In the same year, an agreement known as Hydari Agreement was signed between Sir Akbar Hydari, the then Governor of Assam and the Naga National Council which proposed to grant greater autonomy to the Nagas. The last point of the Agreement stated, "The Governor of Assam as the Agent of the Government of the Indian Union will have special responsibility for a period of ten years to ensure the due observance of this agreement; at the end of the Period, the Naga National Council will be asked whether they require the above Agreement to be extended for a further period or a new Agreement regarding the future of the Naga people would be arrived at".[110] This part of the Agreement, however, created a controversy. Their leader A.Z. Phizo, interpreted this point as a right to demand separation from India after the expiry of ten years. Meanwhile, India attained independence on 15 August, 1947 and the Naga Hills district and the Tribal Area became a part of free India. Phizo, who was elected as the president of the NNC in 1949, became adamant on his claim for having a separate independent country for the Nagas. Initially, he with support of other members of the NNC, followed the line of a non-violent democratic movement, i.e. boycott of election, boycott of government service, non-cooperation with government in all official works.[111] This having proved a failure, the NNC resorted to an armed struggle to achieve the goal. The Assam Rifles and the Assam Police were pressed into service forcing Phizo and several followers to go underground in the Tuensang Area. Thongdi Chang, whom Phizo appointed as commander-in-chief, organised armed gangs in the Tuensang area.[112] Finally, on 22 March, 1956, the underground workers declared the establishment of a Federal Government at Phensinyu village, near Kohima.[113]

The strong winds of this militant movement soon blow over the Phom territory. Several young men of the community left home to join the underground workers.[114] The Indian security forces were deployed in the Phom areas to flush out the rebels. A number of Phom villages were virtually under seize of the armed forces. Almost all the government schools of the area were closed down for months.[115] It was precisely in this situation of chaos Phizo left for London in 1956 leaving the charge of the movement to younger leaders.

It was due to the tireless efforts of the moderate Naga leaders the

Naga Hills-Tuensang Area was united in 1957 and Nagaland attained statehood in 1963. However, the undergrounds were still opposing the formation of the state within the Indian Union and continued their activities. A cease-fire was signed in 1964 which brought an end the hostility for the time being. Following this several rounds of talks were held between the Naga rebels and the Government of India. Sadly, the peace talks failed by 1967 as the underground Nagas continued their demand for an independent country for the Nagas.[116]

In 1975, the historic Shillong Accord was signed between the underground leaders and the Government of India. It provided a ray of hope of a permanent solution to the vexed Naga problem. The euphoria soon turned into a nightmare. A section of the militants who were in foreign lands at that time did not accept the Accord. A group of them led by Issac Swu, T. Muviah and Khaplang, rejected the Shillong Accord and formed a breakaway faction named "Nationalist Socialist Council of Nagaland" (NSCN) on 31 January, 1980. These rebel leaders once served as lieutenants of Phizo. But, now they severed all relations with the Federal Government set up by Phizo.[117] In 1988, a further division of NSCN took place. Khaplang, once a close associate of Muivah and Issac, formed a new faction known as Nationalist Socialist Council of Nagaland (Khaplang).[118] The NSCN-K was initially quite active in the Phom areas. But, from the last part of the twentieth century the NSCN-IM slowly stepped in which resulted in occasional group clashes between the supporters of the rival groups. Many civilians and militants lost their lives as a direct consequence of the factional clashes. The Government of India announced cease-fire in Nagaland in 1997 following some kind of understanding with the opposing militant groups.[119] Yet, peace has not returned completely.

It can be inferred now that following the establishment of Longleng administrative centre the modern system of administration began to take root in the traditional Phom society. Till the time of the formation of Naga Hills-Tuensang Area (1957) the people did not have the opportunity to take part in state politics. The formation of the Tuensang District Regional Council and the Area Councils facilitated their participation in the democratic process of the state. The introduction of election system in the areas provided the people an opportunity to exercise their franchise. The assembly elections made them politically more conscious. They have realised that their problems cannot be solved through armed struggle. The Non-Governmental Organisations (NGOs) which came into existence have been rendering valuable services for rapid advancement of the society by introducing numerous reforms. Yet, the most burning issue of the state, viz. militancy has still remained unsolved despite efforts made by the Centre and the State Governments.

NOTES AND REFERENCES

1. Elwin, Verrier, *Nagaland,* p. 27.
2. *Tuensang District Regional Council, Who is Who* 1973, p. 1.
3. Kumar, B.B., *An Introduction to the Naga Tribes*, p. 8.
4. The 'Naga Tribal Area' means the area along the eastern frontier of 'India' which was not part of 'British India' or of Burma or of any foreign state, more precisely the area lying between the erstwhile Naga Hills District and Burma and which later came to be known as the Tuensang Frontier Division of NEFA (1954). Luthra, P.N., *Nagaland from a District to a State,* p. 18.
5. Elwin, Verrier, *Op. cit.,* p. 29.
6. Luthra, P.N., *Op. cit.,* p. 8.
7. Interview held with Anyak Phom (79), retired *Do-Bhashi,* at Longleng on 11-04-2001.
8. Elwin, Verrier, *A Philosophy for NEFA,* p. 3.
9. *Tuensang District Regional Council, Op. cit.*
10. Elwin, Verrier, *Nagaland,* p. 3.
11. "The North-East Frontier Area (Administration) Regulation 1954, Regulation No. 1 of 1954", cited in Luthra, P.N., *Op. cit.,* p. 81, see Appendix.
12. In April 1945, Pawsey, the D.C. of the Naga Hills district helped to establish the Naga Hills District Council. However, in 1946 at a conference of the tribal representatives the name of the Council was changed to Naga National Council. Anand, V.K., *Conflict in Nagaland: A Study of Insurgency and Counter-Insurgency,* p. 62.
13. Zhimomi, Kuhoi K., *Politics and Militancy in Nagaland,* pp. 33 & 35.
14. *Ibid,* p. 50.
15. *Ibid,* p. 67.
16. Mankekar, D.R., *On the Slippery Slope in Nagaland,* p. 60.
17. Elwin, Verrier, *Nagaland,* p. 65.
18. 'The Naga Hills-Tuensang Area Act, 1957', cited in Luthra, P.N., *Op. cit.,* pp. 83-84, see Appendix.
19. Elwin, Verrier, *Nagaland,* p. 65.
20. 'The Naga Hills-Tuensang Area (Administrative) Regulation, December, 1957', cited in Luthra, P.N., *op. cit.,* p. 87, see Appendix.
21. *Report on the First General Election,* 1963, p. 2.
22. Singh, Chandrika, *Emergence of Arunachal Pradesh as a State,* p. 109.

23. *10 Years' Progress in NEFA: A Brief Account of Administrative and Development Activities in North-East Frontier Agency Since Independence*, p. 16.
24. Interview held with Anyak Phom (81), *Op. cit.*, on 08-12-2003.
25. Singh, Chandrika, *Political Evolution of Nagaland*, p. 67.
26. Jasokie, J.B., 'Nagaland from District to State', in the *Silver Jubilee Souvenir, 25 Years of Nagaland Legislative Assembly*, pp. 60-61.
27. Atsongchanger, Mar (complied), *The Historical Memoranda of the Nagas and Their Neighbours*, pp. 78-84. The Naga militants who still remained adamant on their demand for a separate independent state for the Nagas, outright rejected the sixteen-point proposal. Violence therefore, continued unabated and in the process a few prominent Naga leaders lost their lives at the hands of undergrounds militants.
    The Inner Line Regulation of 1873 is still in force in Nagaland but Dimapur and its surrounding foothills fall out of the inner line. Bareh, H. (ed.), *Nagaland District Gazetteers, Kohima District*, p. 10. Under this Regulation a person from outside of Nagaland is prohibited to enter the state without obtaining a pass from the Deputy Commissioner or of such other officer who are authorised to grant such pass.
28. Singh, Chandrika, *Political Evolution of Nagaland*, p. 69.
29. Jasokie, J.B., *Op. cit.*, p. 71. A Phom gentleman named Pauting Phom was included as a member of fifteen-man delegation.
30. Elwin, Verrier, *Nagaland*, p. 83.
31. Singh, Chandrika, *Political Evolution of Nagaland*, p. 77.
32. 'The Nagaland (Transitional Provisions) Regulation, 1961', cited in Luthra, P.N., *Op. cit.*, pp. 92-95, see Appendix. The Interim Body and the Executive Council functioned as the legislature and the Cabinet for Nagaland respectively during this three-year transitional period.
33. Jasokie, J.B., *Op. cit.*, p. 74.
34. Yaden, L.L., 'Impact of Adult Franchise', in B.B. Kumar (ed), *Modernization in Naga Society*, p. 73.
35. Maitra, Kiranshankar, *The Nagas Rebel and Insurgency in the North-East*, p. 51.
36. *Silver Jubilee Souvenir, 25 Years of Nagaland Legislative Assembly*, p. III.
37. Singh, Chandrika, *Political Evolution of Nagaland*, p. 86.
38. Interview held with Hepong Phom (83), ex-Interim Body Member and ex-Regional Council Member, at Longleng on 19-11-2003.
39. 'The Nagaland (Transitional Provisions) Regulation, 1961' in Luthra, P.N., *Op. cit.*
40. 'The Nagaland Village and Area Councils Act, 1978', *Nagaland Gazette*, 31 March, 1979, Part-V, p. 45. There were twenty-four government recognised Phom villages in 2001. Two more such villages, namely Noksosang and Alayung, were added to the list on 11 July, 2002. *The Warrior*, Vol. 31, September, 2002, No. 9, p. 39.

41. 'The Nagaland Village and Area Councils Act, 1978', *Op. cit.*
42. Interview held with four Village Council Chairmen, viz. S. Pangjei of Bhumnyu, T.C. Nyamnyei Semdok of Sakchi, B. Angshai Phom of Yongam and A. Hamlang of BUra Namsang on 14-03-2004, 22-01-2004, 07-09-2002 and 25-01-2004 respectively.
43. 'The Nagaland Village and Area Councils Act, 1978', *Op. cit.*
44. *Nagaland 2003,* p. 66.
45. Ao, A. Lanunungsang, *Rural Development in Nagaland,* p. 165.
46. 'The Nagaland Village and Area Councils Act, 1978', *Op. cit.*, p. 50.
47 Noklang, C. Amop, *Phom Day: Basis for Peace in Nagaland,* p. 51. There was a recent case which took place in February 2003 at Yongam village. In this case two villagers named Netu and Velei made rival claims over a plot of land covered with palm tree. To strengthen his claim Velei laid a piece of stone as per traditional practice of the village and swore in the name of the sun, the moon, the earth and eating up little soil and declared that if he is guilty of making a false claim he would be cursed. In return Netu also took a similar vow in presence of all those present fixing coming harvest season as the deadline. Strangely, before the commencement of harvesting season the mother of Velei expired and Netu was declared the legal owner of the disputed land.

    The major part of the Phom customary laws and usages explained here are based on B. Henshet Phom ed. book: *The Phom-Naga Customary Laws* and also interviews.
48. Interview held with H. Toshi Phom (47), Longleng Ad hoc Town Committee Member and the Treasurer of LTSU, at PPC Colony Longleng on 12-01-2003.
49. 'The Nagaland Village and Area Councils Act, 1978', *Op. cit.,* pp. 48-49.
50. Sema, Hokishe, *Emergence of Nagaland: Socio-Economic and Political Transformation and the Future,* p. 170.
51. *History of Tuensang Town, Golden Jubilee,* 1948-1998, p. 11.
52. Interview held with Hepong Phom (83), *Op. cit.*
53. 'The Nagaland Village and Area Councils Act, 1978', *Op. cit.,* p. 51.
54. Interview held with Hepong Phom (83), *Op. cit.* Ngaman Phom (Longleng AC), Ango (Tamlu AC), N. Wokshing Phom (Tamlu AC), K.C. Longli (Tamlu AC), Y. Heong Phom (Longleng AC), Hadong Phom (Tamlu AC), Pukyong Phom (Longleng AC) and Kanglong (Tamlu AC) were some of the Vice-Chairmen of the Longleng and the Tamlu Area Councils. *Phom Day, Golden Jubilee,* 1952-2002, 5-6 June, 2002, *Bushah Laitap,* p. 26; *Nagaland Gazettes,* No. 8, 31 July, 1967; No. 13, 30 November, 1973.
55. *Nagaland Gazette,* 30 November, 1965, Part IV.
56. Furer-Haimendrof, Christoph von, *Return to the Naked Nagas,* p. 250.
57. 'The Nagaland Village and Area Councils Act, 1978', *Op. cit.,* p. 55. *Nagaland Gazette,* No. 24, 31 March, 1967.
58. *Nagaland Gazette,* 31 March, 1979, Part-V, p. 53.

59. Furer-Haimendrof, Christoph von, *Op. cit.*
60. *Nagaland Gazette,* 31 March, 1979, *Op. cit.*
61. Interview held with Y. Heong Phom (56), ex-Vice-Chairman of Longleng Area Council and the Vice-Chairman of Longleng Ad hoc Town Committee, at Block Colony, Longleng on 27-11-2001.
62. *Nagaland Gazette,* 31 March, 1979, *Op. cit.*
63. *The Nagaland Code*, Volume IV, p. 189.
64. 'The Sixteen-Point Agreement', Appendix E of Kuhoi K. Zhimomi's *Politics and Militancy in Nagaland*, p. 178.
65. *Ibid,* p. 79.
66. *Tuensang District Regional Council, Op. cit.* As per Article 371-A of the Constitution (Thirteenth Amendment) Act, 1962, a Regional Council for the Tuensang district consisting of thirty-five members was to be established. 'The Constitution (Thirteenth Amendment) Act 1962', in Mar Atsongchanger (compiled) *Op. cit.*, p. 116.
67. *Ibid*, pp. 116-117.
68. *Nagaland Gazette,* 30 November, 1965, Part IV. Hepong Phom (1964-69), Yongnaya (Konyak) (1964-69), Nyakshingnyu (Anyak Phom) (1964-69, 1969-73), Thanglong Konyak (1969-73), Oditemba (1964-69, 1969-73), Mongshet (1968-69, 1969-73) and Keyi Phom (1969-73) were the members of the Tuensang District Regional Council from the Phom areas. Interview held with Hepong Phom (83) on 19-11-2003 and 24-04-2005, *Op. cit.; Tuensang District Regional Council, Op. cit.*, pp. 2-28.
69. Sema, Hokishe, *op. cit.*, p. 171; Interview held with Hepong Phom (83), *Op. cit.*
70. *Tuensang District Regional Council, Op. cit.*, p. 2.
71. 'The State of Nagaland Act, 1962', in P.N. Luthra, *Op. cit.*, p. 106, see Appendix.
72. *Findings of Election Department Nagaland,* p. 85.
73. *Ibid,* p. 100.
74. *Ibid,* p. 122.
75. *Handbook, General Election, 1998 to the Legislative Assembly and Lok Sabha of Nagaland,* pp. 2-3.
76. *Results of the General Assembly Elections of Nagaland* (Fourth Edition), p. 73.
77. *The Warrior*, Vol. 27, March 1998, No. 3, p. 28.
78. Interview held with B. Hayu Phom (59), President, 'Nagaland People's Front' Political Party, Longleng district, at Oushok Colony on 07-06-2007.
79. *Ibid.*
80. Interview held with Y. Heong Phom (56), *Op. cit.*
81. *Ibid.*
82. *Ibid.*
83. *Nagaland 2003*, p. 65.
84. Ezung, Achumi, 'Naga Women and the Need for 33 per cent Reservation',

printed in the Proceedings of a seminar entitled 'Status of Naga Women: Emerging Trend', Longleng 2012, p. 2.
85. *Speeches of Neiphiu Rio*, Chief Minister, Nagaland, 'On the Occasion of Inauguration of Longleng District on 26.01.2004', in *Speeches of Neiphiu Rio,* (January-December, 2004), Kohima, p. 30.
86. Tour Diary of S.J. Duncan, D.C. Naga Hills 1951, Public Records, file No. 61.
87. Interview held with Anyak Phom (79), on 11-04-2001, *Op. cit.*
88. The researcher consulted some official letters in possession of the family of Late Hamnyei (Hamyei), Head *Do-Bhashi.*
89. Elwin, Verrier, *A Philosophy for NEFA*, p. 4.
90. 'The Naga Hills-Tuensang Area (Administration) Regulation 1957', in Luthra, P. N., *Op. cit.*, pp. 89-90.
91. Longleng remained a subdivision under the care of an Assistant Commissioner Grade II for quite some time. There were three types of subdivisional headquarters, first type was headed by an Additional Deputy Commissioner, the second type by an Assistant Commissioner (Grade I) and the third type by an Assistant Commissioner (Grade II). *Nagaland Gazette*, No. 73, 15 April, 1964; *Speeches of Neiphiu Rio, Op. cit.*
92. *The Warrior*, Vol. 32, July 2003, No. 7, p. 29; DAN stands for Democratic Alliance of Nagaland.
93. *The Warrior*, Vol. 33, February 2004, No. 2, p. 30. In the same year, two other administrative headquarters, namely Kiphire and Peren were raised to the status of districts.
94. *Phom Day, Golden Jubilee* 1952-2002, *Op. cit.*, p. 25.
95. *The Warrior*, Vol. 28, August 1999, No. 8. (Two spellings are used for Sakshi, Sakshi for EAC Headquarters and Sakchi as a village. We have used these spellings here to distinguish the two from each other.)
96. Ghosh, B.B. (ed.), *Nagaland District Gazetteers, Mokokchung District*, p. 195.
97. *Ibid.*
98. Ghosh, B.B. (ed.), *Nagaland District Gazetteers, Tuensang District*, p. 153.
99. *Ibid.*, p. 174.
100. *History of Tuensang Town, Op. cit.*, p. 21.
101. Interview held with N. Hamvok Phom (76), *Do-Bhashi*, at Longleng on 15-01-2003.
102. Four aged *Gaon-Buras*, namely K. Panglem of Sakchi, Phongang of Yongam, Chingshen of Bura Namsang and S. Pangjei of Bhumnyu were interviewed by the researcher on 11-01-2004, 08-09-2003, 25-01-2004 and 14-03-2004 respectively.
103. Interview held with Y.B. Angam (47), ex-president of PPC and Public leader, at Longleng on 10-04-2003. The Konyak and the Chang people have been living in the Tobu subdivision of Mon district for a long time. Conflict ensued between them when both the communities laid claim on Tobu as belonging to them. The PPC mediated in the dispute and urged both the

tribes to live peacefully without resorting to bloodshed. Tobu still constitutes a part of the Konyak dominated Mon district.
Every Phom village has a definite land boundary, although there is no land record. Therefore, when the people of a village undertake cultivation in a land or make a claim on a plot of land crossing the boundary of their own, dispute break out between such villages.

104. *Souvenir* published on the occasion of the Seminar on 'Over-View of Backward Areas of Nagaland Since Independence', held on November 16-17, 2001, at Yingli College, Longleng, p. 1.
105. Interview held with H. Toshi Phom (47), *Op. cit.*
106. Interview held with A. Shamthai (38), SIS, President of *Phomla Hoichem*, at Longleng on 02-02-2003.
107. Elwin, Verrier, *Nagaland,* p. 49.
108. Singh, Chandrika, *Political Evolution of Nagaland*, p. 33.
109. *Ibid.*
110. *Ibid,* p. 39.
111. Zhimomi, Kuhoi K., *Op. cit.*, p. 35.
112. Singh, Chandrika, *Political Evolution of Nagaland*, p. 50.
113. *Ibid,* p. 52.
114. Nibedon, Nirmal, *Nagaland: The Night of the Guerrillas,* pp. 48-49.
115. Phom, S. Chaidok, 'Factors Responsible for the Backwardness of the Area with Special Reference to Tuensang and Mon District', printed in the *Proceedings of a Seminar* entitled "Over-view of Backward Areas of Nagaland Since Independence", Longleng, 2001, p. 84.
116. Singh, Chandrika, *Political Evolution of Nagaland*, p. 133.
117. Zhimomi, Kuhoi K., *Op. cit.*, p. 136.
118. Singh, Prakash, *Nagaland,* p. 180. There are now four militant groups including, the Federal Government of Nagaland (FGN), NSCN-IM and NSCN-K.
119. *Ibid,* p. 145.

6
The Phoms : Their Present Status and the Future

The Phom people today are holding a very respectable place among the several Naga tribes of Nagaland. The tribe has undergone slow but steady multifaceted advancement despite numerous hurdles that came in their way. In the words of Hepong Phom, an eminent political leader, "It is like day and night contrast between the past and the present status of our Phom people, and when I look at the changed state of affairs, in the backdrop of the past pictures, it seems as if I am dreaming a magnificent dream of progress".[1] Despite the development that has been achieved, the younger generation of the Phoms believes that they have a long way to go in order to come at par with other advanced tribes of the state. It is perhaps in the fitness of things that the Government of Nagaland has identified this tribe as socio-economically backward.[2]

Fast population growth and absence of corresponding improvement in their livelihood pattern are the new challenges at the dawn of the new millennium. Slow progress of literacy and poor knowledge of family planning have definitely compounded the matter and if strict and practical measures are not taken urgently the situation is likely to drift from bad to worse. The rise in population has put additional pressure on the land. Adoption of scientific measures for growing more food has become necessary for raising the level of production to meet the demands of the growing population. On the other hand, rapid growth of population has indirectly led to other serious problems, i.e. unemployment, drug trafficking, alcoholism, etc. Vast majority of the people in the villages is today living in bare subsistence level.[3]

The Phom people are primarily agriculturists. They are generally unwilling to move out of their land in search of new vocations, if not for government services. Up till now migration of the non-Naga population to the Phom areas has not assumed a menacing proportion. Until a few decades ago, there was a great demand of skilled labour in the area. Therefore, importing skilled labour from outside was encouraged. As such, most of the non-Naga people from other parts of the country came here in search of earning their bread by engaging themselves in petty business or serving as teachers in private schools, or working as porters, drivers, etc., or doing carpentry and masonry works and cutting woods in the forests as hired labourers.[4] However, only a few migrants have settled down here by marrying the Phom women.

On the other hand the younger generations of the Phoms who are generally loathsome in habit are unwilling to do hard physical labour and are becoming more and more dependent on people coming from outside the state. Even the educated youths are desperately after government jobs knowing fully well that all of them can not be absorbed in government service. Thus, those who are unable to join government service have become frustrated and forlorn.[5] Thus, increasing lack of employment opportunities and Centre's doling out money for development purposes, which is unfortunately often misused, has created a milieu of frustrated youths. Needless to say that one important aim of the present education system is to mould and make the young generation fit to stand on their feet. Therefore, the need of the hour is not only to motivate the youths but also to give more attention to technical and job oriented courses in order to generate opportunities of self-employment. The desired Phom youths are to impart the knowledge in different fields like television, computer, cell phone and radio repairing, knitting, weaving and tailoring, electrical works, carpentry, masonry, woodcarving, black smithy, etc. Fortunately, an Industrial Training Institute (ITI) has recently been established at Longleng will surely go a long way to serve the purpose.

Even though education has made rapid stride in Nagaland, the overall educational scenario in the Phom areas has not been on the whole satisfactory. The condition of the government schools is worse; here not only the students even the teachers lack discipline. Students' attendance is poor, whereas many teachers do not regularly turn up for duty but send 'proxy' teachers to perform their duties.[6] Moreover, the government schools, as a rule, lack basic infrastructural facilities. In view of this, a small section of the Phom parents send their children to private schools in Dimapur, Kohima or Shillong for better education. In the prevailing situation good education has become a monopoly of a few Phom students belonging to well-to-do families, whereas all others grow up in a totally stagnating and uninspiring atmosphere.[7]

Comprehending the importance of health and hygiene, the Government of Nagaland has been paying greater attention to health care by setting up hospitals and dispensaries to provide better medical facilities to the people. The State Government spends a large amount of money (next only to education) every month in disbursement of salary to the employees of the medical department.[8] Before the upgradation of the Community Health Centre of Longleng to a District Hospital all the doctors serving here were general practitioners. But, now a few specialist doctors have been recruited to provide improved medical service to the people. Epidemics have been controlled to a great extent. The Phom people have now become more conscious of their food habits. Side by side with the traditional dishes, the Phoms, living in urban centres have taken to north Indian, western and Chinese preparations. In all community feasts cooked items are served along with boiled or roasted items. This newly acquired food habit is, however, found more among the people of high income group than among the masses. Drinking of milk, which was a taboo in the past, is no longer prohibited.[9] Most of the people have at least basic knowledge of modern health care and immunization facilities for their children. They have learnt to live in a clean and hygienic atmosphere.

All the Phom Nagas are now Christians. Christianity has changed their way of life in a short span of time.[10] Christianity had widened their mental horizon. It took them from darkness to light. They are now attracted to a true supreme God whom they worship. It had helped removing their *'pagan like'* habits of drinking wine, sexual laxity, head-hunting and many other social evils, which were rooted in their society for centuries.[11] However, a crisis of identity had ensued in the early years of growth of Christianity. The inevitable conflict between tradition and modernity, between orthodoxy and change started which terribly rocked the Phom society. Those who were converted to Christianity started developing dislike for all the indigenous traits and habits. The age-old woodcarving art, for which the Phoms were so reputed, has been neglected. The traditional dress and costumes of the people were gradually replaced by western dress. Western songs and instruments took the place of their traditional folksongs and dances and musical instruments. All these were aimed at wiping out their rich art and culture of the yester years. The age-old community feeling of the Phoms was slowly evaporating with the discontinuance of the practice of sharing the surplus produce with the members of the community in a feast of merit. Earlier, the idea behind holding the feast of merit was to share a rich man's wealth with his community. In other words the interest of an individual in Phom society was community based and not self-centred as it is today. The present generation of the Phom Nagas has become highly individualistic. The boys are now forbidden by the church leaders to go to the *Bang* and spend the night there.[12] The extinction of such practices possessed the greatest danger to social harmony and cohesion. The Phoms have great creativity and aesthetic qualities which must be promoted and safeguarded.

Fortunately, a section of educated Christian Phoms today are seen trying their best to revive and preserve their rich cultural heritage which are on the verge of disappearance. It is mainly because of the encouragement of the government and also due to the tireless efforts of the Phom Students' Conference and the *Phomla Hoichem,* many of the old social practices have been revived barring those which are socially harmful. These include traditional dance and songs, colourful costumes, *Bangs,* community festivals, games and sports, etc. The Directorate of Art and Culture of the Nagaland Government has taken an important step to publish almost all the myths and folktales of the bygone days of various Naga tribes.[13] Recently, a book entitled *Phom-Naga Customary Laws* has been published by the Longleng District Customary Court.[14]

Thus, it may not be wrong to say that the present Phom culture is primarily a mixture of traditional and western culture. M. Alemchiba Ao wrote about the Nagas in general:

> "In the midst of these changes, it is inevitable that the art of the Nagas would naturally decline, but however the demands of the changes, the moral and cultural foundation of society must be safeguarded, if it is not to be rootless. Otherwise, the rich culture of the Nagas will be lost and they will become a group of people with no culture and tradition."[15]

The Phom land is gifted with varieties of natural resources. Coal, limestone, crude oil, masonry stones, etc., are found in many places of the district. The district is also endowed with forest wealth and water resources. The climate and soil are suitable for the growth of deciduous or evergreen forests. Various species of timber and medicinal plants grow here abundantly. On the whole the nature had been quite kind to the people. But, no step has been taken to harness the natural wealth for the benefit of the people. It is a pity that neither agro nor forest-based modern industries have been set up in the region; no agricultural surplus as such could be sent outside, which is obviously an indication of an underdeveloped economic framework. Little effort has been made to utilize the available resources for manufacturing various articles of day-to-day use. On the other hand their neighbours, the Aos of the Mokokchung district are today in a better position in the field of employment due primarily to their educational superiority and enterprising character. In this respect the Angamis are far in advance in comparison with the Phoms because of their proximity to the centre of political power, Kohima, the state capital. It is high time that the enterprising Phom youths be encouraged to receive necessary training with financial support and other help of the concerned agencies. Investors from outside may also be encouraged to invest capital for which the state government may extend to them special benefits, which may be needed. Long-term plan will definitely prepare the ground for industrial development of the Phom areas besides generating employment opportunities for the people. Villagers shall be benefited by supplying raw materials to feed the industries. The village elders should be given powers to protect the forests and prevent indiscriminate felling of trees and destruction of the rich flora and fauna. The massive deforestation which is going on in the Longleng district will surely create long term ecological problems.

Nowadays hydroelectric power is widely used for commercial purposes, especially to run machines and also in agriculture. It is one of the major sources of power generation for various types of economic activities. Unfortunately, electric power is used here for domestic purpose only and not for productive purposes.

It has been mentioned above that agriculture is the mainstay of the economy of the Phom people. But, no spectacular progress is seen in agricultural production. The Phom cultivators in the present context are neither able to bring about a drastic change in agricultural production nor yield sufficient paddy to meet their domestic requirement for the whole year. Most of the people of Longleng town and many others living at different administrative headquarters, have to buy rice which is imported from Assam.[16] Had the Phom cultivators adopted sustainable method of cultivation, they would have been in a better position to earn a lot more by selling their surplus rice to the people living in the towns. It is true that most of the Phom cultivators are poor, illiterate, un-enterprising and superstitious in nature for which they are usually reluctant to apply modern techniques of cultivation.[17] The agricultural department and the NGOs can surely play a more important role to motivate the farmers so that they can avail of the farmer-friendly methods of cultivation and adopt modern technology to be economically better off and prosperous. One potential area of development is horticulture. The soil is congenial for growth of cardamom, black pepper, ginger, orange, pineapple, papaya, banana, etc., which can be grown in large quantity for commercial purposes. Setting up of a few food processing centres will also improve matters.

It has already been observed in one chapter that as there is no law relating to maximum ceiling of land ownership, major portion of the cultivable lands in Bura Namsang, Yongam, Bhumnyu, Pongo and Sakchi villages are concentrated in the hands of a few wealthy persons, for which, a considerable number of cultivators are made to cultivate others' land on harsh terms and conditions. If this trend continues, there is every possibility of emergence of a landless class of peasantry as is seen in many other parts of the country. Therefore, it has become necessary to formulate laws to prevent concentration of lands. One remedy advocated is that law should be passed empowering Village Councils to distribute cultivable land in excess or disproportionate to one's need among the needy landless clan members of the villages.[18] Such a step will help raising the standard of living of the people as well as removing disparities from society.

Today a large number of cattle, buffaloes and poultry, are imported from outside to meet the demands of the people. There is a great demand of egg and milk among the people living in the administrative headquarters. But, the Phom farmers are unable to meet the requirements owing to short production of the articles.[19] Obviously, avenues are open for the Phom entrepreneurs to start poultry farming, fishery, duckery and cattle farming, sheep breeding and fodder cultivation in a big way as an alternative means of self-employment.

At present in comparison with import, export from Longleng district is very meagre. The main reason of this trade imbalance is that the Phom society is very static with very little surplus production. Considering, the inadequate income generation of the people and lack of alternative employment opportunities, the government of Nagaland has taken certain steps to improve their socio-economic status. The government has opened a number of roads in the district to improve transport facility. In order to solve unemployment problems and also to increase the production of foodstuff, fruits and domesticated animals, etc., the Government of Nagaland has been giving loans with subsidies to the local people. It is partly due to the steps taken by the state government, the production of orange, banana, pineapple, pear, guava, papaya, etc., has increased, which are now enough to meet the demand of the local people. The number of pig has also increased considerably which can meet the demand of pork. A small quantity of the surplus production of timber, bamboo and cane, betel leaf, ginger, etc., is exported from the district. Besides these steps, the Government of Nagaland has appointed a large number of educated Phoms in various government departments. As it is today, with the exception of the government employees, the per capita income of the Phom people is much lower than many other Naga tribes. Therefore, the business community of the district has to mainly depend on the government servants, contractors and the like.[20]

As stated above, road is the only means of transport with different parts of Nagaland. By now almost all the villages have been linked by single-lane motorways. However, the condition of these roads is not up to the mark. Their condition becomes deplorable during the rainy season. This communication handicap is one of the major causes of the backwardness of the area. It is highly regrettable that even after sixty five years of independence the Longleng area is yet to be linked directly with any national highway or by air. The state highway which connects Longleng with Changtongya is, therefore, the lifeline of the district. The condition of the Longleng-Tuensang road and Longleng-Mon road *via* Chompang is so horrible that neither bus nor truck can run safely in these roads. The government spends a large amount of money for the improvement of the roads. For example, a sum of Rs. 5.90 crore was sanctioned in 1999 under the Non-Lapsable Pool of Central Resources for the improvement of the 34 km. Longleng-Changtongya road.[21] At present, Dimapur (in Dimapur district) is the only place in Nagaland which is linked by rail and air. The nearest railhead of the Longleng district is Amguri (in Assam) situated at a distance of ninety-one kms. from Longleng town. Thus, the extension of rail road to the lower ranges of the district (Tamlu and nearby areas) will definitely stimulate passenger and commercial traffic of the region.

The poor condition of the roads has affected the economy in another way. A passenger travelling from Longleng to Dimapur now has to pay an amount of Rs. 280 (two hundred eighty only) in night bus and Rs. 350 (three hundred fifty only) in Tata Sumo as fare which is undoubtedly much higher than the normal fare. Similarly, the movement of goods is also very expensive. For instance, one full truckload of sand which costs rupees one thousand at Amguri or Haluating is currently purchased at about rupees eight to nine thousand by the people of Longleng.[22] For the same reason it becomes uneconomical to send raw materials from the district to other places.

Being a backward tribe of the state, the Phoms are nowadays taking full advantage of the reservation facilities available to them instead of trying to develop their own merit and calibre. This tendency to over-depend on the government policy for all time to come is absolutely harmful as it is likely to stall and retard the mental and physical power of the new generation. The anxiety and apprehension of the Naga intelligentsia is reflected in the former Chief Minister's speech delivered in connection with the 46th General Session of the Phom Students' Conference:

> "However, I want to remind the Phom people that these special measures are only to help them in catching up with the other forward tribes, who are the early starters. These special concessions should not be allowed to induce in them a sense of complacency, and to keep them backward permanently."[23]

It is, therefore, widely felt that the present generation of the Phoms must work hard and try to develop a spirit of meeting new challenges. The Chief Minister further observed:

> "... the Phoms are comparatively late starter in the area of education and socio-economic development process due to historical and locational disadvantages. But I am confident that the resurgent Phoms will have no problem in catching

up with the rest of Nagaland within a few decades from now."[24]

In pursuance of the above policy one important step taken in recent years by the Government of Nagaland is to communitise or empower the people at the grassroots. The system has already been implemented in respect of primary and middle education. Under this system, the respective School Management Committees are given the responsibility of managing primary and middle schools under their jurisdiction; whereas the government's responsibility is limited to provide fund for the purpose.[25] The extension of this system to other fields like health, water and power supply, etc., will be a welcome step.

Happily, the position of the Phom women has improved quite a lot since independence. They are no longer subjected to bondage at home or in the fields but are allowed to take a more active part in social festivities. They have full freedom to study and work or start business like the menfolk. They not only have voting rights, but also are free to take part in politics. Crimes like suicide, physical and mental torture, dowry death, forced marriage, etc., are almost nil in Phom society.[26] In all community festivals the women are now seen singing and dancing freely with the males. Despite this, the century old social rigidity and customs are so deep rooted that no Phom woman can actually rise above the barriers. Primarily for this reason the Phom women are not yet seen contesting for membership in State Legislature or becoming members of the Village Councils or act as *Do–Bhashis* and *Gaon–Buras*. It would perhaps take some more time for the Phom women to assert their right both in spirit and in practice.

Like many other hill people of north-east India the method of solving disputes by the Village Court (*Pangshen*) in Phom society is simple, but highly effective. In trying cases the village elders are guided by the basic principle that the offender must not go unpunished for the offence he had committed. Naturally, in this method of trial even an ordinary person expects to get justice without spending money. In the village everyone knows each other very well and therefore, the antecedents of the persons in disputes are known to the members of the court. Usually, a case is tried by interrogating both the parties involved in the dispute without taking help of mediators, and circumstantial and other evidences are taken into account before passing verdict on the case.[27] This system of dispensing justice remains by and large unchanged over the years.

Days of headhunting and inter-village feuds are over and peace has started returning to the hills. But, the peace process has been halted by growing militancy during the last few decades. Undoubtedly, the spurt of militancy in the recent years is also, to a great extent, an outcome of the lack of adequate economic opportunities at the local level. Thus, armed clashes have been going on from time to time among the various insurgent groups which have slowed down the pace of progress and development in the area.[28] We can quote here a line of Verrier Elwin, "As mankind moves forward to the fulfilment of its destiny, it will fail unless it can banish fear and suspicion, hatred and the spirit of revenge; separateness and xenophobia are today spiritually out of date; to be 'modern' is to love and to unite."[29] Rapid socio-economic development is not possible in a society which lacks peace, political stability and security of life and property. As long as violence continues, people whether Indian or foreigner, will be unwilling to come here, whether as tourists, visitors or investors. In the prevailing situation even the local people are afraid or unwilling to invest money for fear of extortion by the militants. Although a ceasefire has been agreed upon recently between the Government of India and militant factions led by the NSCN(IM) and NSCN(K) paving way for several rounds of parleys, yet no immediate end of insurgency is at sight. Outside the government certain steps are taken by various Non-Governmental Organisations like the Phom People's Council, the Baptist Church Council, the Eastern Nagaland People's Organisation, etc., urging the militants to shun violence and come to terms with the Centre in the larger interest of the people.[30] A political solution to the vexed Naga problem is the only answer and for this violence must be stopped at all cost.

Undoubtedly, the future of the Phom people lies in their commitment to build a society which is progressive and forward looking, a society where peace and prosperity reach the doorstep of everybody. The Phom people must look ahead to reach greater height of development in order to attain a place of pride among all other Naga tribes of the state. The observation of Hokishe Sema, though made in the context of the Naga people as a whole, is also applicable in case of the Phoms:

> "As we look ahead to the future of Nagaland we see that

now there is no place or scope for insurgencies in its life. An era of productive peace has to be ushered in so that the fruits of economic planning and development can be shared by all its people. They have missed the fruits of many years of economic planning and development. Nagas must now take active part in the national mainstream. They should no longer entertain the idea of keeping themselves isolated from the mainstream of national life. The new generation of Nagaland should think in terms of what they can give to their country and not what they can get."[31]

NOTES AND REFERENCES

1. Interview held with Hepong Phom (86), ex-Interim Body Member and ex-Regional Council Member, at Longleng on 24-04-2005. The observation made in Nagamese is translated into English by this scholar.
2. Government Notification No. OM, No. AR/8/9/79(PT-11) dated 16-8-1979, collected from the Additional Deputy Commissioner's Office, Longleng. The Ao, the Angami, the Lotha, the Sema, etc., tribes of Nagaland are counted as advanced tribes of the state.
3. Interview held with forty Phom individuals, eight each from Sakchi, Bhumnyu, Yongam, Bura Namsang villages and Longleng town during 2003-05.
4. Interview held with B. Hayu Phom (59), President, 'Nagaland People's Front' Longleng district, at Oushok Colony on 07-06-2007.
5. *Ibid.*
6. *The Warrior,* Vol. 36, June 2007, No. 6, p.13.
7. Islam, Nurul, 'Over-view of Backward Areas of Nagaland Since Independence with Special Reference to Educational Status of Phom Area', printed in the Proceedings of a Seminar entitled *"Over-View of Backward Areas of Nagaland Since Independence"*, Longleng, 2001, p. 40.
8. For instance, as per the records available in the Sub-Treasury Office, Longleng, an amount of Rs. 98,55,559.00 and another sum of Rs. 17,11,318.00 had been sanctioned for disbursement of salary of the employees of the education and medical departments respectively for the month of December 2002.
9. Interview held with forty Phom individuals, *Op. cit.*
10. Henshet, B., *The Phom-Naga Indigenous Religion: A Socio-Philosophical Perspective,* p. 9.
11. Sema, Hokishe, *Emergence of Nagaland: Socio-Economic and Political Transformation and the Future,* p. 53. The observations of Hokishe Sema about the Nagas in general are also applicable in the case of the Phoms.

12. *Ibid*, p. 55.
13. For details see *Folk Tales from Nagaland.*
14. Phom, Henshet, B.(ed), *The Phom-Naga Customary Laws*, Longleng, 2005.
15. Ao, M. Alemchiba, *The Arts and Crafts of Nagaland,* p. 119.
16. Interview held with T. Ponglong Phom (52), Chairman of Sub-divisional Chamber of Commerce Unit Longleng, at Longleng on 12-10-2003.
17. Interview held with forty Phom individuals, *Op. cit.*
18. *Ibid.*
19. Interview held with T. Ponglong Phom (52), *Op. cit.*
20. The researcher gathered this information from a few shopkeepers of Longleng town in January 2008.
21. *Nagaland (1993-2002), A Decade of Stability, Progress and Development,* p. 45.
22. The researcher collected the information from a few shopkeepers of Longleng town in January 2008.
23. *Speeches of Neiphiu Rio,* Chief Minister, Nagaland, January-December 2005, p. 2.
24. *Ibid,* p. 1.
25. *Nagaland 2002,* p. 113.
26. Jha, B.N. and Chakrabarty, P., 'Socio-Educational Status of Phom Community', research paper presented in a Seminar held at Yingli College, Longleng on 9-10 July, 1997.
27. Interview held with four Village Council Chairmen, viz. S. Pangjei of Bhumnyu (14-03-2004), T.C. Nyamnyei Semdok of Sakchi (22-01-2004), B. Angshai Phom of Yongam (07-09-2002) and A. Hamlang of Bura Namsang (25-01-2004).
28. Zhimomi, Kuhoi K., *Politics and Militancy in Nagaland*, p. 141.
29. Elwin, Verrier, *Nagaland,* p. 104.
30. Interview held with B. Hayu Phom (59) *Op. cit.* The Naga *Hoho,* a very powerful and influential social organization of Nagaland, which is taking a very active interest in social and political reconstruction of the tribal societies in other parts of the state, however, has no solid base in the Phom areas.
31. Sema, Hokishe, *Op. cit.,* p. 192.

7

Conclusion

The twentieth century has been an important period for the Phom people as the wind of change blew over the entire area touching almost every sphere of their society and economy. In the hindsight this change turns out to be a boon and curse for them. The people, who lived in near isolation for several centuries after their migration to the present sites of settlement, were exposed to the outside world only in the nineteenth century after coming in contact with the rulers. Towards the end of the nineteenth century the colonial authority annexed the Phom villages of the present Tamlu subdivision to the erstwhile Mokokchung subdivision of the Naga Hills district in order to protect the area from the raids of the villagers living on the other side of the Dikhu river, whereas the territory to the east of the Dikhu river was placed in the category of loose political control for poor prospect of revenue collection. These villages were, therefore, neither subjected to payment of revenue nor had their security become a responsibility of the government. As a first step towards administrative consolidation the age-old practice of head-hunting was abolished in the Tamlu area, though inter-village feuds continued among the Phom villages in the eastern part of the Dikhu river. Slavery, another primitive institution of the people, came to an end as a result of the steps taken to reorganise the Phom society.

With the gradual annexation of all the Phom areas a novel system of administration began to take root in the Phom areas. Earlier, all matters relating to the village government, law and justice, external affairs, border trade, etc., were decided independently by the Village Councils (*Pangshen*). The sovereign power enjoyed by the villages declined when the British began to recognise the *Barriks* and appointed *Gaon-Buras,* the loyal agents of the colonial administration, to look after the village administration without, however, disturbing their customary laws. As a result of this arrangement the power and prestige of the *Anghs* also declined. The basic features of the village government introduced by the British are still in existence notwithstanding new laws being enacted by the present government for convenience of administration. The Village Council now deals with all matters relating to disputes according to the customary laws. The *Do-Bhashis,* a native administrative agency created by the colonial authority, has been assisting the officers to settle disputes and maintain law and order.

Christianity spread among the Phoms from the third decade of the twentieth century and by the end of the century almost all the Phom people were baptized. Simultaneously, the educational scenario began to change. There were only three primary schools in the entire Phom area, the percentage of literacy being almost nil at the time of independence. A number of government and private schools were established since then. Today, there is no Phom village without a school. The percentage of literacy of Longleng district and the number of educated persons in government service have registered a steady increase. The arts college at Longleng is catering to the needs of higher education for the post-matriculate students. The educated Phoms have worked to develop the Phom language with the Roman script.

With the introduction of modern education and growth of Christianity the Phom people began to lose faith in superstitious beliefs. Their rational outlook had made them more forward-looking. As a result, the priest and the *thibu* lost their place in society. The practice of observing funeral ceremony in the most barbaric way and hosting feast of merit no longer exist now. At one time the *Bang* was considered as an important institution of the village. But, it has now become a mere cultural symbol of the past.

The second half of the twentieth century witnessed rapid growth of the Phom population. Famine and epidemic have been controlled. A noticeable change has taken place in the dietary habit of the people. They have learnt to take various new items of food which were unknown to them earlier. Until the first half of the twentieth century all the houses of the Phom areas were thatched, but today a large number of hill type and RCC buildings are seen in the Phom areas.

The traditional dress and ornaments excepting shawls and *mekhalas* were losing popularity among the Phoms from the time they came in contact with western culture. The old style of haircutting and tattooing, wearing traditional ornaments, loincloth, waist wrapper, etc., are discarded altogether. The Phom youngsters are now more attracted to western songs and music than their old folk songs, dances and musical instruments. In comparison with the olden days the condition of the Phom women has improved a lot, though they are still being deprived of inheriting land and landed properties, becoming members of Village Council and enjoying headship of their clan.

Agriculture, as elsewhere in Nagaland, remains the principal occupation of the Phoms. They have learnt to grow varieties of cash crops and vegetables. Terrace cultivation is gradually replacing the *jhum* system of cultivation. But owing largely to non-application of modern technology a vast majority of the cultivators are still not able to produce enough paddy to meet their annual requirement. The Phom people have acquired the knowledge of domesticating some animals and birds, a practice which was unknown to them earlier. They have started rearing improved breeds of cattle and poultry, but are still not in a position to meet the growing demand of meat.

Barring the Tamlu area, the Phom villages had no roads at the time of independence. But, at present almost all the villages are linked by motor-able roads. Moreover, the Longleng district has three state highways connecting different places of Nagaland. Postal communication, which was so under-developed at the time of independence, has developed slowly and by the end of the twentieth century nine post offices were set up in the Phom areas. Longleng was linked with telephonic network only in 2004. By the end of the last century all the villages were electrified.

Before independence the Phom villages used to depend on the Geleki *duar* for selling the hill products to the people of the plains. The *duar* was normally kept open for business but was closed down temporarily by the British following an outrage committed by the Nagas in the area. The natural and agricultural products are still sent out from the Tamlu sub-division through this *duar*. But, the export of the district in comparison with import is quite unsatisfactory. The replacement of brass plates and the barter system by money economy, establishment of new administrative set up, extension of transport and banking facilities, etc., have led to the increase of business activities of Longleng district.

Not till the formation of the Villages Development Boards (1980), the active participation of the people at the grassroots level development activities did not start in the real sense. The formations of VDBs have helped to check the influence of the intermediaries and root out corruption to a certain extent. However, the overall development, individual or community, has not been satisfactory.

With the attainment of independence the Phom dominated areas became an integral part of the Indian Union. It marks the beginning of increasing contact of the Phom people with the rest of the country. The improvement of transport and communication as well as various other factors has accelerated the process of interaction of the Phom people with other Naga people of the state. This has helped to remove their isolation. A sense of broader Naga identity has grown and loyalty to the state has overtaken clan loyalty. Although insurgency remains the most burning problem of the region, a vast section of the underground workers have realised the futility of an armed struggle and have started returning to the national mainstream.

The colonial authority was indeed responsible for the backwardness of the region. Very little development works were initiated by the earlier rulers for the benefit and welfare of the people. In the same manner the nationalist leadership did little to bring these people to the mainstream of the freedom movement. A vast majority of them, therefore, had neither any idea of anti-imperialist struggle which was going on in other parts of the country, nor any opportunity to break the self-imposed isolation. Consequently, when the Phoms were fighting against each other, some other Naga tribes, viz. the Aos, the Angamis, the Lothas, the Semas, the Rengmas, etc., took advantage of the comparative peace prevailing in their lands to tread the path of development. So, a generation gap has taken place among the Phoms in comparison with the advanced Naga tribes. Though a number of measures are taken by the present government for their welfare, certain irritants like corruption, communication handicap, lack of adequate infrastructure, insurgency, antipathy to hard physical labour, etc., have stood in the way of progress. The result is that in comparison with the steps taken and money spent for the development of the region, the overall result has not been up to the mark. Now is the time for New Delhi to give these people a just and rightful place in the process of national reconstruction. Non-participation or non-involvement of any group or community, however backward or remotely situated may be, in India's future progress, will have serious consequences of regression and withdrawal.

The rapid change and development, which had taken place elsewhere in the north east, have made the Phom people realize and think seriously as to why they are unable to catch up the progress made by their fellow Naga tribes. Like their counterparts in other districts of Nagaland they have a dream of building a progressive society. They want to reap the fruits of development without nursing its roots and body. They have a vision of a bright prosperous tomorrow. To achieve this goal they need to take steady and calculated steps with firm determination and perseverance. The Phom people have passed through a long period of trials and tribulations and it is time for them now to march ahead towards a new world of peace and prosperity.

In the midst of rapid change in the socio-political scenario cracks have been witnessed in several spheres of the Phom society. For example, the society has sharply been divided into the rich and the poor, literate and illiterate, urban and rural, employed and unemployed, etc. This gap can be minimized by discouraging the migration of the educated section of the people from their native villages to the urban centres. Undoubtedly, this elite class can take a more active part in enlightening their fellow villagers. The Phom people have to assert their identity and resist exploitation. In this respect the non-governmental organizations can also play a vital role to plug the loopholes in their path to progress and development.

Arguably, the last sixty-five years after independence was a period of progress and decay for the Phom people. While on the one hand the people had witnessed certain degrees of development in social and economic spheres, symptoms of erosion in their traditional way of lives have become quite perceptible which had produced disastrous and paralysing effects on them. The impact of modern civilization has been felt on all aspects of their arts, crafts and culture. Far from bringing immediate benefits, the colonial and partially post-colonial periods had done more harm than good to them, by exposing them to the cross-currents of modern civilization. In their quest for gaining something 'new' they had lost something 'old'. In the process of transition from old to the new they have accepted something what they have found attractive and lovable, but discarded something, which had rich cultural values.

Now while looking ahead to the future, the present generation of the Phom-Nagas must learn to love and preserve their rich cultural heritage. They should try to make a re-evaluation of the years of transitional crisis in order to understand the damage caused to them by the Christian missionaries or through personal dislike and neglect.

They should try to understand that the lack of interest in one's originality and blind love for things which are new and modern, are greatest dangers to complete disappearance of their cultural identity. For centuries they have expressed their joys and jubilations through their songs and dances and there is no reason why these should be discarded in their attempt to be 'modern' and 'civilized'. An amalgamation of their traditional art and culture with modern and western culture will definitely add to the enrichment of both.

Glossary

Abor	:	Independent Naga villages located in the remote hills.
Angh	:	Hereditary village chief who used to control village administration and external policy.
Bang/Morung	:	Bachelors' dormitory; a traditional institution of the Phom people.
Barricks	:	Village elders elected by the people to look after the village administration.
Basha	:	A house having wooden post, double *tarja* bamboo mat wall and CGI sheet roof.
Bham	:	A family of banyan tree.
Bhum	:	Cloud.
Bihu	:	Spring festival.
Bori	:	Naga villages bordering on Assam.
BushahLaitap	:	A history book.
Bushong	:	A log drum.
Ching	:	Village.
Chong Kahvang	:	Terrestrial god.
Chunga	:	Bamboo piece used for storing water.
Dalchini	:	Cinnamon.
Dao	:	A multipurpose chopping knife.
Dhania	:	Coriander plant.
Do-Bhashi	:	Government interpreter possessing knowledge of the local language and also of Nagamese.
Duar	:	Gate; mountain pass.
Gaon-Bura	:	Village chief appointed by the Government.
Genna	:	A day/days when the people abstained from doing certain works.
Hamba	:	An honourable title bestowed upon a man who had taken at least one human head.

Jhum	: Shifting cultivation.
Kaḥvang	: Terrestrial god.
Kala sada	: Black tobacco.
Khel	: Sub-division of a village or town.
Kochu	: The arum; a bulbous vegetable which grows underground.
Kotoki	: An envoy of the Ahom king posted at frontier gates or passes.
Nyamnyu/Laya, Langnyu, Langha and Langla	: Different shaped brass plates used occasionally as coins.
Mekhala	: A long skirt worn by women.
Mithun	: Indian bison.
Pan	: Betel leaf.
Pangshan	: Village government.
Panji	: Sharp and pointed bamboo spike planted on the path to resist the enemies from pursuing.
PhomlaHoichem	: Phom Women's Union.
Rotti	: Bread.
Samber	: Particular specie of deer.
Shah	: Dialect
Shang Kahvang	: God of lightning, rain, sunshine, etc.
Shem	: Huge log drum.
Shiching	: *Shi* means dog and *ching* means village. It is a place where dog rears the departed souls.
Thibu	: Person having knowledge of medicine and magic.
Yimching	: Village of the souls.
Yow	: Girls' dormitory.
Yiupa	: Helper.

Select Bibliography

A. Primary Sources

I. Unpublished Documents

1. **Assam State Archives and Secretariat Records Office, Dispur, Guwahati:**
   Modification of the Inner Line of the Sibsagar district, 1901, Assam Secretariat General Department, Foreign-A Oct, Nos. 2-43.
2. **State Archives, Kohima:**
   — Angpan and Totang VS Phum (Report), dated 11.6.09, General Department, file no. 269.
   — Annual Administrative Report of the Mokokchung Sub-division for the year 1920-21, General Department, file no. 342.
   — Diary of A.E. Shuttle Worth, Sub-Divisional Officer of Mokokchung for the month of October 1895, Secret Department, file no. 439.
   — Letter from F.C. Daukes, Secretary to the Chief Commissioner of Assam to the Officiating Deputy Commissioner, Naga Hills, 30th May, 1893, Political Department, file no. 43.
   — Note on including the Trans-Dikhu tribes within an area of Political Control, 1889-90, Political Department, file no. 14.
   — Raid by the Phum village of Hukpang against Orangkhung (Report), 1910, Sub-Divisional Officer, Mokokchung, General Department, file no. 290.

— Raid on Ourangkong, Report of S.D.O., Mokokchung, 20.7.1919, General Department, file no. 333.

— Report of the head taking of a man of Kamahu by Party of Tangsa man, 7.10.10, General Department, file no. 276.

— Slavery in the Un-administered Area between Assam and Burma, 1916, General Department, file no. 324.

— The Policy to be Adopted in Dealing Trans-Dikhu villages, 21.11.91, Political Department, file no. 183.

— Tour Diary of C.R. Pawsey, Sub-Divisional Officer, Mokokchung for the months of April and May 1928, Secret Department, file no. 452.

— Tour Diary of C.R. Pawsey, Sub-Divisional Officer, Mokokchung for the month of December 1929, Secret Department, file no. 452.

— Tour Diary of E.D. Savi, Sub-Divisional Officer, Mokokchung for the month of January 1897, Secret Department, file no. 44.

— Tour Diary of S.J. Duncan, Deputy Commissioner, Naga Hills for May-June 1950, on Column Duty-Phomching Column, Public Records, file no. 61.

— Tour Diary of S.J. Duncan, Deputy Commissioner, Naga Hills for February-March 1951, Public Records, file no. 61.

— Tour Diary of S.J. Duncan, Deputy Commissioner, Naga Hills 1951, Public Records, file no. 61.

3. Miscellaneous Records:

— Abstract of Proceedings of the Tuensang District Regional Council, Fourth Session (3rd to 8th June, 1965), Collected from Hepong Phom, ex-Interim Body Member and ex-Tuensang District Regional Council Member.

— Official correspondence/letters in possession of the family of Hamnyei Phom, Head DB.

— Resolution passed in the second session of the Tuensang District Regional Council held on 28th and 30th April, 1964. A copy of Resolution was collected from Hepong Phom, ex-Interim Body Member and ex-Tuensang District Regional Council Member.

4. Respondents of Questionnaires:

— Abenthung, Junior Engineer (Power), Longleng Sub-Station, 17-06-2003.
— E. R. Huskha Yeptho, SDO, Irrigation and Flood Control, Longleng, vide letter No. I & FC/LLG/ACT-19/2002-03/68, 9 April, 2003.
— H. Lakphak, Sectional Officer (SO) PWD R/B, Longleng, 10-03-2003.
— Karuna Kanta Deka, Assistant Manager, State Bank of India (SBI), Longleng Branch, 25-03-2002.
— M. Imti, In-charge Nagaland State Transport (NST), Longleng, 15-02-2003.

II. Published (English):

1. Documents, Reports, Accounts, Memoirs, etc.

Annual Administrative Report 1998-99, Department of Forest, Ecology and Environment and Wild Life, Government of Nagaland, Kohima, year not mentioned.

Annual Administrative Report 1992-93, Department of Forest, Government of Nagaland, Kohima, year not mentioned.

Annual Administrative Reports 1995-96 and 1999-2000, Department of Rural Development, Government of Nagaland, Kohima, year not mentioned.

Annual Administrative Report 1981-82, Nagaland Forest Department, Government of Nagaland, Kohima, year not mentioned.

Annual Administrative Report 1985-86, Planning and Coordination Department including Department of Economics and Statistics, Town Planning, Organisation and Evaluation Unit; Government of Nagaland, Kohima, year not mentioned.

Annual Report 1995, Holistic Child Development India, Nagpur, year not mentioned.

Atsongchanger, Mar (compiled), *The Historical Memoranda of the Nagas and Their Neighbours,* Guwahati, 1995.

Census 1951, *Assam, Naga Hills District Census Hand Book, Shillong, 1952.*

Census 1971, *Nagaland, District Census Handbook,* Tuensang

District, Series 15, Directorate of Census Operations, Nagaland, Kohima, 1978.

Census of India 1951, *Assam, Manipur and Tripura,* Volume XII, Part I-A, Shillong, 1954.

Census of India 1981, *Nagaland, District Census Handbook,* Tuensang District, Series 15, Directorate of Census Operations, Nagaland, Kohima, 1982.

Census of India 1991, *Nagaland, District Census Handbook,* Tuensang, Series 18, Part XII-A & B, Directorate of Census Operations, Nagaland, Kohima, 1993.

Census of India 2011, *Primary Census Abstract—Nagaland, Directorate of Census Operations in Nagaland, Kohima.*

Census of India 1961, *Nagaland,* Volume XXIII, Part II-C, Delhi, 1969.

Citizens' Charter, *Health and Family Welfare Department, Government of Nagaland, Kohima,* 2002.

Classified List of Post Offices in North Eastern Circle (corrected as on 1st April, 2003), The Chief Postmaster General, North Eastern Circle, Shillong, year not mentioned.

Evaluation Report on the Impact of Block Programmes in Nagaland, Government of Nagaland, Kohima, Publication no. 2: 1975.

Festivals of Nagaland, Directorate of Information and Public Relations, Government of Nagaland, Kohima.

Findings of Election Department Nagaland, Chief Electoral Officer, Kohima, year not mentioned.

Folk Tales From Nagaland, Directorate of Art and Culture: Nagaland, Kohima, 1989.

Handbook, General Elections 1998 to the Legislative Assembly and Lok Sabha of Nagaland, Chief Electoral Officer, Nagaland, year not mentioned.

Imchen, Panger (ed.), L. Kijung Ao The Longest Night (An Outline Biography of the first Naga Missionary), Dimapur, year not mentioned.

List of Health/Medical Units in Nagaland, Department of Health and Family Welfare, Government of Nagaland, Kohima, 2000.

Naga Assembly News, No. 20, January-June 1996, Government of Nagaland, Kohima, year not mentioned.

Nagaland 1993-2002, A Decade of Stability, Progress and

Development, Directorate of Information and Public Relations, Government of Nagaland, Kohima, year not mentioned.

Nagaland 1963-1969, Directorate of Information and Publicity, Government of Nagaland, Kohima, year not mentioned.

Nagaland Forest Statistical Book 1979, Chief Conservator of Forest, Government of Nagaland, Kohima, year not mentioned.

Nagaland Rural Development in Action, Department of Rural Development, Government of Nagaland, Kohima, 1984.

Primary Health Care Delivery System in Nagaland, Department of Health and Family Welfare, Government of Nagaland, Kohima, 2001.

Report on Census of Minor Irrigation Schemes in Nagaland 1994-95, Department of Irrigation and Flood Control, Government of Nagaland, Kohima, year not mentioned.

Report on Census of Minor Irrigation Schemes in Nagaland 2000-2001, Department of Irrigation and Flood Control, Government of Nagaland, Kohima, year not mentioned.

Report on Census of Minor Irrigation Schemes in Nagaland 1987-88, Department of Irrigation, Government of Nagaland, Kohima, year not mentioned.

Report on Fourteenth Quinquennial Livestock Census 1987, Department of Veterinary and Animal Husbandry, Government of Nagaland, Kohima, year not mentioned.

Report on Seventeenth Quinquennial Livestock Census 2003, Department of Veterinary and Animal Husbandry, Government of Nagaland, Kohima, year not mentioned.

Report on the First General Election 1963, Chief Electoral Officer, Government of Nagaland, Kohima, year not mentioned.

Report on the General Elections to 10th Nagaland Legislative Assembly 2003, Chief Electoral Officer, Government of Nagaland, Kohima, year not mentioned.

Report on Thirteenth Quinquennial Livestock Census 1982, Directorate of Veterinary and Animal Husbandry, Government of Nagaland, Kohima, year not mentioned.

Results of the General Assembly Elections of Nagaland (Fourth Edition), Directorate of Economics and Statistics, Government of Nagaland, Kohima, 1998.

Singh, R.D.N. and Zeliang, T. (ed.), *Development Profile of Animal Husbandry in Nagaland,* Government of Nagaland, Kohima, 1991.

Souvenir 1980-2005, Commemorating 25 Years of Village Development Board, Department of Rural Development, Government of Nagaland, Kohima, year not mentioned.

Speeches of Neiphiu Rio, Chief Minister, Nagaland, January-December 2004 and January-December 2005, Directorate of Information and Public Relations, Government of Nagaland, Kohima, year not mentioned.

Speeches of S.C. Jamir, Chief Minister, Nagaland, 2000, Directorate of Information and Public Relations, Government of Nagaland, Kohima, year not mentioned.

Statistical Hand Book of Nagaland 1965, Planning and Co-ordination Department, Statistical Branch, Government of Nagaland, Kohima, year not mentioned.

Statistical Hand Books of Nagaland 1968, 1981, 1996, 2001 and 2011 Directorate of Economics and Statistics, Government of Nagaland, Kohima, 1969, 1982, 1997 and 2002.

Survey of Area and Production of Horticulture Crops in Nagaland 1985-86, Directorate of Agriculture, Government of Nagaland, Kohima, year not mentioned.

The Nagaland Code, Volume IV (Second Edition), Government of Nagaland, Department of Justice and Law, 1995.

Tuensang District Regional Council, Who is Who 1973, Government of Nagaland, Place and year not mentioned.

Village Development Boards Model Rules 1980 (Revised), Department of Rural Development, Government of Nagaland, Kohima, 1989.

Village Level Development Indicators (As on 31.03.1997), Directorate of Economics and Statistics, Government of Nagaland, Kohima, 1999.

Village-wise Index of Development (As on 1st April, 1983), Directorate of Economics and Statistics, Government of Nagaland, Kohima, 1987.

10 *Years' Progress in NEFA: A Brief Account of Administrative and Development Activities in North-East Frontier Agency Since Independence,* Shillong, 1957.

2. *Bulletin, Journal, Document, etc. published by the Government of Nagaland, Kohima*

Basic Facts, Nagaland (A document published yearly by the Directorate of Information and Public Relations, Government of Nagaland, Kohima), for the years 1997, 1999, 2000, 2002, 2004 and 2006.

Nagaland (A yearly journal published by the Directorate of Information and Public Relations, Government of Nagaland, Kohima), for the years 1986, 1998, 2002 and 2003.

The Warrior (A monthly bulletin published by the Directorate of Information and Public Relations, Government of Nagaland, containing detailed accounts of Government policies and programmes announced and implemented from time to time).
Vol. 27, March 1998, No. 3.
Vol. 28, August 1999, No. 8.
Vol. 29, April 2000, No. 4.
Vol. 30, November 2001, No. 11.
Vol. 31, September 2002, No. 9.
Vol. 32, July 2003, No. 7.
Vol. 32, August 2003, No. 8.
Vol. 33, February 2004, No. 2.
Vol. 33, April 2004, No. 4.
Vol. 33, September 2004, No. 9.
Vol. 34, January 2005, No. 1.
Vol. 36, June 2007, No. 6.
Vol. 40, April 2012, No: 12,

3. *Gazette (published fortnightly by the Government of Nagaland, Kohima):*

Nagaland Gazette, No. 73, 15 April, 1964.
......................, Part IV, 30 November, 1965.
......................, No. 21, 15 February, 1966.
......................, No. 24, 31 March, 1967.
......................, No. 8, Part-I, 31 July, 1967.
......................, No. 13, 30 November, 1973.
......................, No. 23, 15 March, 1978.
......................, Part-V, 31 March, 1979.

B. SECONDARY SOURCES

(a) Books (English)

Aier, Yajen, *A Brief History of Education in Nagaland During the Last 25 Years: From 1947 to 1972,* Kohima, year not mentioned.

Aier, Yajen, *Growth of Education in Nagaland*, Guwahati, 1999.

Alemchiba, M., *A Brief Historical Account of Nagaland,* Kohima, (First Edition), 1970.

Allen, B.C., Gait, E.A., Allen, C.G.H. and Howard, H.F. (ed.), *Gazetteer of Bengal and North-East India,* New Delhi (reproduced), 2001.

Anand, V.K., *Conflict in Nagaland: A Study of Insurgency and Counter-Insurgency,* Delhi, 1980.

Ao, A. Lanu (ed.), *Naga Cultural Attires and Musical Instruments*, New Delhi, 1999.

Ao, A. Lanunungsang, *Rural Development in Nagaland,* New Delhi, 1993.

Ao, M. Alemchiba, *The Arts and Crafts of Nagaland,* Kohima, 1968.

Ao, Tajenyuba, *British Occupation of Naga Country,* Mokokchung, 1993.

Bareh, H. (ed.), *Nagaland District Gazetteers, Kohima District,* Kohima, 1970.

Bareh, H.M., *Encyclopaedia of North-East India,* Vol. VI, Nagaland, New Delhi, 2001.

Datt, Ruddar and Sundharam, K.P.M., *Indian Economy,* New Delhi (48th Revised Edition), 2003.

Devi, Lakshmi, *Ahom-Tribal Relations: A Political Study,* Guwahati (Second Edition), 1992.

Elwin, Verrier, *A Philosophy for NEFA*, Itanagar (Third Reprint), 1988.

Elwin, Verrier, *Nagaland,* New Delhi (Reprint), 1997.

Elwin, Verrier, *The Art of the North-East Frontier of India*, Itanagar, 1988.

Elwin, Verrier, *The Nagas in the Nineteenth Century,* Bombay, 1969.

Furer-Haimendorf, Christoph von, *Return to the Naked Nagas,* New Delhi, 1976.

Gait, Edward, *A History of Assam*, Gauhati (Fourth Edition), 1990.

Ganguli, Milada, *A Pilgrimage to the Nagas,* New Delhi, 1984.

Ghosh, B.B., *History of Nagaland,*.New Delhi, 1982.

Ghosh, B.B. (ed.), *Nagaland District Gazetteers*, Mokokchung District, Kohima, 1979.

Ghosh, B.B., *Nagaland District Gazetteers*, Tuensang District, Kohima, 1981.

Henshet, B., *The Phom-Naga Indigenous Religion: A Socio-Philosophical Perspective,* Longleng, 2000.

Horam, M., *Naga Old Ways and New Trends,* New Delhi, 1988.

Horam, M., *Naga Polity,* Delhi (Reprint), 1992.

Horam, M., *Social and Cultural Life of Nagas (The Tangkhul Nagas),* Delhi (Reproduced), 1992.

Hutton, J., *Report on Naga Hills,* Delhi, 1986.

Hutton, J.H., *The Angami Nagas,* place of publication not mentioned, 1969.

Imnayongdang, *Levels of Rural Development in Nagaland: A Spatial Analysis,* Meerut, 1990.

Konyak, A. Yanang, *From Darkness to Light*, Guwahati, 1986.

Kumar, B.B., *An Introduction to the Naga Tribes*, Meerut, 1997.

Kumar, B.B., *Society and Culture in a Corner of Nagaland,* Meerut, 1998.

Luthra, P.N., *Nagaland from a District to a State,* Shillong, 1974.

Mackenzie, Alexander, *The North East Frontier of India,* New Delhi (Reproduced), 1999.

Maithani, B.P. and Rizwana, A., *Decentralised Development: A Study of Village Development Boards in Nagaland,* Hyderabad, 1991.

Maitra, Kiranshankar, *The Nagas Rebel and Insurgency in the North-East,* New Delhi, 1998.

Mankekar, D.R., *On the Slippery Slope in Nagaland*, Bombay, 1967.

Michell, John F., *The North East Frontier of India,* Delhi (reprint), 1973.

Mills, J.P., *The Ao Nagas, Kohima* (Third Edition), 2003.

Nibedon, Nirmal, *Nagaland: The Night of the Guerrillas*, New Delhi, 1983.

Noklang, C. Amop, *Phom Day: A Basis for Peace in Nagaland,* Mokokchung, 2002.

Philip, P.T., *The Growth of Baptist Churches in Nagaland,* Guwahati (Second Edition), 1983.

Phom, Henshet B. (ed.), *The Phom-Naga Customary Laws,* The Longleng District Customary Court, Longleng, 2005.

Rao, V. Venkata, 'Modernization of the Naga Society', in B.B. Kumar (ed) *Modernization in Naga Society*, New Delhi, 1993, pp. 45-54.

Roy Burman, B.K., *Towards Poverty Alleviation Programmes in Nagaland and Manipur,* Delhi, 1984.

Saleh, Swabera Islam, *Nagaland's Economy in Transition Since 1964,* New Delhi, 1989.

Sardeshpande, S.C., *The Patkoi Nagas*, Delhi, 1987.

Sema, Hokishe, *Emergence of Nagaland: Socio-Economic and Political Transformation and the Future*, Sahibabad, 1986.

Sema, Piketo, *British Policy and Administration in Nagaland 1881-1947*, New Delhi (Second Edition), 1992.

Shakespear, L.W., *History of the Assam Rifles,* New Delhi (First Indian Reprint with an Introduction), 1980.

Singh, Chandrika, *Emergence of Arunachal Pradesh as a State,* Delhi, 1989.

Singh, Chandrika, *Political Evolution of Nagaland*, New Delhi, 1981.

Singh, Prakash, *Nagaland,* New Delhi (Fourth Edition), 1995.

Smith, William C., *The Ao-Naga Tribe of Assam,* New Delhi (Reproduced), 2002.

Stracey, P.D., *Nagaland Nightmare,* Calcutta, 1968.

Yadon, L.L., 'Impact of Adult *Franchise*', in B.B. Kumar (ed) *Modernization in Naga Society*, New Delhi, 1993, pp. 71-79.

Zhimomi, Kuhoi, K., *Politics and Militancy in Nagaland*, New Delhi, 2004.

(b) Published (in Phom language)

Babu Oukshokching Baptist Attoi, Silver Jubilee Bushah Lai *(Silver Jubilee History Book)* 1959-1983.

Phom Baptist Christian Association, *Golden Jubilee 1953-2003, Bushah Laitap* (History Book), Longleng, 2003.

Phom Day, *Golden Jubilee 1952-2002,* 5-6 June, 2002, Bushah Laitap.

(c) Papers, Articles, Booklets, Newspapers, etc.

Babu, S.V., 'Reorganisation of Dobashis in Naga Hills', *the Proceedings of North East India History Association, 21st Session, 2000,* pp. 230-232.

Bhattacharya, P.K., 'Economic Evolution of the Naga Society – A Glimpse', *the Highlander,* Vol. III, No. 2, September 1975, pp. 1-9.

Borooah, N., 'The School Report', *the Souvenir,* The Silver Jubilee 1972-1997, Government High School, Longleng, pp. 35-36.

Chungpang, Namchei L., 'Over-view of Backward Community of Nagaland Phom', printed in the *Proceedings of a Seminar* entitled "Over-view of Backward Areas of Nagaland Since Independence", Longleng, 2001, pp. 76-81.

Ezung, Achumi, 'Naga Women and the Need for 33 per cent Reservation', printed in the Proceedings of a seminar entitled 'Status of Naga Women: Emerging Trend', Longleng, 2012, pp. 1-3.

History of Tuensang Town, Golden Jubilees (establishment of the Town), 1948-1998.

Islam, Nurul, 'Over-view of Backward Areas of Nagaland Since Independence with Special Reference to Educational Status of the Phom Area', printed in the *Proceedings of a Seminar* entitled "Over-view of Backward Areas of Nagaland Since Independence", Longleng, 2001, pp. 37-41.

Islam, Swabera, 'An Overview of the Backward Areas of Nagaland – Suggestions for Economic Development', printed in the *Proceedings of a Seminar* entitled "Over-view of Backward Areas of Nagaland Since Independence", Longleng, 2001, pp. 3-10.

Jasokie, J.B., 'Nagaland from District to State' in the *Silver Jubilee Souvenir,* 25 Years of Nagaland Legislative Assembly, Nagaland, 1989, pp. 54-74.

Jha, B.N. & Chakrabarty, P., 'Socio-Educational Status of Phom Community', paper presented at a *Seminar* held at Yingli College, Longleng on 9-10 July, 1997.

Joseph, C., 'Socio-Economic Development in Tuensang District of Nagaland', paper presented at a Seminar entitled "Socio-

Educational Status of Phom Community", held at Yingli College, Longleng on 9-10 July, 1997.

The Nagaland Post, Dimapur.

Oottukalathil, Joseph, 'Education, the Means to Development and the Contribution of the Catholic Church in Tuensang District', printed in the *Proceedings of a Seminar* entitled "Over-view of Backward Areas of Nagaland Since Independence", Longleng, 2001, pp. 64-67.

Phom, N. Chingyam, 'Pre and Post Independence Socio-Economic and Historical Background of Nagaland: Especial Reference to Tuensang', printed in the *Proceedings of a Seminar* entitled "Over-view of Backward Areas of Nagaland Since Independence", Longleng, 2001, pp. 68-75.

Phom Naga Since 1942: A Tribute to Late Shri M. Hamyei, Rtd. Political Assistant to Deputy Commissioner, Longleng, 2002.

Phom, O. Kongyan, 'Health and Hygienic Problems of the Backward Areas of Nagaland – An Observation', printed in the *Proceedings of a Seminar* entitled "Over-view of Backward Areas of Nagaland Since Independence", Longleng, 2001, pp. 42-43.

Phom, S. Chaidok, 'Factors Responsible for the Backwardness of the Area with Special Reference to Tuensang and Mon Districts', printed in the *Proceedings of a Seminar* entitled "Over-view of Backward Areas of Nagaland since Independence", Longleng, 2001, pp. 82-85.

_______, 'Growth and Development of Modern Education in Phom Community', paper presented in a *Seminar* entitled "Socio-Educational Status of Phom Community", held at Yingli College, Longleng on 9-10 July, 1997.

Rahman, Abdur, 'The Place of Female in Phom Society', paper presented at a *Seminar* entitled "Socio-Educational Status of Phom Community", held at Yingli College, Longleng on 9-10 July, 1997.

25 Years of Nagaland Legislative Assembly, Silver Jubilee Souvenir, Government of Nagaland, 1989.

(d) Interview

I. Interview held with individuals mentioned below:

— A. Shamthai (35), Sub-Inspector of Schools (SIS),

President of *Phomla Hoichem,* at Longleng on 02-02-2003.

— Anyak Phom (79), retired *Do-Bhashi,* at Longleng on 11-04-2001 and 08-12-2003.

— Apisangpa (70), retired *Do-Bhashi,* at Bahok Colony, Longleng on 20-05-2004.

— B. Hayu Phom (59), President, 'Nagaland People's Front' Political Party, Longleng Division, at Oushok Colony on 07-06-2007.

— H. Toshi Phom (47), Member of Longleng Ad hoc Town Committee and the Treasurer of Longleng Town Students' Union (LTSU), at PPC Colony, Longleng on 12-01-2003.

— Hepong Phom (83), ex-Interim Body Member and ex-Tuensang District Regional Council Member, at Longleng on 19-11-2003 and 24-04-2005.

— Kongyan Phom (40), Medical Officer, at Longleng on 05-02-2003.

— L. Shaupang Phom (78), retired government employee, at Longleng on 01-12-2003.

— Lima Hamyei (56), Head Assistant (HA) to Deputy Commissioner (DC) Longleng, at Longleng on 14-09-2003.

— N. Hamvok Phom (76), *Do-Bhashi*, at Longleng on 15-01-2003.

— P. Oyemth Phom (30), teacher, at Longleng on 15-01-2004.

— T. Ngecham, Forest Guard, at Longleng on 30-05-2004.

— T. Ponglong Phom (52), Chairman of Subdivisional Chamber of Commerce Unit Longleng, at Longleng on 12-10-2003.

— Y. B. Angam (47), ex-President of Phom People's Council (PPC) and public leader, at Longleng on 10-04-2003.

— Y. Heong Phom (56), ex-Vice-Chairman of Longleng Area Council and the Vice-Chairman of Longleng Ad hoc Town Committee, at Block Colony, Longleng on 27-11-2001.

— Y. Pangong (49), Upper Divisional Assistant (UDA),

Sub-District Industries Centre (DIC), Longleng, at Longleng on 30-01-2003.

II. Interview held with some persons in groups belonging to the following villages, namely Bhumnyu (2004), Bora Namsang (2004), Sakchi (2004) and Yongam (2002-05), and Longleng town (2004) regarding the subjects mentioned below:

— 40 (forty) cultivators,08 (eight) each from 04 (four) villages and Longleng town regarding the system of cultivation, food habit, animal husbandry, etc.

— 04 (four) aged *Gaon-Buras,* namely S. Pangjei of Bhumnyu (14-03-2004), Chingshen of Bura Namsang (25-01-2004), K. Panglem of Sakchi (11-01-2004) and Phongang of Yongam (08-09-2003), on matters relating to village administration.

— 04 (four) Secretaries and four female members of the Village Development Boards, viz. V. Chingtuk (15-09-2002) and Yongpen (08-09-2002) of Yongam; M. Pheknyu Phom (14-03-2004) and E. Nami Phom (14-03-2004) of Bhumnyu; H. Longshem (24-01-2004) and N. Shaoang Phom (19-01-2004) of Bura Namsang; and Y. Buchei (11-01-2004) and T. Menyu Phom (11-01-2004) of Sakchi about activities of Village Development Boards.

— 04 (four) senior persons, namely Yingsak Phom of Sakchi (12-01-2004), Phongang Phom of Yongam (29-03-2003), W. Longnyi Phom of Bura Namsang (14-01-2004) and Z. Bushem Phom of Bhumnyu (14-03-2004) regarding housing pattern, etc.

— 04 (four) Village Council Chairmen, viz. S. Pangjei of Bhumnyu (14-03-2004), T.C. Nyamnyei Semdok of Sakchi (22-01-2004), B. Angshai Phom of Yongam (07-09-2002) and A. Hamlang of Bura Namsang (25-01-2004) regarding powers and functions of Village Council.

Index